Russian Decorative Arts 1917–1937

Vladimir Tolstoy

RIZZOLI
NEW YORK

Russian Decorative Arts 1917-1937

Russian Decorative Arts

1917-1937

Vladimir Tolstoy

RIZZOLI
NEW YORK

First published in the United States of America in 1990 by
RIZZOLI INTERNATIONAL PUBLICATIONS, INC.
300 Park Avenue South, New York, New York 10010

Library of Congress Cataloging-in-Publication Data
Tolstoi, Vladimir Pavlovich.
    Russian decorative arts, 1917–1937 / Vladimir Tolstoy.
      p.   cm.
    Translation of: Art décoratif soviétique, 1917–1937; originally
published in Russian.
    Includes index.
    ISBN 0-8478-1242-1
    1. Decorative arts—Soviet Union—History—20th century.
I. Title.
NK975.T6   1990
745'.0947'09041—dc20   90-52612
                                       CIP

Translation by Michael Taylor and Nina Bogin
Design layout by Mary McBride
Composition by David E. Seham Associates, Inc.
Printed and bound in Switzerland

Contents

Introduction

The development of the decorative arts in the Soviet Union was, in these troubled times (1917-1937), intimately linked to historic events. Each stage in their evolution seemed to correspond to a new social force. Since decorative art reflects the society which engenders it and for which it is designed, it therefore projects not only a faithful image of the economic and technical factors of a given period, but also, as we will see, of the abiding mentality. The decorative arts also serve instructive purposes. "The artistic source should help to inspire work, to embellish everyday life, and to uplift mankind," was what the program of the Communist Party of the Soviet Union proclaimed.

The artist's task was thus to enhance the environment as well as to establish mankind as the object's master rather than its slave. It is important to remember that while a work of art depends solely on the artist who creates it, a work of decorative art is shaped by the many different people involved in its production. Only a few branches of the decorative arts are able to escape this general rule.

Industrial production is, accordingly, highly complex. After the artist's creation of a piece of work, it is the turn of the engineers, technicians, economists, and production managers to decide what course its career will then take. Before the Revolution, different forms of production existed in Russia, from cottage industries to mass production. A few years before 1917, the decorative arts were swept by a series of contradictory socio-economic influences. The porcelain, faïence, glass, and textile industries, run by a handful of owners, were subject to the laws of competition. Since the clientele was limited to the middle classes, the production had by necessity to respond to their tastes which were as traditional as they were mediocre. On the other hand, the Imperial Porcelain Factory in Saint Petersburg, the Gardner Factory in the Moscow region, the Giraud, Moussy-Gougeon, and Tsindel textile factories in Moscow and a few other companies which catered to the upper classes, merely produced imitations of Western European fashions. The Russian-Byzantine style also had its moment of glory, first in architecture, then in jewelry produced by the Sopojnik, Sazikov, and Khlebnikov firms. This particular fashion was introduced somewhat artificially by means of massive subsidies provided to industrial designers. A curious combination of ornamental motifs drawn from old manuscripts and household objects of the seventeenth century, it did not take into consideration either the function or the shape of the object. The apartment of the "average Russian" displayed an over-abundance of furniture and tableware in order to exhibit the owner's wealth. Despite the great tradition of folk art which had always been the pride of our country, bad taste abounded.

Faced with the destruction wrought by industrial production, the intelligentsia, inspired by such Western European artists as John Ruskin and William Morris, began to support traditional art forms. The idealization of manual work as compared to mechanized production could be clearly seen in the activities of such folk art workshops as the Talashkino studio. Inspired by Savva Mamontov and Elena Polenov at Abramtsevo, original examp' ℮ of peasant art were preciously preserved so as to keep intact the true source of popular creativity. Victor Vasnetsov, Vassly Polenov, Ilya Repin, Valentin Serov and Mikhail Vrubel were among the talented artists of the era who shared this belief. Some of them, through experimentation, were able to give new life to handicraft production. Vrubel, for example, was able in his majolica pieces to anticipate certain achievements in modern ceramics thanks to his painterly use of colors. As early as the end of the last century, an upheaval in the activity of the *zemstvos* (local councils) took place in most of the Russian provinces, the Ukraine and the Caucasus, in order to remedy the crisis in creativity. The crafts arts were studied attentively, and apprenticeship and production workshops were organized, raw materials were supplied, and sales channels were created. Replacing mechanized production by manual means remained, however, both illusory and limited.

Though from a strictly artistic viewpoint, handicrafts and industrially produced objects had lost many of their truly traditional characteristics, traditional work can still be seen in the Russian kerchiefs produced in the Ivanovovo-Vosnessensk, Chouia, and Pavlovsky Posad factories of the Moscow area. Nor had traditional folk art disappeared from the painting of Khokloma, the ivory carvings of the North of Russia, the sculpted toys of Bogorodskoye, the ceramics and rugs of Central Asia and the Caucasus, and the hammered gold objects made in the village of Kubatcha. In this period preceding the Revolution, some of the significant premises of the evolution to come in the domain of the decorative arts were developed. In fact, the arts industry had already entered a phase in which mass production of clothing, dishes, and cloth had become a major concern.

It had become impossible to satisfy the ever-increasing demand for these products; only the new possibilities offered by machines could remedy the situation. A handful of members of the Russian avant-garde had already begun to discuss the problem in these terms, following the path already taken in the domain of architecture. Indeed, it was during this same period that eminent designers such as Lanceray, Kuznetsov, N. and E. Danko, Tchekhonin, and others, became the industrial directors of a number of art and handicrafts firms. The idea that only by coordinating the arts and industry could a renewal of the artistic culture of the twentieth century be achieved was beginning to gain ground. However, the government's policies at that time did not make it possible to solve all the problems of mass producing art objects.

It is obvious that after October 1917, the struggle to change the existing mentality was an arduous one, as was a genuine approach to the issue of a "true and authentic proletarian culture." This issue was first raised in a directive issued by the Central Committee of the Bolshevik Russian Communist Party, *Concerning the Proletkult,* in 1920, and subsequently in the Central Committee's 1925 resolution, *Concerning Party Policies in the Field of Literature and Art.*

The October Revolution was quite diversely reflected in art. The immediate response to the realities of the Revolution took the form of posters, decorations for propaganda trains, propaganda porcelain, producing revolutionary celebrations, and so on. This was followed by a radical and profound change in artists' consciousness thanks to totally new approaches to the production of decorative art. In a conversation with Clara Tsetkin, Lenin discussed this in the following terms: "The awakening of new forces, their effort to create a new art and culture in the Soviet Union, is a very good thing. The impetuous rhythm of their progress is both understandable and necessary. We must make up for centuries of neglect; this is our ardent desire."

The first years following the Revolution involved the laying of the foundations of a truly mass culture and art. The realities of the situation made it imperative for artists to find a more intimate approach to the life of the people and the day-to-day experiences of the workers.

For the first time in history, the problem of how to modify man's everyday environment was debated. "Finally, the whole natural milieu must be reconstructed," wrote Lunacharsky in 1922, in his article entitled "Art as Production." ". . . Naturally, the present situation is one of extreme cultural poverty. . . . Nevertheless, we cannot simply overlook the problem of production in the domain of the arts. On the contrary, we must immediately buckle down to the task of dealing with such problems with increasing determination."

A conflict then arose between Lenin and a certain number of artists, whose goal was expressed by Pletnov, one of the Proletkult leaders, in these terms: "In the new world, the visual arts must be productive, or not exist at all."

According to the partisans of Proletkult, "the proletarian artist must be simultaneously artist and worker." For Lenin, as he noted in the project of the resolution submitted to the Proletkult Congress of 1920, "Marxism has not rejected in the least the significant achievements of the bourgeois era, but has, on the contrary, assimilated and reworked all that was valid at the moment of the two-thousand-year-old evolution of human thought and culture. Only a far-reaching effort starting out with this basis and continuing in the same direction, inspired by the practical experience of the proletarian dictatorship as the last battle against exploitation of any sort, can be understood as an effective advance in proletarian culture."

Fresco on the revolutionary propaganda train *The Red Cossack*, 1920.

AGITPROP

Fresco on the revolutionary propaganda train *V.I. Lenin*, intended for literary instruction, 1918.

Propaganda Trains and Boats

T he October Revolution gave birth to an original artistic phenomenon, the decoration of trains and boats whose mission was to spread propaganda throughout Russia. ". . . Artistically painted and colored, [they] are so many traveling libraries . . . cinema studios, mobile tribunes, pedagogical tools. . . . It is a gigantic undertaking, almost fantastic . . . and, in the springtime, when the rivers thaw, literary boats go off on the vast waterways of the Republic, down the Volga and its tributaries, down the Dniestr . . ."[1] Trains, using hastily repaired railroad lines, passing villages devastated by the war and abandoned fields, traveled to the farthest corners of the nation, only just liberated from the White Guards and foreign troops, and were welcomed often by illiterate peasants who listened with avid attention to the fiery speeches of the orators, and were fascinated by the painted frescoes, the exhibitions and the film documentaries.

The role of the decorators was capital. Few sketches, alas, have been preserved; only archive photographs give an idea of the uniqueness of their work. Nevertheless, the authors of some fifty compositions have been identified.

The circumstances themselves created the originality of the decoration. At first, the cars were simply plastered with posters which were inevitably damaged by rain, snow, and so forth. The posters were then replaced by oil paintings executed directly onto the side of the train. These paintings, similar in spirit to revolutionary posters, depicted the convulsive events of the time. They had all the characteristic features of propaganda: brevity and expressivity of form, contrasting colors, the capacity to draw immediate attention. The close relationship between image and text and the evident message contained in these compositions evoked popular Russian imagery (*luboks*). Moreover, they had an element of satire which verged on caricature. Their large size was determined by the form of the decorated object (train cars, river boats), and the themes, usually heroic, were similar to monumental painting.

Designed to reach an uneducated population, the messages were necessarily simple and effective, images often replacing words. Time was precious, and the execution of such paintings was often hasty. Artists representing all the different tendencies of the time took an active part in the preparation of this type of propaganda during late 1918 and early 1919. Lenin (President of the Council of People's Commissars) gave much importance to the mission of the propaganda boats and trains. It was he who had prepared the instructions for organizing the mission.[2]

Kalinin traveled seventeen times on the train called *The October Revolution,* and Krupskaya went on board *The Red Star.*

The trains were painted in the workshops of the decoration department of the IZO (Visual Arts Section of the People's Commissariat for Education). According to Burov, who directed the Department of Propaganda Trains and Boats created in 1919 by the Central Executive Committee of Russia,[3] "The sides of the train cars were covered with Futurist and symbolic paintings which depicted enormous monsters devouring the Revolution. Most of these images were incomprehensible and merely served to confuse the local population. The organizers had no experience in this domain, it was as if the artists had been given complete license to do whatever they wanted."[4]

Let us not forget that among the people involved in this new genre were painters, illustrators, masters of poster art and caricature, and painters of Palekh icons. It is not difficult to imagine the richness and diversity of styles.

The first Lenin Literary and Military Train, considered by Burov to be an experiment, left Moscow on August 13, 1918, for Kazan and the territories recently liberated from the Czechoslovakian counter-revolutionaries. An account was given in the press: "Proudly bearing the slogan 'Working people of all nations, unite!' above the sleek back of the traincars, our train pursued its path. . . . Its unusual aspect, the decorated cars, the foliage and posters drew the attention of peasants who stopped their work to follow the train with their eyes. First stop at the Liubertsy station, where a crowd of people jammed the platform. The train was overrun by the spectators avid to see the posters and read the revolutionary slogans. . . . Laughter and jokes could be heard from the depot, plastered with Cubist posters. This new tendency caused much merriment among the peasants."[5]

What appears to be this very train can be seen in a handful of photographs. The walls of the train were painted from top to bottom, ornamented with workers, peasants, and soldiers of the Red Army, with contrasting shades of color accentuating the outlines against the irregular surface of the freight coaches. The second *Lenin N·1 Literary and Formative Train* left on December 26, 1918, for the Northwest and the regions liberated from German occupation. Some of the cars from the experimental train were apparently included.[6]

It has been possible, thanks to archival sources, to identify the artists of certain frescoes. One of the coaches bears a strong resemblance to the work of Tchekhonin, by the dynamism and boldness of the composition and the precise graphics. The painting, rendered with great expressivity, depicts the silhouette of a worker against an immense red banner. Another coach bears the slogan, "The Soviet government leads the people toward the light," and evokes the work of Osmiorkin. Certain of the paintings are close to the satirical sketches of the period representing generals and members of the bourgeoisie; they differ only by their size. One of the

Fresco on the revolutionary propaganda train *The Red Cossack*. 1920.
Fresco on the revolutionary propaganda train *The Red Flag*. 1921.

Fresco on the revolutionary propaganda train *V.I. Lenin*. intended for literary instruction, 1918.

cinematographic coaches deserves to be described: access to the car was through a sort of classical portico, while the exterior walls were decorated in an ordinary poster style with outsized busts of workers and peasants against a sunrise.

In early 1919 a third train was decorated, probably by Chevaldycheva and Artiukhova, students, during the winter of 1918-19, in the second Free Workshops (the former School of Painting, Sculpture, and Architecture) in collaboration with Pomansky, Etcheistov, and Kozlov, among others, a team led by D. Moor. Named *The October Revolution,* this train left Moscow for the first time on April 29. Under the supervision of M.I. Kalinin, it crisscrossed the country until the spring of 1920.[7] One of the coaches depicted a giant, representing Russia, sweeping the earth of the Revolution's enemies. This same theme, treated in a different manner with a female protagonist, had been drawn by D. Moor.[8] A great many photos of this train exist. The decoration consisted mainly of symbolic and allegorical scenes. Terrifying monsters, symbols of capitalism, writhe in flames; the Revolution, represented by a worker, proudly carries a banner, or, if symbolized by a warrior, shoots an arrow. Meanwhile, the flames of the worldwide revolution outline extraordinary silhouettes. Sometimes mountain peaks spread out at the feet of a worker and a Red Army soldier who stride forward bearing the banner of the hammer and sickle.

Realized in the spirit of old Russian frescoes, another work shows the combat between the White Guards and the soldiers of the Red Army mounted on fantastical horses, in the style of depictions of St. George slaying the dragon. The background landscape is also reminiscent of icon painting. We must remember that all these images included captions, with the words incorporated directly into the

Frescoes on the revolutionary propaganda train *The October Revolution*,
intended for literary instruction, 1919.

composition. There is ample testimony concerning the impact these trains made on the population. Political officers took surveys and noted down the various reactions in notebooks; this may be the reason that allegorical pictures gave way to themes which expressed Soviet reality in more concrete terms. This transition occurred much later on in the other artistic categories. The new tendency was prevalent in the work of the Visual Arts for Propaganda Collective which was directly dependent on the Trains and Boats for Propaganda Section of the Central Executive Committee, consisting of Guerassimov, Kotchergin, Kostianitsyne, Melnikov, Feinberg, Pomansky, Markitchev, Pachkov, Vinogradov, S. Tikhonov, N. Tikhonov, and others.[9]

Fresco on the revolutionary propaganda train *The Soviet Caucasus.*
V. KOSTIANITSYN. Fresco on the revolutionary propaganda train *The Red Cossack.* 1920.

A. GUCHTCHIN. Fresco on the revolutionary propaganda train *The October Revolution*, 1920. A. YANTCHENKO. Fresco on the revolutionary propaganda train *The October Revolution*, 1920.

D.I. MELNIKOV. Fresco on the revolutionary propaganda train *The Red Cossack*. 1920.

With Nivinsky as artistic director, from the end of 1919 onward, this collective realized the great majority of commissioned frescoes. The work was done in close collaboration with the editorial commission of the Section, directed by Karpinsky,[10] which decided the fresco themes. Each subject was developed into a small scenario,[11] and submitted to a jury. It was the jury's job to see that the design was politically convincing and accurate in its depiction of clothing, gestures, tools, weapons, etc. The folklore of the different regions the trains were to pass through was also incorporated into the paintings. Burov announced at one such meeting that "sketches of a Futurist nature would be rejected."[12] Discussions also bore on the general composition of the train. For *The Red Orient,* for example, the artists of the Collective had to insure harmony between the colors, the texts, the decorations, and the lighting effects. While the compositions and portraits were usually painted directly onto the sheet metal, the emblem of each republic was executed in glass and lighted from inside. Each train had its own banner which was decorated during the voyage with branches and red flags.

The Red Orient was one of the first trains to be painted by the Collective. Painted in Oriental style by Vinogradov, Gutchin, Tikhonov, Iakimtchenko, Sapalov, Soborova, Ovechkov, and Pachkov, it left Moscow in January of 1920 bound for Turkestan.[13]

One of the most beautiful trains was *The Red Cossack* which left Moscow on April 9, 1920, in the direction of the Donet and the Kubar regions. The civil war

Fresco on the revolutionary propaganda train *The October Revolution,* intended for literary instruction, 1919.

N.N. POMANSKY. Frescoes on the revolutionary propaganda train *The Red Cossack*. 1920.

was still being fought in these parts of the country, and the slogans written on the sides of the coaches exhorted the population to join the ranks of the Red Army. The red cossacks were brightly painted and picturesque, while the enemy was given grotesque attributes. The main characters towered imposingly in the foreground; next could be seen the crowd, and in the far background, the place of action. In Pomansky's decoration of the cinematographic coach, there is no evidence of abstraction; the satire is without finesse, recalling the imagery of popular *luboks:* a worker cossack frightens away a general, a bourgeois, and a kulak.

One of the coaches is inscribed thus: "The Tsarist government brought oppression, vodka, and the whip to the people." The phrase is illustrated by a scene which takes place in a cabaret, where a drunken cossack is being savagely beaten by a general. Melnikov depicted cossacks on horseback, advancing two by two toward the spectator. Each group is separated from the next by a coach window; the faces, clothing, and gestures are clearly individualized. The accompanying inscription reads: "Cossacks, join the ranks of the Soviet Army!" The frescoes painted by Glazunov, master of the Palekh technique, are easily recognized by the richness of their colors. Tikhonov, Nicolayev, and Pomansky were responsible for the lettering of the slogans and the executions of the emblems and coats of arms. The Collective was responsible, in 1919 and 1920, for the decoration of four trains: *The Soviet-Sverdlov Caucasian, The Ukrainian-Lenin Train, The Red Cossack* painted a second time, and the second *The October Revolution,* and, in 1921, of *The Red Standard. The October Revolution* is undoubtedly the train that best represents the Collective's style.

We know the names of the artists who contributed to this last train: the bridge scenes are by Gussov; Melnikov painted "If You Want to Wipe Out Epidemics, Fight Dirt First"; the "Telephone" is by Tikhonov; "Learning" by Soborova; and "Let Work Begin in the Factories," the most decorative of the frescoes, by Kostianitsin.

Kotchergin's decorations for the cinematographic coach harked back to the allegorical style of the first propaganda trains, covered with monsters representing famine, desolation, and ruin. Here, famine tries to strangle a group of workers, its enormous wings taking up the whole upper part of the coach, and in the background, in the shadow of those monstrous wings, are abandoned factories, while the agitated silhouettes of capitalists, generals, and the Czar can be seen against a lighter background.

During this same period, other trains were decorated in Ekaterinburg by artists from the political section of the Third Army on the eastern front, including Labass, Lakov, and Plaksin.

A flotilla of boats and canal barges was also used for literary and educational purposes. Tychler and Kozintsova-Erenburg remember having decorated two of these, in collaboration with the students of the Exter Studio. Vividly colored geometrical figures covered the hull of one boat so that, seen from afar, it was like one great ornamental design. The other boat, painted from sketches made by Krüger, used motifs from Ukrainian folk art. The names of these boats have not come down to us, though one of them may have been *The Bolshevik*. The boat called *Dawn* and two canal barges followed the banks of Lake Onega and the network of rivers that included the Mariinsk, the Svir, and the Volkhov. *The Mikhail Kalinin, The Volodarsky, The Torch of Socialism-Sverdlov, The Orinoko* and the canal barges *Kama* and *Oka* navigated along the Volga River. *The Red Star* and its accompanying canal barges were decorated by the Collective, under the aegis of the Central Executive Committee. According to Voskressensky,[14] the ornamentation of *The Red Star* was inspired by the traditional decoration of the nineteenth-century river boats and barges of the Volga River, and played on contrasts between white and red. Architects were also called upon to work on the interior decoration of boats and trains. The Central Executive Committee organized an internal competition for the interior and exterior decoration of a houseboat which was to be used as a theater and exhibition hall.

For this competition, Ossipov, Korchunov, Efimov, and Roerberg submitted designs. The winning entry was Roerberg's sketch of an old-fashioned barge ornamented with all sorts of neo-classical decorative and architectural elements (horns of plenty, pilasters, cornices, balustrades, and obelisks).

Although their duration was relatively short, about three years in all, the propaganda trains and boats brought together a great number of first-rate artists and remain without a doubt one of the major episodes in socialist artistic culture.

NOTES

1. TsGAOR (National Central Archives of the Revolution). Folio 1252, file 101, leaf 1.
2. See *"Main Lines Concerning the Educational Value of Propaganda Trains and Boats."* V.I. Lenin, *Complete Works*, Volume 40, p. 72.
3. See: N.K. Krupskaya, *Lenin's Guiding Lines in the Cultural Domain*. Moscow, 1934, pp. 237-238.
4. *Propaganda Trains and Boats of the Central Executive Committee*. Moscow, 1920, p. 9.
5. "On the Red Train." *The Evening News*. newspaper of the deputy workers and soldiers Soviet. N° 68, October 9, 1918, p. 1.
6. TsGAOR, folio 1252, file 101, leaf 1.
7. According to archive documents, the name *The October Revolution* refers to two different trains. The decoration of the first train was begun in the beginning of 1919, while the second train, painted by a different team of artists, was done in the summer of 1920. Both trains were directed by Kalinin. The second train continued its voyages until 1923. (TsGAOR, folio 1252. Ts GA RSFSR, folio 2313.)
8. The artist D. Melnikov confirms D. Moor's participation on other decorative train projects. He remembers seeing several coaches painted by Moor in 1919, on the side track of the Iaroslav Station in Moscow.
9. According to the documents in TsGAOR (folio 1252) and in TsGA RSFSR (folio 2313), the following artists also participated in the decoration projects: T. Gussev, S. Pitchugin, N. Sapalov, S. Sergueev, B. Takke, A. Guchtchin, A. Iakimtchenko, M. Eberman, A. Glazunov, A. Soborova, N. Nicolayev, S. Yagujinsky, P. Spassky, A. Yantechenko, M. Dobrov, Prokhorov, Rybakov, A. Belsky, I. Grandi.
10. A. Viatcheslav (1880–1966). Doctor of economic sciences, writer, Party propagandist.
11. For example, for the decoration of one of the coaches of the train *Lenin* sent to the Ukraine in 1920,

Fresco on the revolutionary propaganda train *The Red Orient*. 1920.

Karpinsky gave the following subject: "The main slogan 'Long life to the Red Army!' is written at the top in large letters. On the left side, bearing large black banners and little red flags, Makhno's partisans flee the White Army. One of the bandits carries a hen under his arm, another is making away with a baby pig, a third with an accordion; the fourth has a liquor bottle sticking out of his pocket. In the background, his rifle at his feet, another bandit holds a woman in his arms. On the bottom, in small letters, is written: 'Makhno's bandits pillage the peasants but flee the White Army.' On the right, The Red Army, in ordered ranks, advances on the fleeing White Army. Make the red stars on the caps and hats conspicuous. Behind the Red Army are the male nurses. Make the badges on their armbands conspicuous. Then come the ambulance cars and the convoy. Give special attention to the weapons and uniforms. Below the previous line, in tiny letters: 'The Red Army is the armed fist of the people who fight for their freedom.'" (TsGAOR, folio 1252. File 116, leaf 36.)* Makhno: Ukrainian anarchist leader (Translator's note).

12. See TsGAOR, folio 1252, leaf 4.
13. See TsGAOR, folio 5508, leaf 8.
14. V. Voskressensky. *Forty years ago—The Art of Cinema*. 1959, pp. 109-18.

Revolutionary propaganda boat *The Red Star*. 1920.

N. KOLLI. *The Red Corner*.
Revolution Square in
Moscow, first anniversary of
the October Revolution.

Revolutionary Celebrations

Of all the different artistic modes used for propaganda, decoration for revolutionary celebrations appears to be one of the most important, not only for its scale but also for its political significance. On the day such celebrations took place, artists of all ages took part in the decoration of the city and the preparation of the processions. This artistic genre had its particular slogan: "Art of the masses." Painters, illustrators, architects, musicians, and theater directors presented their work in the streets and public squares, drawing several thousand spectators. These artists had to take into account the starkness of daylight, the perspective of the streets, the vastness of the public squares, and the diversity of the architecture, all of which required a greater precision of form as well as more intense colors. The principal quality of these works of art was immediately to capture the spectator's attention. The heroic revolutionary themes required art of monumental proportions and favored generalization to detail.

In Russia, the Ukraine, the Urals, the Caucasus, the Baltic countries, Siberia, in every part of the nation in which Soviet power was being installed, revolutionary celebrations were held. The most important of these took place in Petrograd and in Moscow to commemorate the first anniversary of the Revolution. The artists who were responsible for the decorations came both from the traditional academies as well as from the more "left-wing" artistic tendencies. Buildings were covered with flags, banners, posters, garlands, flowers, and immense painted murals. Arches of triumph, statues, monuments, and obelisks were erected on public squares and at intersections. From outlying districts, the crowds marched in endless processions, bearing banners and signs and converging on the center of the city. Floats and cars served as mobile platforms for singers, musicians, and artists. Orators standing on tribunes harangued the crowd. Short plays were presented. At night, there were fireworks, spotlights, and bonfires.

The decoration was in perfect harmony with the architectural characteristics of each city. The celebrations which took place in Petrograd, a city of somber and classical beauty, were reminiscent of those held during the French Revolution and the Paris Commune, or of feast days in Russian cities during the eighteenth and nineteenth centuries.

For the first anniversary of the October Revolution, the architect Rudnev decorated the parade ground, where celebrations had formerly been held and where the tombs of the heroes of the Revolution were now aligned. He had conceived a composition at once spatial, architectural, and pictorial. The tiered funerary monuments, still unfinished, were covered with a frieze showing a funeral procession. Above this rose a red obelisk, surmounted by the traditional figure symbolizing Glory. Flags, tapestries, and decorative panels added dynamism and originality to the setting.

As can be seen today from the few sketches that remain, Rudnev's design rejuvenated the attributes of classical art and traditional forms.

For the same celebration in Petrograd, Langbard decorated the Palace and the Work Square, Shchuko decorated the Tauride Palace, Plitman decorated the Engineer's Building, Simakov decorated the Finland Station, Schwartz decorated the Baltic Station and its square, Serafimov decorated Senate Square, Regelson decorated Mikhaïlov Square, and Savitsky decorated the Academy of Sciences.

Lecht and Gerardov adapted their decorations admirably to the architecture of the city. Against the facade of the Rozhdestvensky Soviet, they hung an immense triptych showing the silhouettes of a worker, a peasant, and a Red Army soldier. The Proletkult artists, responsible for the decoration of the Smolny Institute, had hung between the columns of the main portico tapestries on which were painted large figures. Triangular hangings embellished the ornamental facade.

Dobuzhinsky decorated the Admiralty with vast red tapestries; Petrov-Vodkin draped Theater Square with large panels attached to the galleries of the Mariinsky Theater and the Philharmonic. These canvases showed traditional Russian heroes from epic poems and folk tales: Stepan Razin and his band, Mikula Selianinovitch, Ivan the Czarevitch and the Fire Bird, Vassilissa the Wise and the witch Baba Yaga.

G. SAVITSKY, E. SIMONOV, V. KUTCHUMOV, sketch for the decoration of the Academy of Sciences, on the Neva side, first anniversary of the October Revolution.

Kustodiev ornamented former Ruzheynaya Square with banners and large emblems representing the workers and the symbols of their different professions.

Diderichs and Alvang transformed Sampsoniev Bridge (today S. Razin Bridge) into Stepan Razin's epic flotilla. Boats attached to the bridge piers seemed to float as their sails billowed in the wind.

Stahlberg and Sokolov decorated Troïtsky bridge by accentuating diagonal lines, while the architect Ovsiannikov preferred rectangular forms for Anitchov Bridge.

Arches of triumph inspired by the traditional architecture of Russian cities of the eighteenth and nineteenth centuries were also erected, in classical style or in modernized baroque.

Savitsky erected an arch of triumph on Vassiliev Island at the corner of Grand Boulevard and First Line. Langbard did the same in front of the Work Palace, Chukhayev in front of Lieutenant Schmidt Bridge, Bucholtz on Grand Boulevard, and Belogrud on the Lateral Canal near Novokamenny Bridge. In order to radically change the habitual appearance of the streets and squares, certain decorative ensembles deliberately broke with the city's architectural style. It was in this spirit that Sterenberg decorated the Palace Quay, the Hermitage, and the Winter Palace on the Neva side; that V. Lebedev ornamented Politseisky Bridge; Puni and Boguslavskaya, Liteiny Avenue and part of the Okhta; Kozlinsky the other part of the Okhta and Liteiny Bridge; and Guminer, Znamensky Square.

This was an entirely new experience, on a scale that was more than grandiose

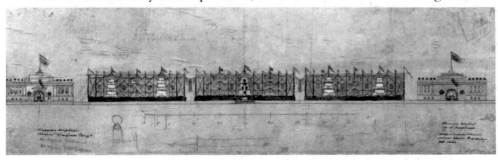

B. KUSTODIEV, sketch for the decoration of the parade ground of Petrograd,
first anniversary of the October Revolution.
K. PETROV-VODKIN, panel sketch, "Mikula Selianinovitch" for the
decoration of Theater Square in Petrograd, first anniversary of the October Revolution.

E. STAHLBERG, P. SOKOLOV, decoration of Trinity Bridge in Petrograd, first anniversary of the October Revolution.

for the era. In accordance with a project designed by Altman, the northwest side of Palace Square was covered with green canvases, and all along their length were printed the large letters of the slogan, " Workers of the World, Unite!" The colored surfaces and geometric figures in relief, placed at the foot of Alexandrov Column, transformed this classical monument surmounted by an angel into an abstract and expressive construction which served as a rostrum for the speakers. Immense painted panels representing a worker, a peasant, and a sailor imposed their bright colors and the deliberate primitivism of their forms on the sumptuous and intricate decor of the Winter Palace as well as on the severe, classical beauty of Central Headquarters. This same contrast can be seen in the decoration of Politseisky Bridge, realized by Lebedev, or in that of the monument to Alexander III in Insurrection Square, which was surmounted for the occasion with an enormous, bright-colored cube. Certain artists used allegorical figures from classical tradition: Liberty was personified by a woman in a tunic, bearing a torch; Victory of the Revolution by a Greek goddess, etc. Other classical symbols such as altars, chariots, and laurel wreaths were also employed. Much of the work was also done in pseudo-Russian style. Liberated Russia was personified by a woman dressed in national costume (in *sarafan* and *kokochnik*), and a worker by a valiant knight from Russian epics.

The panels designed by Volkov, Smukrovitch, Heller, Savitsky, and Kutchumov showed workers going about their jobs.[1] In Moscow, unlike Petrograd, decoration of the city did not involve adapting or masking existing architecture or even replacing the old with the new. Moscow, with the diversity of its streets and squares where each era had left its imprint, offered far more artistic possibilities.

Every district of the city was decorated to celebrate the first anniversary of the Revolution. Particular attention was paid to Theater Square, Revolution Square, Okhotny Promenade, Tver Street, the Kremlin Towers and above all, Red Square—in a word, the entire center of the city, where all the processions converged. During these festivities, Lenin inaugurated the commemorative plaque on the collective tomb of the heroes of the Revolution, designed by the sculptor Konenkov.

Soviet Square was decorated by Ivanov, after a project design elaborated by

V. BAVANOV-ROSSIN, sketch of a panel for the decoration of Insurrection Square in Petrograd, first anniversary of the October Revolution.
A. DIDERICHS, V. ALVANG, sketch for the decoration of Sampspnievky Bridge in Petrograd, first anniversary of the October Revolution.

B. KUSTODIEV, sketch for a panel, *Work*, for the decoration of the parade
ground in Petrograd, first anniversary of the October Revolution.

L. RUDNEV, panels, *Funeral Procession*, for the decoration of the Petrograd
parade ground, first anniversary of the October Revolution.

V. and A. Vesnin. The Moscow Soviet, designed by Kazakov, the late eighteenth-century police station across from it, the classical forms of the obelisk commemorating the first Soviet constitution, designed by Ossipov, the purple flags with the gold letters RSFSR (Republic of Russia), the garlands of flowers hung across Tver Street, and the posters, formed a tableau in which "there was a kind of triumph that was both sumptuous and severe."[2]

In Moscow, artists of different tendencies did not always respect architectural or artistic styles. Two sketches for the panel by Guerassimov called *The Master of the Earth*, designed to decorate the building which had formerly housed the municipal Duma (today the Central Lenin Museum), have been found.

The panel by Chernychev called *Science and Art Bring Their Talents to Work* was hung on this same building; it shows allegorical compositions and characters borrowed from everyday life.

Facing the former Duma, the Provisioning Committee building (the former Grand Hotel of Moscow) was decorated in the same manner, with seven panels by Feinberg, Sergueev, and Pomansky.

The decoration of Theater Square (today Sverdlov Square) was similarly eclectic, the collective result of several artists representing a variety of tendencies. On the square, the Metropole Hotel was entirely covered by an immense panel by Zakharov, entitled *Workers of the World Unite!* Opposite this, in the square, a rostrum had been erected and decorated by Siv with huge flowers. Maly Theater was hung with a panel by Kuznetsov called *Stepan Razin and His Band*, painted in the folk-art *lubok* style. As for Nezlobin Theater (today Central Children's Theater), its Cubist decoration was by Kuprin.

If we also consider the various statues and monuments erected on this same square, we can see how eclectic the decoration of Moscow really was. It seemed to be an exhibition of work by individual artists rather than a decorative artistic ensemble.

Two panels by Osmiorkin, showing a carpenter and a house-painter, hung from the facade of the Deputy Workers' Soviet Theater (formerly Zimin Theater) on the Dmitrovka Street side. The laconic style and asymmetry of these panels made them easily adapted to the composition of red flags, drapes, flowers, and plants which decorated the Theater. From the Monastery of the Passion to Okhotny Promenade, Tver Street (today Gorky Street) was hung with red panels, flowers, and posters. On the fence surrounding the telegraph construction site, the young artists Lakov and Grünberg had painted a frieze consisting of several compositions in shades of carmine, green, black and gray, joined by the overall theme of "The Birth of the New World."

The Stenberg brothers played an important role in Soviet decorative art. On

S. MERKUROV, monument to the memory of K. Tumiriazev, 1923.

the building of the Soviet of the Economy, their decoration used Russian folk-art motifs. For the Central Post Office, they had designed asymmetrical compositions in which the emblems of the postal service and telegraph stood out in relief against the building's facades. Colossal plaster sculptures were used to embellish the building of the Maritime and River Transportation Authority; the sculptures represented a worker and a sailor.

Other cities were also the sites of similar festivities in honor of the first anniversary of the Revolution.

Rabinovitch, Lecht, and Tychler worked in Kiev and Kharkov; Labass and Lakov in Ekaterinburg; Krylov, Chegal, Ovsiannikov, and Pokarzhevsky in Tula; Guerassimov in Kozlov; Savinov, Utkin, Kravtchenko, Konstantinov, and Karev in Saratov; Fechin, Gavrilov, and Chebotarev in Kazan; Dmitriev in Minsk; Sudeikin, Arapov, and Aladzhalov in Baku; Skulme in Riga; and in Vitebsk, Dobuzhinsky, Pen, Falk, Malevitch, Lissitsky, and Chagall, as well as the young "left wing" artists of the OuNOVIS group.[3]

D. OSSIPOV, obelisk on Sovietsky Square in Moscow, first anniversary of the October Revolution.

Their means were restricted and the materials used were cheap. At the very best, artists had calico, plywood, plaster at their disposal, and a limited palette of colors. The short-cut to success was via bright and contrasted colors. "The October festivities were a veritable triumph of colors."[4] Mayakovsky's dream of a new proletarian art in which "artists would transform the gray dust of the cities into multicolored rainbows" was coming true.

However, because of work that was either too schematic, formalistic, or hermetic, the revolutionary message was sometimes misunderstood by the people for whom it was intended. The press was the platform for the abundant criticism concerned with this problem.

For example, Piotrovsky wrote: "The columns of participants seemed most often to be perplexed and nonplussed by the red and black cloth which had been draped across Politseysky Bridge by Lebedev; nonplussed by the green veils and orange cubes strewn across Altman's whimsical inventions along the boulevard and the Palace Square column, and nonplussed again by the enormous figures bearing hammers and rifles along the Petrograd piers. . . . It was in 1918 that everyday life and art experienced a brutal rupture."[5]

In April of 1919, a decision was handed down by the Executive Committees of the Moscow and Leningrad Deputy's Soviets forbidding the Futurists to participate in the decoration of cities for festivities of any sort. Several reasons were given, among which was their extremism. Certain projects planned for the May 1st celebrations were cancelled.

The sumptuous festivities of the first anniversary of the Revolution were not repeated. In the following years, because of the civil war, decorations were more modest in conception. Only flags, portraits, flowers and electric bulbs were used.

N. TCHERNYCHEV, decoration of the former duma of Moscow, panel entitled
Science, first anniversary of the October Revolution.
Decoration of the Little Theater of Moscow, first anniversary of the October Revolution.

Float of the International Union of Circus Artists for the Moscow parade on the first anniversary of the October Revolution.

In addition to the decoration of the cities, their streets, and their squares, a great number of parades, theater performances, and concerts were organized.

Automobiles or floats bearing symbolic figures led the parades. The cars belonging to the International Union of Circus Artists and the Metalworkers' Union carried enormous globes symbolizing the earth and illuminated by the light of Communism. In the procession through the Krasnaya Presnia quarter, a float carried peasants and soldiers in chains, with Liberty discarding the chains of slavery. On Red Square, scarecrows symbolizing kulaks were burned. In many quarters of Moscow, emblems of the former regime were burned during the speeches or beneath the fireworks. The demonstrators were both spectators of and actors in the festivities.

Theater performances were held in the streets, parks and public squares. Traditional themes of celebrations and village fairs were used. Poems were read, tight-rope-walkers and jugglers performed. Simultaneously, theater, music and singing circles were being created in factory, school and army barracks clubs, with active participation in carnivals and street fairs. In the years 1919-1920, within the framework of a certain architectural landscape, performances on a grandiose scale took place, employing thousands of people for walk-on roles. A new form of popular theater was born.

The main theme was almost inevitably the October Revolution, the crowning victory of the people's age-old battle for freedom. Only the libretto was written

N. TYRSA, sketch of a decorative panel in Petrograd, first anniversary of the
October Revolution.
N. ALTMAN, sketch for the decoration of the courtyard of the Winter Palace,
of staff headquarters, and of the Alexander Column.

Float for the May 1, 1919, parade in Petrograd. Revolutionary propaganda float,
Alliance between the City and the Country, for the May 1, 1919, parade in Moscow.

in advance; the rest of the text was improvised during rehearsals or even during performances.

Meyerhold's direction of Mayakovsky's *Mistero-Buffo* had a great influence on the evolution of such performances. The theme of the battle between two enemy worlds, the system of images reflecting symbolic social types rather than individual characters, and the synthesis of heroic pathos and caustic satire were elements that could already be distinguished.

The first mass performance, which was almost entirely improvised, was given in Petrograd in 1919. This was *Rejoicing for the February Revolution,* directed by a detachment of Red Army soldiers under the guidance of Vinogradov. One of the most successful evenings occurred on November 7 in Palace Square. Two platforms made up the stage, with the Winter Palace as a backdrop. One of the platforms was occupied by the actors playing the roles of the Czar, Kerensky, the ministers and generals, while workers and soldiers stood on the other platform. Such performances always ended with a grandiose climax.

On May 1, 1920, *The Mystery of Liberated Labor,* based on a scenario by P. Arsky, was given near the Petrograd Stock Exchange. (Directors: Annenkov, Kugel, Maslovskaya; actors: Dobuzhinsky, Annenkov, Shchuko; music by Verlich.) In addition to the professional actors, a great number of soldiers had walk-on parts, making a total of some 2000 participants in all.

L. KHOKHLOVA, caricature of an "emancipated" woman realized for the political carnival, 1929.

The Stock Exchange gate had been adapted in such a way as to allow a change of decor. In the first act, it represented a fortress in which Napoleon, the Pope, a Turkish sultan and other "great men of the world" were feasting and carousing. The people invaded the fortress which gave way to a symbolic "tree of liberty" around which all peoples were united. Red Army soldiers traded their rifles for work tools. Slaves paraded to the music of Chopin's Funeral March. The parade of the oppressors was accompanied by gypsy music, drowned out at times by the *Marseillaise* or other revolutionary songs. During the *Reign of Light,* excerpts from *Lohengrin* were played.

The Stock Exchange served as the theater for an even more grandiose performance, entitled *Toward the Worldwide Commune.* This performance took place on June 19, 1920, in honor of the celebration of the Third International. The commissar was Andreeva, the head director, Mardzhanov, the director of the first part, Petrov, of the second part, Radlov, and of the third part, Soloviev. Music was by Verlich. Altman contributed one of the projects for the decor of the Stock Exchange, with columns draped in red and an assemblage of prisms, diamond-shapes, and other geometrical figures in blue and green. A gilded sphere was to be placed beneath the attic. This extravagant project, however, was not used. The Stock Exchange was decorated with hangings, emblems, and the usual slogans.

This theatrical performance was remarkable for its thorough use of space. Thus, after the scene representing the victory of the Revolution (symbolized by the fall of a two-headed eagle which was replaced by the gilded letters RSFSR [Republic of Russia]), the scenic space grew progressively larger. The Stock Exchange square became the site of great animation—flames shot off from the rostrum's columns, and battles between the Red Army batallions and the enemy were held on illuminated bridges. Authentic canons, automobiles, and torpedo boats floodlighted the scene with projectors from where they were stationed at the Fortress of Peter and Paul. Violet rays of light across a curtain of smoke accentuated the tragedy of the scene in which women wept on the tombs of fallen heroes. The climax occurred with a display of fireworks during the final triumphant procession of the liberated masses.

A. PLITMAN, sketch for the decoration of the courtyard of the Engineers' Palace in Petrograd, first anniversary of the October Revolution.

The use of an authentic site as a theater set was repeated in the production of *Blockade of Russia* on June 20, 1920. The play was organized by Andreev, directed by Radlov, with Fomin supervising the architectural aspect, Khodassevitch the decoration, and Tchekhonin the calligraphy. The play took place on Kamenny Island; the riverbanks had been converted into a huge amphitheater seating 8000 people. The play culminated with a flotilla of ships and a thousand flags of different colors brandished by all the soldiers at once.

On November 7, 1920, another vast production, *The Taking of the Winter Palace,* took place in Petrograd in Uritsky Square. It was organized by Tiomkin, directed collectively by Evreynov, Petrov, and Kugel, with decorations by Annenkov. The action took place on two enormous platforms built on either side of the Staff Headquarters arch. "The provisional government" was represented with a palace decor on one of the platforms, while on the other, soldiers and workers stood against a background of factories and buildings with lighted windows. There were 6000 participants in all. The battle scene took place in silhouette against the illuminated facade of the Winter Palace. At the final moment, a multitude of automobiles appeared with soldiers bearing torches, and the cruiser *Aurora* fired a salvo.

After the civil war, in the years 1922 and 1923, the main theme of the celebrations changed to the struggle to revive industry. Allegorical figures gave way to manufactured products, such as gigantic locomotives, boats, cars, shoes, or pencils. Parade participants carried products, or drove real cars, or carried diagrams.

Toward the middle of the 1920s, festivity decorations were also increasingly centered around political satire. Their targets were capitalists, popes, generals, social democrats, and all the other international enemies of the proletariat, represented by grotesque figures, either flat and cut out in plywood, or in relief. The action took place in short plays given on open trucks.

Float of *The Red Guard* factory for the May 1, 1925, parade in Leningrad.
Stage-set for a theater performance, *The Taking of the Winter Palace*, Palace Square, Petrograd,
third anniversary of the October Revolution.

Decoration of Theater Square in Moscow for May 1, 1921.

Industrial propaganda and political satire were often combined in farcical comedies full of folk humor. Several examples come to mind: highly caricatured representations of the Triple Entente are seated in an enormous rubber shoe produced by The Red Triangle factory; a capitalist crouches under the heel of a gigantic boot produced by The Runner factory; on the burner of The Red Guard factory, a Polish *pan* is being roasted; an immense pair of scissors manufactured by The Bolshevik factory closes on a figure representing international capitalism; the millstones of a mill crush Poincaré and MacDonald; coffins bearing capitalism, alcoholism, religious rites, and so on, are taken to the cemetery. Ilf and Petrov, in their book *The Golden Calf,* mention just such a coffin bearing the inscription, "Death to Bureaucracy."

In these years between 1921 and 1925, the decoration of cities included something new: three-dimensional constructions. The first one was erected on May 1, 1921, on Theater Square in Moscow. It served as a booth for Soviet of the Economy posters.

In 1925, for the eighth anniversary of the Revolution, the main podium on Uritsky Square in Leningrad was a three-dimensional construction representing the Communist Worker's Party boat, which appeared to be floating on a sea of participants. The mast was the Alexandrov Column.

The organization of the celebrations in honor of the tenth anniversary of the Revolution was given particular attention. The main themes were spelled out in slogans, texts, and diagrams, as in the decoration of Tauride Palace by Belogrud. Or they were adapted into decorations such as that of Equality Bridge in Leningrad, realized by Lialin, with three-dimensional constructions representing pylons and such symbolical images as a ruined palace, a toppled two-headed eagle, or the rising sun of Liberty. Trotsky decorated the former Kchessinskaya Palace in Leningrad. He had a tower erected, at the foot of which was a plaster frieze. The theme of this bas-relief was "From Imperialist War to Civil War." Although the composition was classical, the dynamic rhythm was close to that of a poster.

Ivan Fomin's design for the decoration of Insurrection Square was also an attempt to find new forms of expression. The proposed theme was the "abolition of the autocracy," represented by Trubetskoy's monument to Alexander III. Fomin's idea was not to hide the sculpture behind panels but rather to enclose it inside a cage. A spiral tower was to be built next to it, symbolizing the idea of permanent evolution.

Katonin's decoration of Alexander Nevsky Square and Rudnev's decoration of the parade ground also bear witness to the desire to introduce grandiose elements in three dimensions (factory blueprints, cars, blocks).

The 1927 celebrations were based on the achievements of the Soviet govern-

A. OSMIORKIN, panel entitled *The Carpenter,* for the decoration of the theater of the Deputy Workers' Soviet.

E. KATONIN, decoration of
Red Square in Leningrad,
tenth anniversary of the
October Revolution.

ment and of the international working class. The decorators were thus increasingly inclined to use actual examples of industrial products or living emblems. The parade participants wore costumes decorated with a letter; when lined up, they formed the name of a factory.

In 1927, political satire was still in wide use. The workers of the Triokhgornaya Factory in Moscow paraded with the shroud of the international bourgeoisie and the coffin of the Second International. The Rubber Factory was symbolized by an enormous globe in chains. Chinese students carried a dragon that was ten meters long to symbolize the hydra of the counterrevolution in China. A place was reserved in the parade for "champions"—Mussolini, champion of delinquency; Chamberlain, champion of hypocrisy, etc.

A tradition of posters, parades, and theater performances thus came into being. In 1929, for the inauguration of Gorky Park, a parade on a grandiose scale was organized in Moscow. It comprised some fifty floats, using political themes and theater techniques. Many young artists, including Buchelev, Kopzlovskaya, Sevortian, Starodub, Samorodsky, Shchukin, and Kheifits, participated in the preparations directed by I. Rabinovitch. Each float had its own theme. The hold of the "Boat of British Imperialism" was filled with poor immigrants from the colonies; there were also "Capitalist France," decorated by Khokhlova, "Yellow Journalism," decorated by Maguidson, "The Marriage of the Pope and Musso-

I. FOMIN, decoration of Insurrection Square in Leningrad, tenth anniversary of the October Revolution.
N. TOTSKY, decoration of the Kchesinsky Palace in Leningrad, first anniversary of the
October Revolution.

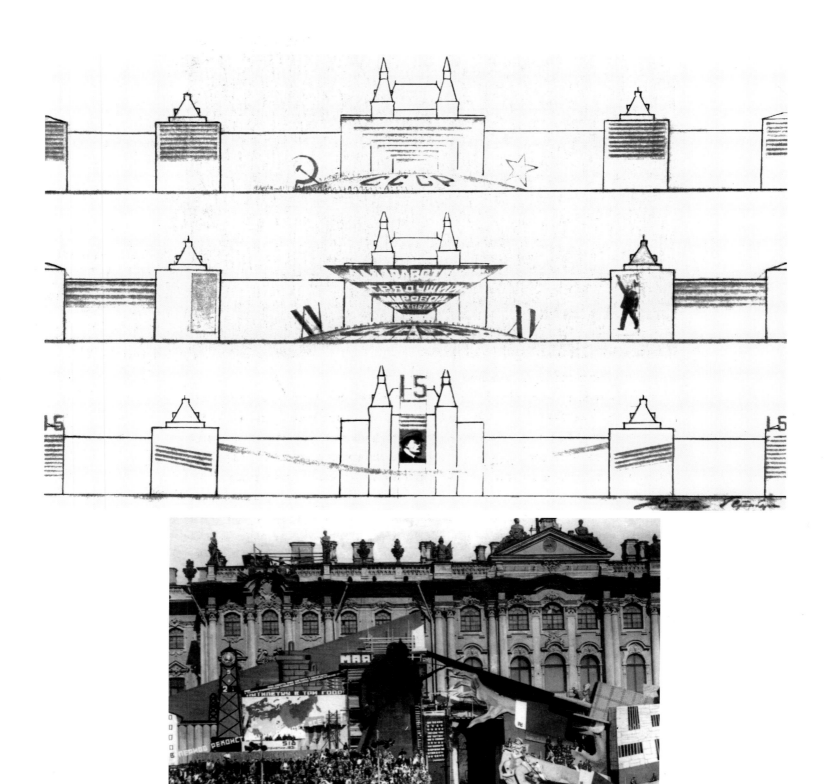

V. STENBERG, G. STENBERG. The decoration of Red Square in
Moscow for the fifteenth anniversary of the October Revolution.
Decoration of a podium on Uritsky Square in Leningrad by the
Plastic Arts section of the Workers' Youth (Plastic Arts of Working Youth) Brigade,
under the direction of M. Brodsky and L. Karateyev, for May 1, 1931.

Carnival in honor of the inauguration of the Central Park of Culture and Leisure in Moscow, decorated by the students at Vhutemas (College of Arts and Crafts) under the direction of I. Rabinovitch, 1929.

lini," also decorated by Maguidson.

On June 8, 1929, in Uritsky Square in Leningrad, Radlov and Khodassevitch directed the play *The Giants' Revue,* which dealt with the theme of success in the city's factories. Once again, this was a production on a grand scale, using a real-life stage set as in the years 1918-1920, with the difference that in the years 1927-1929, gigantic, grotesque marionnettes replaced the actors, and radio replaced the spoken voice.

In honor of the Sixteenth Congress of the Communist Party, a theatrical performance was organized in Moscow's Gorky Park. Romas and Chestakov were responsible for the decor, Radlov for the direction of the play. The entire park plus part of the Moscova served as the stage set. The "actors" were played by gigantic marionnettes, 26 to 32 feet high, which changed shapes during the course of the play. The rubber-balloon kulak struggling with a tractor slowly withered into a pile of rags; the magnificent marionnette representing the Pope exploded in a burst of fireworks. The fascists were represented by gorillas carrying bombs.

At the end of the 1920s and at the beginning of the 1930s, festivities continued to be organized by the same group of artists consisting of the Stenberg brothers, Ladur, Romas, Rublev, Iordansky, Rodyonov, Mussatov, Trochin, and S. Siv in Moscow, and of Brodsky, Karateyev, and Rayevskaya in Leningrad. The improvised decorations of the years 1918-1920 gave way to the professionalism of the years 1925-1935. In May 1933, in the square facing the Bolchoi, Rodionov, Mussatov, and Trochin staged a tableau called "The Success of Industrialization in the

Parade commemorating the first anniversary of the October Revolution.

Soviet Union." They built a gigantic model of a rolling mill in red, black, and white colors. The illusion of molten metal was given by the interplay of blinking lights. To simulate sparks, fireworks went off at the place where the saw bit into the metal. The accompanying music imitated the screech of the saw. A radio speech gave a commentary on the different branches of industry.

It was in 1933, during the celebrations of the Revolution, that film screens appeared for the first time. The central theme of the festivities was the canal linking the Baltic Sea to the Barents Sea. This was illustrated by many different aspects of art—theater, music, literature, cinema.

During the 1930s, the dynamic of color took on a particular significance.

A. MATVEYEV, statue of Karl Marx in Petrograd, 1918. SIPAISKY, statue, Lassimo.

Flagbearing Workers, Uritsky Square, Leningrad, thirteenth anniversary of the
October Revolution.
N. MUSSATOV, B. RODIONOV, N. TROCHIN, decoration of Sverdlov Square,
Moscow, May 1, 1933.

The Stenberg brothers, who decorated Red Square on several different occasions, explained their attraction to the color red and the richness of its tones: "This color creates a new treatment of material and enforces its artistic action. Our decorations are based on the combination of color, calligraphy, and carefully laid out horizontal and vertical surfaces."[6]

In addition, the use of lighting effects was expanded. The committee for the fifteenth anniversary of the Revolution ordered optical equipment, color projectors, illuminated signs over the Moscova, a giant screen for slide projections, and lastly, a monumental illuminated number "15" suspended from a balloon at a height of one thousand feet. On May 1, 1933, Romas and Pigarev decorated Komintern Square in Moscow with an enormous sphere which represented the Earth turning on its axis. Lit by three projectors, the sphere was covered with mirrors whose reflections illuminated the entire square.

During the 1930s, the artists of the Plastic Arts section of the Worker's Union were responsible for both industrial and satirical themes. Their decorative compositions were, however, often overloaded with details which weakened their artistic qualities and diminished their propaganda impact.

On May 1, 1931, in Leningrad, Akichin and Guerassimov of the Plastic Arts section of the Workers' Youth group were able to unite industrial and satirical themes in a composition in which the waters of the Dnieprogres dam swept away grotesque characters representing fascism, capitalism, the Pope, and kulaks.

On May 1, 1932, Liskovitch used the same theme to show a big marionnette made of plywood, representing a capitalist, drowning in the Circular Canal, in Leningrad, against a background of banks and ruined consortiums. During the 1930s, Moor became the head of a group of Moscow decorators. Their specialty was constructions like "The Geneva Merry-Go-Round," with marionnettes representing the Pope and the other participants in the Geneva Conference going round and round. Moor was also responsible for decorating Pretchistenskaya Square (Kropotkinskaya) and the Palace of the Soviets using anti-religious themes, and Malaya Dmitrova Street (Chekhov Street).

At this same time, plywood sculptures also began to be used, representing heroic workers, peasants, and Red Army soldiers. These were simple monumental sculptures, such as *Workers Holding the Banner* on Uritsky Square in Leningrad (1930) or *The International* by Kuznetsov on Red Square in Moscow.

Decorative panels now gave way to immense photographs or photo-montages. Store windows were decorated and used as showcases. In 1932, the stores on Gorky Street in Moscow were decorated with satirical drawings by Moor, Denis, and Efimov. Paintings showing the construction, culture, and history of the Soviet

V. KHODASSEVITCH, E. ENEI. *The Capitalist*. political performance in Leningrad. Tenth anniversary of the October Revolution.

E. LISKOVITCH, caricature on the Obvodny Canal, Leningrad, May 1, 1932.
Celebratory decoration of Insurrection Square, Leningrad, fourteenth anniversary
of the October Revolution.

Detail of the decoration of Revolution Square, Moscow, for the May 1, 1930, festivities.

M. SAMORODSKY, sketch for the decoration of Sverdlov Square, Moscow, for the
eighteenth anniversary of the October Revolution.
Poster, "Kukrynksov," 1941.

Union were also shown. In 1933, the same store windows exhibited models of new buildings, schools, quays, and subway stations. Paintings by famous Soviet artists were exhibited on Kuznetsky Bridge. The second half of the 1930s saw the advent of carnivals, farmer's markets, and village fairs. Gymnastic performances were organized too.

During World War II, revolutionary celebrations expressed the gravity of the events with military parades, aircraft demonstrations, and triumphant fireworks.

During the different stages of its evolution, the decoration of revolutionary celebrations had always been a faithful representation of each epoch as well as a synthesis of the main forms of art.

NOTES

1. We are able to form an idea of what most of these panels looked like thanks to the sketches preserved at the Russian State Museum, the Museum of the Revolution, and the Leningrad Historical Museum. These sketches were published and analyzed in an article by V.P. Tolstoy, "Material for the History of the Art of Propaganda During the Civil War," in the *Information Bulletin of the Institute of Art History of the Academy of Sciences of the Soviet Union* (1953 - N· 3). Also in the book by the same author, *Soviet Monumental Painting* (Moscow, 1958).
2. See V. Kerjentsev, "After the Celebration," in *Art.* 1918, n· 6, p. 3.
3. The most famous project was undoubtedly that of the decoration of a tramway with the slogan, "Work shall be Sovereign." It was realized by Tseitlin in Malevitch's studio for the May 1, 1919, festivities. The asymmetrical composition of geometrical figures in primary colors is characteristic of Suprematism. As for Lissitsky, he created a most interesting and dynamic project for a tribune.
4. See A.A. Sidorov, "Two Years of Russian Art and Artistic Activity," in *Creation.* 1919, N· 10, p. 38.
5. A.I. Piotrovsky, "The Anniversary" in *For the Soviet Theater.* Leningrad, 1925.
6. "The Artists and their Work," *Bulletin of the Central Committee of Artists of the Moscow Soviet Concerning the Organization of Celebrations for the Fifteenth Anniversary of the Revolution.* Moscow, 1932, p. 19.

D. MOOR, decoration of Malaya Dmitrovka, Moscow, May 1, 1932.

V. MOVTCHANISR, tower of the Yakhrole lock on the Moscow canal, 1938.

Lenin Square, Erevan.

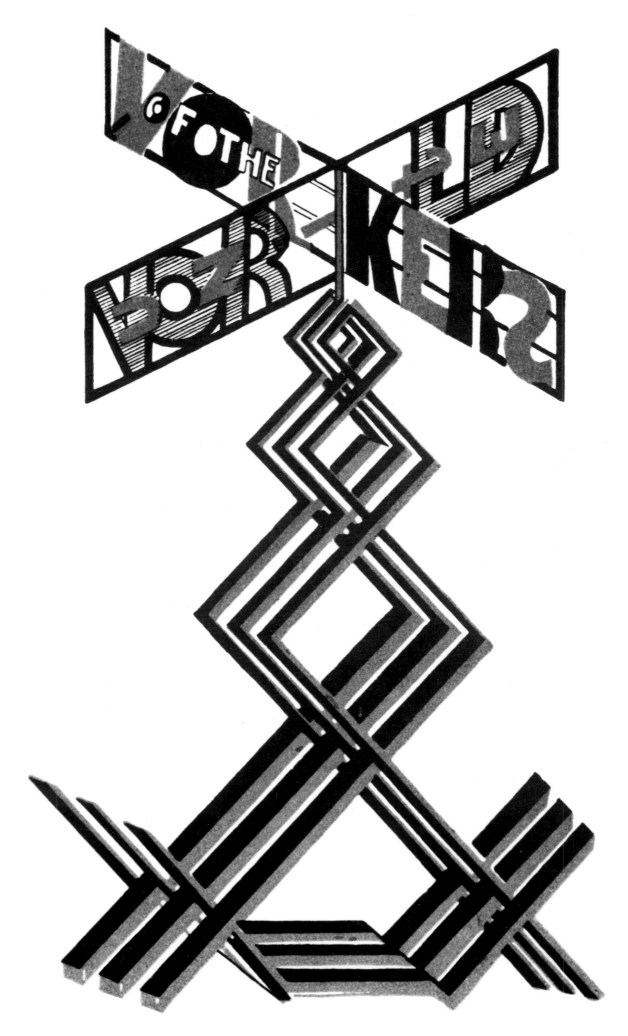

G. KLUCIS, podium for haranguing, 1922.

Exhibitions and Fairs

Placed at the service of propaganda, public relations, and advertising, the art of exhibitions was enriched by contemporary innovations in the fields of architecture and decoration. Dominated by a central theme, exhibitions used dramatic arts and performance techniques, occasionally reinforced by the use of photography, cinema, radio, music, and even of urban parks. Nevertheless, the exhibited object remained the essential factor. It was for this reason that exhibition art went beyond the limits of the decorative arts, proof of its ability to serve as a means of synthesis. During the years 1920–1930, exhibitions of visual arts were not particularly original.[1] In fact, the important goal during these years was to familiarize the public with industrial innovations, automobiles, agricultural equipment, and so on. Naturally, during exhibitions designed to reach a large audience, the role of the artist was of great importance—hence the interest in international exhibitions, exhibitions of the national economy, etc.

The Permanent Exhibition of Industry of the Soviet of the Economy, held in Moscow from 1918 to 1924, was the first exhibition of such importance. It was a strange combination of the old and the new, with scientific innovations presented by archaic means.

In the Mining Industry section, with a decor by Orlov, traditional display cases, glass covers, numerous painted panels (sometimes hung upside down), photographs, and diagrams created a museum-like atmosphere. In several rooms, display cases and booths were arranged in a strictly symmetrical manner.

The walls, ceiling, and tables of the Fabrics of Moscow and Silk Fabrics pavilions were uniformly covered with fabric, as were the mannequins. It was all very boring. It was necessary to invent new types of displays. Only the Agricultural Machines booth had an original presentation. Above the agricultural equipment, the plows, and a small airplane, the map of the electrification of Russia hung next to several slogans. Real objects and symbols were seen side by side, in greater size and with more colorful graphics.

In 1922 and 1923, Soviet Russia participated in a number of international fairs—Koenigsberg, Leipzig, Tallin, Riga, Lyons, Frankfurt, Helsinki—with displays of furs, skins, linen, propaganda porcelain, handicrafts, and industrial products. The Russian booth at the Lyons fair in 1923 and the pavilion at the Riga exhibition, the first in the form of a traditional Russian boat, the second inspired by the architecture of wooden churches, were both decorated with pseudo-Russian motifs dating from before the Revolution. In contrast, the Soviet pavilion at Frankfurt (1923) was innovative both by its architecture and its interior decoration. In 1923, the Exhibition of Agriculture and Industrial Crafts opened in Moscow. Russia, the Ukraine, Bielorussia, the Caucasus, and Central Asia participated [2] in this political and cultural event. This exhibition had been conceived by the Presidium of the Central Executive Committee, and its mission, as formulated by the tenth Congress of the Russian Soviets, was to "display" our fundamental achievements in the domains of the reconstruction, strengthening, and development of agriculture . . . under the direction of the Worker's and Peasant's Force."

The interior architecture of the open-topped booths, scattered over a vast space, was carefully worked out for the first time. According to a plan devised by Joltovsky, the pavilions were arranged here and there on a lawn planted with assorted varieties of plants. This was the central axis, modest for such an immense and colorful exhibition. Each pavilion was remarkable. In the Far East pavilion, a mast with billowing sails and several nomad tents suggested the sea, the taïga, and the Far North. Golossov was responsible for the architecture, Frantsuz for the interior decoration.

Models of ultra-modern factories were exhibited in the Makhorka-Tobacco pavilion (architecture by Melnikov, interior decoration by Frantsuz). Other pavilions, such as The News, The Red Field (interior decoration by Exter, sculpture by Mukhina, architecture by Gladkov), and Dobroliot were arranged as decorative advertising kiosks displaying the latest in modern communications as witnessed by the radio mast and the airplane propeller used as decorative elements. [3]

In contrast, in traditional architecture styles designed by Exter, Nibinsky, the Stenberg brothers, and Gutchtin, the frescoes and bas-reliefs of certain pavilions were used as symbols of agriculture: wind mills, mill wheels, electric motors, geological maps, and pictures showing work in the fields. The facades of the Improvements and Field Cultivation pavilions and the entrance arcade to the Foreign Section (architecture by Shchuko, interior decoration by Exter) were designed in this manner.

The interior decoration was somewhat less interesting. The decorators employed two basic aspects of traditional presentation: the "museum" type and the "store" type, at times suggesting shopping arcades or covered markets. In other pavilions, such as the Far East pavilion, such methods were in direct contrast to the new forms of interior architecture. The reason for this discrepancy was undoubtedly a lack of coordination between independent decorators.

The participation of the USSR in the International Exhibition of Decorative Arts and Modern Industry, held in Paris in 1925, was a watershed in Soviet exhibition art. It is true that the organizers' requirements were clearly stated: "All imitation, copying, or forgery of any type of traditional style will be systematically

N. ALTMAN, sketch for the decoration of the Alexander Column in Petrograd, first anniversary of the October Revolution.

K. MELNIKOV, Makhorka Pavilion, Moscow, 1923.
Right-hand page: A. EXTER, V. MUKHINA, B. GLADKOV, model of the "Izvestia" and
"Krasnoy Nivy" pavilion, Agricultural Exhibition, Moscow, 1923.

excluded. . . . The era of railroads, automobiles, airplanes, and electricity requires new forms . . ."

The Soviet section[4] was located in the Grand Palais, in the USSR Pavilion, as well as inside an arcade and in a dozen kiosks on the Esplanade des Invalides. The USSR pavilion contained a mast bearing the Republic's initials, a kind of "propaganda machine," in Tugenhold's words, of a surprising modernism.[5] The Gossizdat Hall, designed by Rabinovitch in the style of a reading room, was particularly successful. Open books were arranged on shelves and low tables, while the center of the room contained glass display cases with sufficient space around them for the public to circulate freely. This room was a tribute to the 1920s and the pathos of the battle against illiteracy and the struggle of the masses to attain culture. One of the new procedures of exhibition techniques was to use interior architecture to emphasize the ideology intrinsic to the exhibited objects. The decision to arrange the furniture in symmetrical fashion was in accordance with the graphic arts booth built along a central axis, with large panels placed on either side so that the public had a maximum amount of viewing space. Simple lines and colors—red, gray, and black—were employed, and the arrangement of the objects gave a pleasant rhythm to the ensemble.

D. STERENBERG, sketch for a panel for the decoration of the little bridge on the winter canal in Petrograd.

El Lissitsky distinguished himself on two occasions with the Exhibition of Polygraphic Art in Moscow in 1927 and the Journalism Exhibition in Cologne in 1928. An architect, designer, draughtsman, photographer, as well as typographer—and, of course, painter— he also proved to be an excellent organizer. He played a determining role in the creation of the art of exhibitions, inaugurating the profession of exhibition decorator following the success achieved by these two exhibitions.

The Polygraphic Art Exhibition, held in the former central pavilion of the 1923 Soviet of the Economy, was opened to the public in August of 1927. This hexagonal building consisting of vast rectangular and symmetrical rooms, containing chancels, recalled a three-naved basilica.

Determined to create a new organization of space and to neutralize particular architectural elements of the central pavilion, Lissitsky located within the three naves of one of the rooms the History of Typeface and Printing, Graphic Arts, and Production Procedures sections. In order to lessen the effect of the room's gigantic size, the booths reached to only half the ceiling height and were arranged in diagonals, staggered rows, or triangles in order to avoid a rigid symmetry. The beams were hidden by a false ceiling with alveoli, a procedure still used to this day. The booths, furniture, and exhibition panels were mostly rectangular in form, a judicious choice from an aesthetic point of view as well as for technological or functional reasons, since it allowed for a practical and simple installation of a variety of elements. Trapezoidal surfaces and parallelograms were frequently used during

K. MELNIKOV, project for the USSR pavilion at the International Exhibition
of Decorative Arts, Paris, 1925.

EL LISSITSKY, polygraphic industry section at the Polygraphic Exhibition in Moscow, 1927.

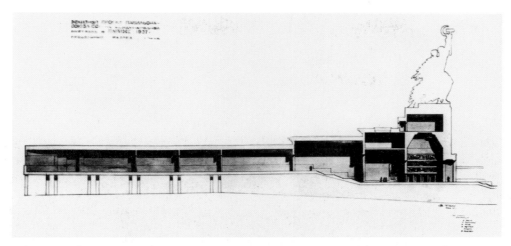

this period in art and architecture (project proposals, blueprints, furniture, graphic arts). Thanks to this exhibition and to the Paris exhibition, new concepts came into use: outdoor constructions, contrasts between the heavy mass of an edifice and the apparent fragility of its base, simplicity of form, painted surfaces replacing draped fabrics.

The following year, the International Journalism Exhibition took place in Cologne. One thousand square meters were set aside for the Soviet Union in the wing of the States pavilion. The team of decorators, directed by Lissitsky, initially intended entirely to renovate this old-fashioned building, but the project was rejected by the organizers. The facade was simply ornamented with the hammer and sickle and the letters USSR, a relatively new procedure at the time.

The trapezoidal interior, equipped with direct and indirect lighting, was well adapted to an exhibition. The decorators broke up the symmetry by dividing

TOP: B. IOFAN, project for the USSR pavilion at the International Exhibition, Paris, 1937. BOTTOM: N. SUETIN, competition project for the second hall of the USSR pavilion at the International Exhibition, Paris, 1937.

EL LISSITSKY, project for the arrow of the mast in the USSR pavilion at the
Press Exhibition, Cologne, 1928.

ALEXEYEV, ALEXEYEVA, sketch for the decoration of Okhotny Ryad,
Moscow, first anniversary of the October Revolution.

the space into zones centered around the most important pieces being shown. These included a monumental photographic frieze as well as a presentation of newspapers, difficult to exhibit, which the decorating team was able to display at its true value. The three-dimensional compositions had such names as The Star or The Sickle and Hammer. The booths themselves were occasionally in the form of a human silhouette, a rotary printing-press, or a capital letter (R for the radio booth, etc.).

Naumov and Teplitsky decorated the Red Army and the Press booth with five convex panels covered with local military newspapers. Each panel was surmounted with the silhouette of an identical red soldier and the newspapers gave the illusion of being rolled directly off the rotary presses, symbols of the mobility of the press and its availability to the masses.

The photographic frieze, realized by Lissitsky and Senkin, evoked life in the USSR. The art of photo-montage was directly inspired from the cinema. Used at first as an advertising technique, it became an important element in political post-

Blueprint of the USSR
pavilion at the Press
Exhibition, Cologne, 1928.

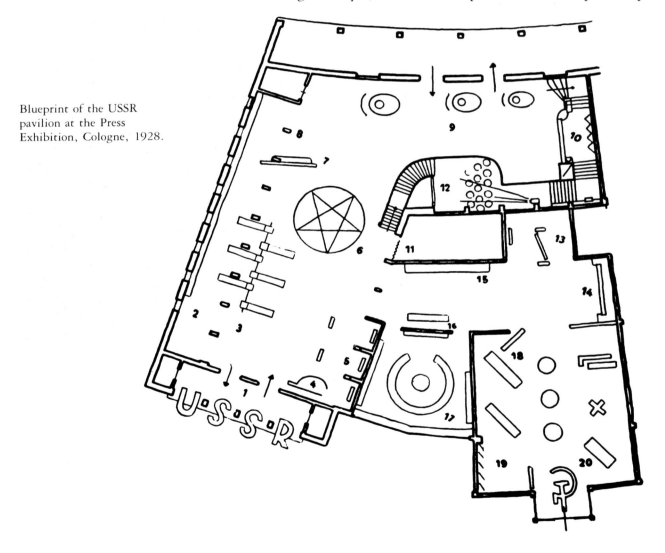

EL LISSITSKY, central hall of the USSR pavilion at the Press Exhibition, Cologne, 1928.

I. RABINOVITCH, government publications room, USSR pavilion, International
Exhibition of Decorative Arts, Paris, 1925.

EL LISSITSKY, lateral section of the USSR pavilion, Press Exhibition, Cologne, 1928.

EL LISSITSKY, S. SENKIN, frieze for the USSR pavilion, Press Exhibition, Cologne, 1928.

A. NAUMOV, L. TEPLITSKY, decoration, *The Red Army and the Press*, USSR pavilion, Press Exhibition, Cologne, 1928.

ers during the 1920s. Thanks to its size (9 ½ × 1 ¼"), to its images that were both static and dynamic, and to the tragic or amusing subject matter, this photomontage entered perfectly into the exhibition context.

Compared to most of the other installations, the Soviet booths turned out to be particularly innovative. Only the Polish and German booths came up to their standard.

Under Lissitsky's direction once again, this new art was given additional opportunities to perfect itself in Stuttgart (Film-Photo, 1929), in Dresden (Hygiene, 1930), and in Leipzig (Furs, 1930).

In the second half of the 1930s, decorators involved in exhibitions began to be replaced. Suetin, whose project for the International Exhibition in Paris of 1937 had been selected, replaced Lissitsky, whose name gradually disappeared from such manifestations. This in itself does not explain the changes that took place in Soviet exhibitions. The arrangement of the exhibition halls altered; there were now the same number of exhibition rooms as subjects being presented. The total surface was calculated in accordance with the exhibition material, and an obligatory itinerary for viewing the exhibits was established. The architects, often forced to conceive an exhibit based only on a project proposal or theme, without knowing where the exhibit would occur nor what materials would be used, created neutral spaces or had to work within the framework of traditional installations, such as successions of rooms. In addition, exhibition furnishings were required to be in keeping with the exhibition and its theme. Booths suddenly became vases or fountains filled with fruit, vegetables, or objects. Shelves were in the form of pyramids or obelisks; decorators resorted to the use of painting, sculpture, and ceramics. The boundary between exhibition art and interior architecture blurred; monumental art (painting, sculpture) replaced innovative interior decoration, and art works increasingly took the place of industrial objects. This can be seen in the Soviet of the Economy exhibition of 1939 in Moscow, where real sheaves of wheat stood next to their replicas in plaster or bronze and where real fruit was piled at the foot of a sculpture representing a farmer.

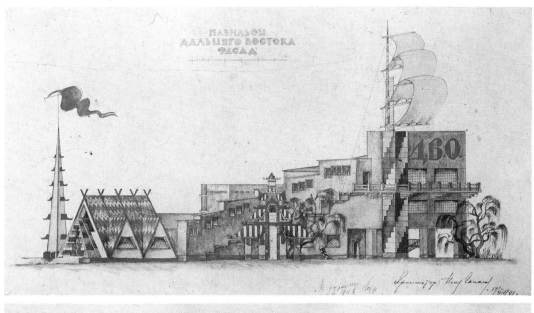

I. GOLOSSOV, project for the Far East pavilion at the Agricultural Exhibition, Moscow, 1923. GOLI, farming podium, Moscow. Gouache and India ink, 1923. GNIMA.

EL LISSITSKY, USSR
pavilion at the Fur
Exhibition, Leipzig, 1930.

B. RODIONOV, V. EFREMOV, decoration, *The Nationalities of the USSR*,
USSR pavilion at the Press Exhibition, Cologne, 1928.
EL LISSITSKY, exhibition, USSR pavilion at the Hygiene Exhibition, Dresden, 1930.

N. SUETIN, I. BUYEV, B. IORDANSKY, entrance hall, USSR pavilion,
International Exhibition, Paris, 1937.

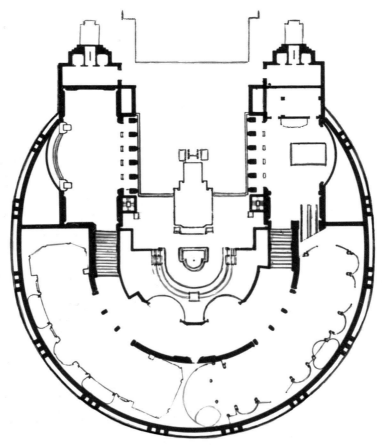

B. IOFAN, K. ALABIAN,
blueprint of the ground floor
of the USSR pavilion,
World's Fair, New York,
1939.

This new orientation required new materials: marble, granite, semi-precious stones, bronze, crystal, stainless steel, carved wood, etc. This principle had been inaugurated in Paris in 1937 with the monumental steel sculpture by Mukhina entitled *The Worker and the Woman Kolhoznik,* a monumentalism which was to illustrate Socialism's victorious achievements.

In 1943 and 1944, a large exhibition took place in Leningrad, retracing "the heroic defense of the city." The exhibition halls, displaying photographs, documents, weapons and some 170 airplanes and tanks, followed a scrupulously chronological order of the events, insisting on their dramatic nature through the use of details such as a daily ration of food or a pyramid of German helmets—accessories used to create an emotional climate. This manner of dramatizing exhibitions was to continue to develop in the USSR in the post-war years.

NOTES

1. The art of exhibiting developed during the 1920s. New methods of exhibiting appeared in museums as of the 1930s, but the experience did not bear fruit as can be seen in the exhibitions held at the Tretyakov Gallery (N. Kovalevskaya, A. Fedorov-Davidov), at the Hermitage (T. Lilova, A. Miller), at the Russian Museum (L. Dindsev), etc.
2. 80,000 objects were exhibited. The participating architects were A. Shchussev, V. Shchuko, N. Lanceray, K. Melnikov, I. Fomin, I. Joltovsky; the painters were A. Exter, B. Johanson, A. Osmiorkin, E. Lissener, A. Rodchenko; the sculptors were I. Chadr, V. Mukhina.
3. The interior decoration of the first two pavilions mentioned was similar to that of theater decors: the ballet with stage set by Exter and music by Scriabin (1922), and the play *The Magnificent Cuckold* with decor by L. Popova (1922).

N. SUETIN, K. RODZHESTVENSKY, exhibition in the circular exhibition
hall, USSR pavilion, New York World's Fair, 1939.

B. VILENSKY, G. GLUCHTCHENKO, Arctic Pavilion at the Agricultural Exhibition, Moscow, 1939.

4. Section commissar: P. Kogan. Artistic director: D. Sterenberg. Organization of the nationalities booth: Ia. Tugenhold, A. Miller. Organization of the Gossizdat booth: I. Rabinovitch. Of the Gostorg booth: D. Sterenberg, A. Rodchenko, A. Poliakov.

At the Grand Palais: architecture booth: D. Sterenberg, B. Ternovets, A. Poliakov. Posters and graphic arts booth: V. Nikolsky, A. Rodchenko. Crafts booth: A. Durnovo. D. Sterenberg. Porcelain booth: D. Arkine. Theater booth: V. Moritz.

In the arcade on the Esplanade des Invalides: The Worker's Club by A. Rodchenko, "The Isba-Library" by Tugenhold, Volter, Poliakov, Sterenberg, Durnovo.

In the kiosks: porcelain, rugs, stamps, books, shawls, fabric, and objects made of ivory, wood, papier-mâché and precious stones. The kiosks were conceived by Melnikov, Exter, Bart, Lebedev.

5. "The Russian Pavilion. . . conceived by the congenial Melnikov, was the confirmation of the aesthetic concepts referred to as 'new tendencies' in the arrangement of exhibition space. Soviet Russia had nothing to sell at the Paris Exhibition; it was interested only in propagating its social ideas and political system, at the expense of commercial interests. . ." in Aloi, R. *Esposizioni architettura-allestimenti*. Milan, 1960, p. XLIII.

"Dobroliot" pavilion at the Exhibition of Agricultural and Traditional Handicrafts, Moscow, 1923.

EL LISSITSKY, entrance hall, USSR pavilion, Hygiene Exhibition, Dresden, 1930.
EL LISSITSKY, USSR pavilion, Fur Exhibition, Leipzig, 1930.

N. SUETIN, USSR pavilion, International Exhibition, Paris, 1937.

N. SUETIN, poster for the exhibition on the heroic defense of Leningrad.
Diorama, *View of the Nevsky.* 1943-1944.

N. SUETIN, trophies hall at the exhibition on the heroic defense of Leningrad, 1943-1944.
N. SUETIN, main hall of the exhibition on the heroic defense of Leningrad, 1943-1944.

B. KUSTODIEV, wall calendar, 1926.

Graphic Arts

Applied graphic art, a cross between graphic art and applied decorative art, covered a diversity of products ranging from theater posters to match boxes. These objects of everyday life were sometimes printed in millions of copies. The functional aspect of the graphic arts made them ideally adaptable to advertising and even to propaganda. In addition, applied graphic art was an important factor in forming public taste. Since this little-studied artistic genre possesses no method of classification nor any clear terminology, we will try to clarify here its basic typographical groups.

The largest sector was that of industrial graphic art, which included posters, advertising leaflets, commercial advertising in the press, labels, catalogs, prospectuses, and wrapping paper.

Theater advertising was another important sector. This included posters for films, exhibitions, theater, and sports events, as well as theater programs and tickets.

Graphic art in the domain of tourism was similar to commercial and theater advertising. It dealt with poster, road maps, suitcase stickers, and transportation maps and schedules.

Another important sector was that of government stationery or official graphic art. This sector included bank notes, bonds, lottery tickets, diplomas, stamps, envelopes, postcards, and postal forms, as well as badges, decorations, and insignias.

Also included in the applied graphic arts were calendars, playing cards, children's games, and educational posters.

Nor was this an isolated artistic genre. It included political posters and designing.

Extremely active immediately after the Revolution, Soviet graphic art underwent periods of greater and lesser intensity according to social and political events. Artists tended to be more involved with theater advertising than with industrial graphic art. At the beginning of the century, artists such as Bakst, Bilibin, Vrubel, Serov, Lanceray and Dobuzhinsky created extraordinary advertising posters.

In March of 1917, a poster competition was organized for the launching of "Liberty Loans." The jury, presided over by Maxim Gorky, selected Kustodiev's project representing a peasant-soldier holding a rifle and surrounded by a crowd of people. But it was after October 1917 that this art form began to be widely used.

Its qualities were ideal for the propagation of the ideas of the Soviet government and for the education of the working people. Equally urgent was the replacement of money and stamps bearing the Czar's portrait. All sorts of revolutionary emblems—standards, banners, streamers—were created spontaneously, the most popular being the plow and the hammer symbolizing the union of workers and peasants. This emblem, based on a design by Khodassevitch in 1918, was used on the Red Army star and on demonstrators' buttonholes. The emblem of the hammer and sickle was created by Kamzolkin for the May 1918 celebrations. In June of the same year, the Commissars' Soviet ratified the Republic of Russia's emblem proposal, which had the hammer and the sickle joined in the center. The sword was eliminated on Lenin's recommendation.

The twenty and forty ruble bills issued by the Provisional Government were replaced by the first bank notes issued by the Soviet bank. These were designed by the Goznak artists, organized along the same lines as the Czarist Press. The People's Commissariat on Education organized a design competition for postal stamps, the Sovnarkom seal, and ruble coins. A number of artists applied, including Altman, Lebedeva, and Tchekhonin. Two new stamps were issued—a brown thirty-five kopeck stamp and a blue seventy kopeck stamp—designed by Zarinch and Ksidias, showing the fall of the old world in a style similar to stamps designed by Lanceray in 1913.

In 1922, another contest was launched for the fifth anniversary of the Soviet State. The theme for the stamps was the victory of work. Dubassov's proposal, showing a worker in the process of engraving 1917–1922 RSFSR on a metal plate, was selected.

Among the most successful projects for stamps during the 1920s were the series issued for the first Agriculture and Crafts Exhibition in 1923, realized by Pachkov; the stamps in honor of Lenin at the time of his death, realized by Dubassov in January 1924, and for the first anniversary of his death, by Zavialov; and lastly, those commemorating the bicentennial of the Academy of Sciences, realized by Alexeev in 1925. In 1922, the Goznak commissioned Chadr to realize the busts of a worker, a peasant, and a soldier, for reproduction on bank notes, bonds, and stamps.

At this time, labels and packages of formerly privately owned firms continued to be printed. Little by little, however, these too were transformed into a means of propaganda. Candy wrappers represented the heroes of the proletariat, and Lenin and Marx were reproduced on the wrappers of Jubilee Candies. In 1924, Mayakovsky designed a candy wrapper for Red Star caramels with satirical drawings and a brief text; in 1920, Elkin decorated a calendar with Marx's portrait.

Film posters were conceived and printed in government or privately-owned workshops. The most interesting were, without a doubt, those designed by Maya-

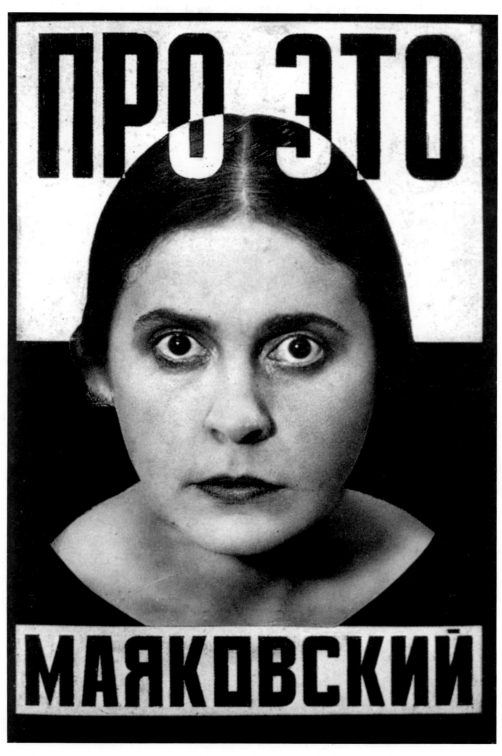

A. RODCHENKO, bookcover for *Of This* by V. Mayakovsky, 6 x 9″ (15 x 23 cm), Moscow, 1923.

A. DEINEKA, poster for the newspaper *Dayoch*, 1929.

S. **TCHEKHONIN**, poster for the Sixth Nijni Novgorod Fair, 1927.

P. STRAKHOV-BRASLOVSKY, poster, 41 x 29″ (105
x 73 cm), *Vladimir Ulyanov Lenin*, 1924-1934.
G. KLUCIS, poster, 57 x 41″ (145 x 104 cm), *The
Nation Must Know Who Its Heroes Are*, 1931.

D. MOOR, military propaganda poster, *The Solemn Vow*.
D. MOOR, military propaganda poster, *The Alert*.

V. STENBERG and G. STENBERG, film poster for *The Decembrists*, 1927.

kovsky, such as *He Wasn't Born for Money,* a film in which Mayakovsky also played the leading role, and the posters by Svarog for *Condensation* (1918) and Apsit for *The Maid of Orleans* (1919). From 1920 on, the Soviet of the Trade Unions organized the first competition of union emblems; the participants included Petrov-Vodkin, Benois, Dobuzhinsky, Tchekhonin, and Favorsky. Some of these projects were exhibited in Moscow in 1921. That same year, the NEP was launched, and it was thus that, thanks to nationalized, private, and cooperative industry and commerce, Soviet graphic art underwent significant development. Labels, packages, advertising posters and stamps were produced in great amounts, even, at times, in a pre-Revolutionary "petit bourgeois" style such as that representing three scantily dressed "graces" on a label commissioned from Samokich-Sudovskaya by the private chinchona firm, Kazimi.

Simultaneously, the avant-garde work of such artists as Moor, Iuon, Bilibin, Roerberg, Mitrokhin, Deyneka, and Lebedev, and Narbut in the Ukraine, continued to flourish. Of the old generation, Kustodiev worked with the most intensity. A painter, engraver, and illustrator, he also designed advertising and theater posters, calendars, stamps, soap labels, and notebook covers, as well as illustrations for fashion magazines. His palette was always highly concentrated, the drawings compact and precise, the compositions clear and decorative. In order to improve the technical and artistic qualities of commercial and industrial advertising, the Central Administration of Industry and the Soviet of the Economy created a special commission designed to attract leading artists and to make advertising more plausible.

Most of the officially printed products were designed by Gruzenberg, a talented architect and artist. His drawings in Indian ink, suggestive of woodcuts, represented attributes of work or symbols of the appropriate institution. Their goal was to allow the uneducated masses to grasp their significance. Pudovkin, who was not yet the renowned filmmaker he was to become, participated on official document projects such as those printed by the People's Commissariat for Health. Gruzenberg also designed stamps, advertising posters, and silver and copper coins. His work was distinguished by its artistic finesse and by a perfected and classical composition. Favorsky, Piskarev, Ilin, and Kravchenko specialized in designs for diplomas, invitation cards, exhibition invitations, different sorts of stamps, and book covers. Ilin's style was characterized by the use of various sorts of calligraphy, employing all the resources of typography. Numerous publishing houses and volunteer associations printed calendars each year. The ones designed by Kustodiev were extremely colorful, while Mitrokhin, Ostrumova-Lebedeva and Gontcharova also produced fine work in this genre. Iakovlev and Kulikov specialized in children's calendars. Advertising posters, however, marked a high point in Soviet graphic art during the 1920s. Such posters owed their inspiration

G. BORISSOV, N. PRUSSAKOV, poster for the film by Boris Barnet,
The House on Trubnaya Square, 53 x 37 1/2" (135 x 95 cm), 1928.

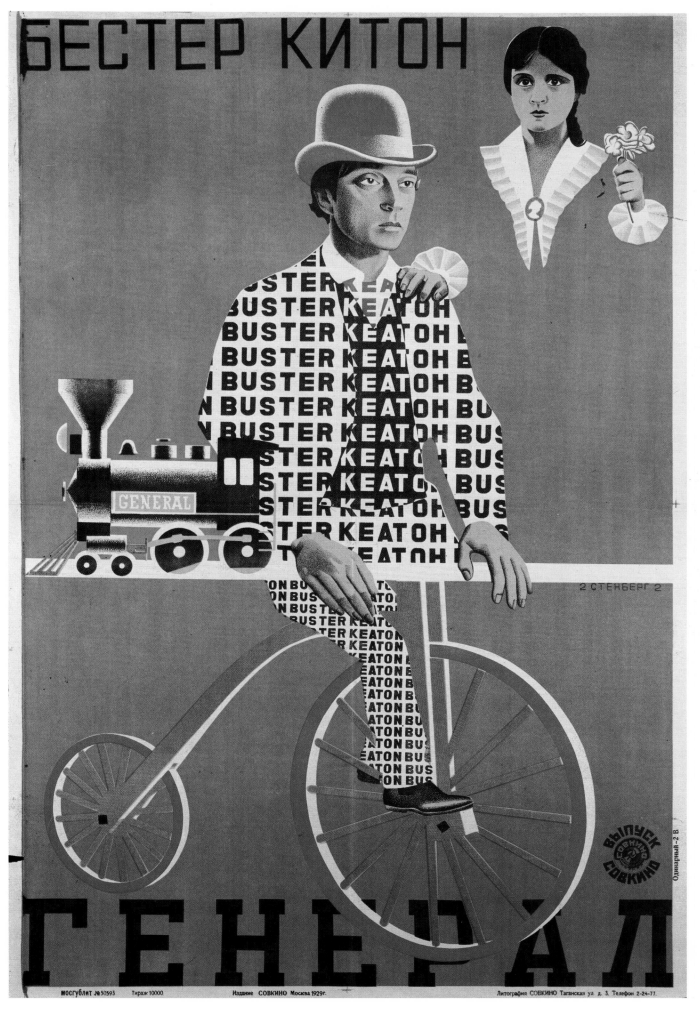

V. STENBERG, G. STENBERG, film poster for *The Mechanic of the "General"* with Buster Keaton.

to Mayakovsky, who was convinced that this was the surest means of influencing the masses. In collaboration with Rodchenko, Stepanova, and Lavinsky, he added poetic texts to posters. In 1933, he created several famous advertising campaigns for Mosselprom ("Nowhere Else Like Mosselprom"), for Resinotrust ("A Better Nipple Can't Be Found—I'll Suck On it Still When I am Old"), and for Gossizdat. These posters were usually executed in two or three colors, with lines of great simplicity and "hatched" calligraphy. Photographs or photomontages were occasionally used. Mayakovsky and Stepanova designed a poster that was both political and promotional for the Gossizdat, which announced that "Educated men will better the lives of the peasants—with Gossizdat manuals, educate your children!" Such efforts coincided with the cultural revolution. Mayakovsky's talent had already been recognized outside of the Soviet Union; in 1925, he received the silver medal of the International Exhibition of the Decorative Arts and Modern Industry in Paris.

Rodchenko, Lissitsky, and Klucis played an active role in the upsurge of advertising posters in the 1920s. Photomontages were readily integrated into their designs, allowing a maximum amount of real material within the limited space of the poster, while the composition's originality reinforced the information being presented.

Deyneka also designed a number of posters, including one for the worker's magazine *Give!* in 1929. The severe lines of the industrial constructions and the rhythmical repetition of the word *Give!* raised up by cranes and seeming to move out toward the spectator gave this poster a remarkable energy and "industrial romanticism."

Among the most successful theater posters is the one realized by Kustodiev in 1926 for *The Flea* at the Grand Theater in Leningrad. This humorous poster showed a general with an enormous head, a flea for his epaulette and, in place of his stripes, the title of the play.

In the middle of the 1920s, a number of artists worked for the Goskino designing film posters. Eisenstein, Vertov, Pudovkin and Dovzhenko were the influential filmmakers of the period, and the posters often revealed the content of the film, such as the one by Lavinsky for *The Battleship Potemkin* in 1925 or by the Stenberg brothers and Ruklevsky for the latter's film, *October,* in 1927. The Stenberg brothers were the authors of a remarkable series of works, in particular two posters for the film *The Mechanic of the "General,"* for the second national circus *Negro-Operetta* and for the music-hall poster of *Where the Glaciers Are.*

This aspect of graphic art became so popular that in 1925 the first exhibitions of film posters were held in Moscow. In 1927, two important exhibitions were held simultaneously, The Graphic Arts in the USSR, in Leningrad, and the Na-

V. STENBERG and G. STENBERG, film poster, *La Parisienne*. 1927.

A. KUPRIN, sketch for a panel, *Art,* for the decoration of the Nezlobin Theater in Moscow, first anniversary of the October Revolution.

V. and G. STENBERG, film poster, 42 x 28″ (107 x 71 cm),
for *The Eleventh*, 1928.
A. NAUMOV, poster, 34 x 50″ (87 x 128 cm), for the film by G.
Fitzmaurice, *Bella Donna*, 1927.

Envelope back with advertising proclaiming the advantages of the Zouev Club.
V. MAYAKOVSKY, candy wrapper, 1924.

tional Polygraphic Exhibitions in Moscow.

We should not forget the active role played by the Mosselprom in the launching of the applied graphic arts in the USSR. At the end of the 1920s, Iuon was head of the artistic bureau, and we know from his notes[1] that work conditions were particularly difficult: paper, cardboard, and paint were hard to come by. Nevertheless, the Mosselprom's artistic bureau left its imprint on the graphic arts thanks to the calligraphy used for hundreds of different labels and packages which reflected Soviet life, culture, events: "The Migration of the Stars," "Krassin's Polar Expedition," "The Expedition to Pamir," "The Pioneer," "The International," "The Peoples of Siberia," etc.

In the 1930s, priority was given to the development of heavy industry, to the detriment of light industry. One of the results was the reduction of work in the applied graphic arts. The only aspect that persisted during these years was advertising for export articles.

A Bureau of Commercial Propaganda was created in 1929 to study, among other things, the experiences of capitalist countries. It is obvious that the absence of advertising in the domain of exportation would have condemned Soviet foreign trade. This new genre drew such artists as Igumnov, Lazusky, and Mansurov, Zhukov and Fomina, who realized a series of posters for the Intourist travel agency entitled *The Caucasus, Winter in the USSR, Leningrad.* The Mosselprom artistic bureau was replaced by the Reklampitcheprom artistic collective consisting of Pobedinsky, Sakharov, A. and B. Zelinsky, Andready, and others.

Film poster art was still going strong. The most interesting work from this period was by Pimenov (*Ball of Tallow,* 1934, *The New Gulliver,* 1935, *The Wedding,* 1936) and Kukryniksov (*Maxim's Youth,* 1935). Belsky's poster for the film *Tchapayev* symbolizes even today the civil war. Zelinsky's poster for *Volga-Volga* also had its hour of glory.

The postage stamps of the 1930s were remarkable for their lack of originality. Since the theme, that of industry, was invariably the same, artistic symbols and metaphors disappeared almost entirely. Only Gan's anti-war series and the stamps issued for the Congress of Iranian Art, designed by Zavialov, were of any interest. During the war, the best series of stamps were those representing medals and decorations of the USSR, designed by A. Mandrussov in the years 1943-1945.

Graphic arts in the nineteen-forties were intended to bolster patriotic feeling: tickets for exhibitions of artists returning from the front, cigarette packages (*Attack!, Tanks, The Red Star*), ersatz rations for soldiers (with anti-Hitler caricatures by Kukryniksov, accompanied by satirical verses by Marchak), information bulletins for the population (Dobroklonsky on the curfew), etc. All such work was real-

A. KRAVTCHENKO, invitation, 1927.

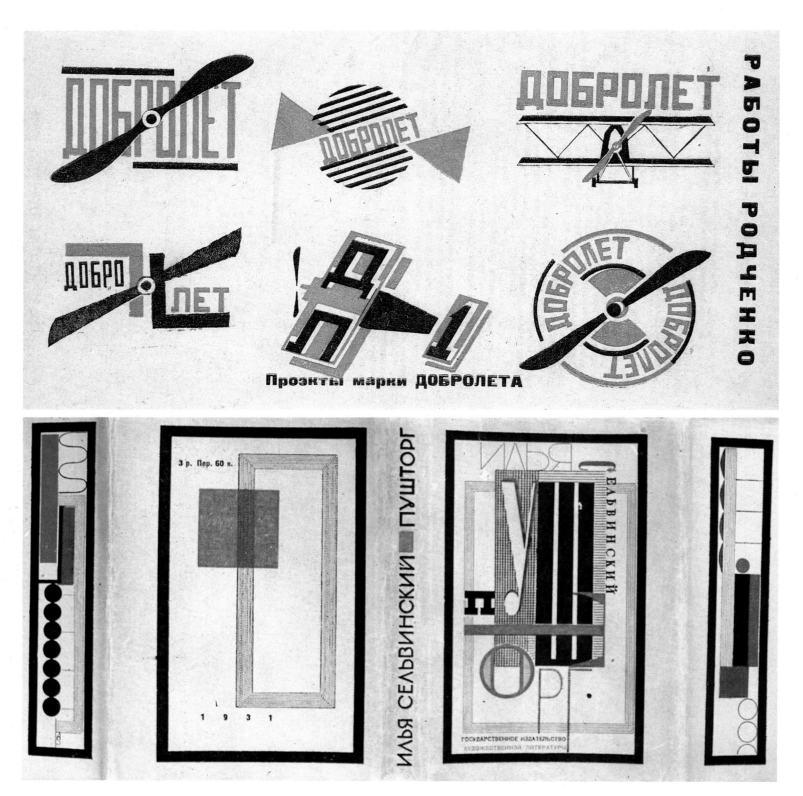

A. RODCHENKO, proposals of logotypes for Dobroliet airlines, reproduced in
Lef, no. 2, 1923. S. TELINGATER, bookcover for the novel *The Fur Counter* by
I. Selvinsky, 5 1/2 x 7 3/4″ (13.7 x 20 cm), Moscow-Leningrad, 1931.

I. SIMAKOV, propaganda poster, *Remember the Hungry*. Magazine cover, *Kasnia Niva*. 1926.

ized by Goznak (State Graphics) artists.

In 1963, the first National Exhibition of Soviet Applied Graphic Art was held in Moscow. The artistic qualities of the graphic arts were at last given the honors which they deserved.

NOTES

1. Iuon, K.F. *On Art.* vol. 2, Moscow, 1959, pp. 190-191.

Cinema magazines, 1926, 1927, 1928.

M. DOBROKLONSKY, *The Target for Killing the Enemy*, leaflet published by the Revolutionary Propaganda Committee of Moscow and by the Artists' Union of the USSR, 1941.

A. RODCHENKO, bookcovers, 5 x 7″ (13 x 18 cm), for a detective novel in ten episodes by Marietta Chaginian (alias Jim Dollar), *Miss Mend or a Yankee in Petrograd*, Moscow, 1924, from left to right: *The Mystery of the Mark, The Challenge is Sent, The Corpse in the Hold, Radio-City, For and Against, The Black Hand, Police Genius, The Yankees Arrive, The Explosion of the Soviet.*

Cyrillic alphabet, text, and lithographs by V. MAYAKOVSKY, 1920.

I. NIVINSKY, advertising poster in favor of newspapers, *Subscribe to the Daily Newspaper Izvestia, to the Weekly Krasnia Niva and the Monthly Novy Mir*, 1924.

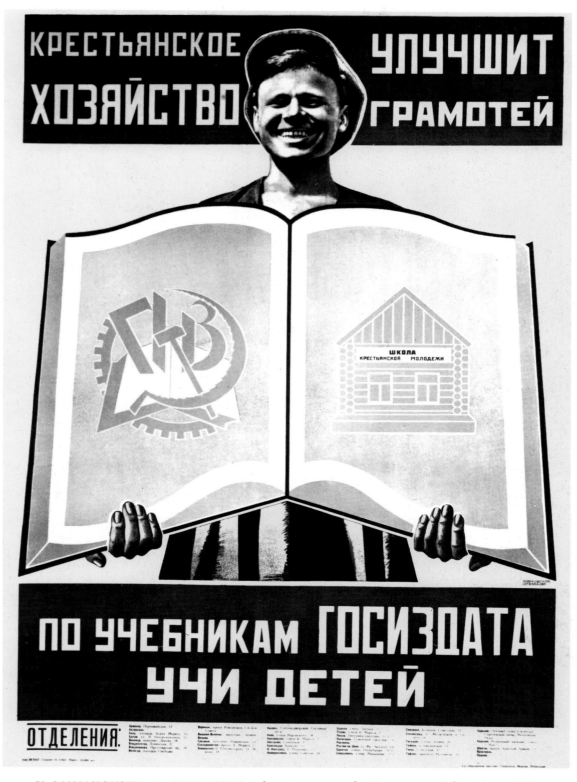

V. MAYAKOVSKY, V. STEPANOVA, advertising poster for Government Publications, 1925.

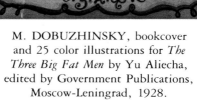

M. DOBUZHINSKY, bookcover
and 25 color illustrations for *The
Three Big Fat Men* by Yu Aliecha,
edited by Government Publications,
Moscow-Leningrad, 1928.

ЭСКИМОС — ШАМАН

119

Six Masks, drawings by V. ERMOLAYEVA, Leningrad, 1930.

Граждане!
берегитесь воров:—
лишившись денег, вы
теряете возможность
приобрести журнал

СМЕХАЧ

цена 15 коп.

БЛОХА

ГОС. БОЛЬШОЙ ДРАМ. ТЕАТР. ФОНТАНКА 65.

SCHMACKHAFT! NAHRHAFT!
GEFRORENE UND LEBENDE
FISCHE AUS DER USSR

100 g FLEISCH VON FRISCHEN FISCHEN ENTHALTEN: (IN GRAMM)					
	FEUCHTIGKEIT	EIWEISS	FETTE	SALZE	KALORIEN
1 KARPFEN	79,0	18,0	2,0	1,1	92,0
2 ZANDER	80,0	18,0	0,5	1,3	79,0
3 HECHT	80,0	18,0	0,5	1,0	79,0

ПЫШКА

художественный
ФИЛЬМ
по Г. мопассану

режиссер
М. РОММ

A. RODCHENKO, cover for the book by the Constructivist Literary Center, *Business*, 5 1/2 x 9″ (13.8 x 22.9 cm), Moscow, 1929. Left-hand page: A. RADAKOV, advertising poster for the newspaper *Smekhatch*. B. KUSTODIEV, theater poster for *The Flea* at the Main Dramatic Theater of Leningrad, 1926. S. IGUMNOV, advertisement boasting the merits of fish imported from the USSR. IOU PIMENOV, poster for the film *Ball of Tallow*. 1934.

N. TIMOFIEVA, sketch for a theater costume, 1925. V.
LEBEDEV, poster demonstrating by its graphic design the use
of Suprematism in popular polygraphic realizations.

A. VESNIN, sketch for a poster for a performance given at the Chamber Music Theater,
Phaedra, gouache on paper, 1922. GNIMA.

V. LEBEDEV, poster, 37 1/2 x 30" (95 x 76.2 cm), 1921.

V. FAVORSKY, engraving in memory of the October Revolution, Ksilogradia, 1928. V. FAVORSKY, engraving in memory of the outstanding events of the years 1919, 1920, and 1921.

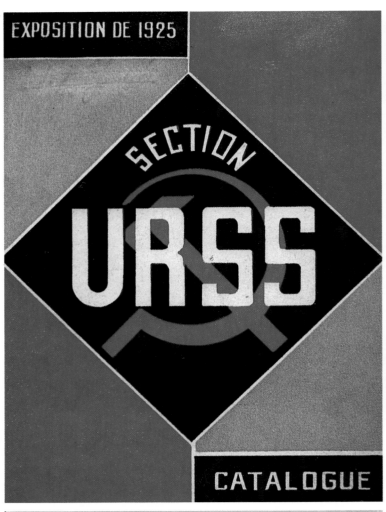

EXPOSITION DE 1925

SECTION

URSS

CATALOGUE

1924

K
U
N
S
T

ISM

US
US
US
US
US
US
US
US
US
US
US
US
US
US

FILM
KONSTRUKTIV
VER
PROUN
KOMPRESSION
MERZ
NEOPLASTIZ
PUR
DADA
SIMULTAN
SUPREMAT
METAPHYSIK
ABSTRAKTIV
KUB
FUTUR
EXPRESSION

1914

А. КРУЧЕНЫХ

ПРИЕМЫ
ЛЕНИНСКОЙ
РЕЧИ

Москва—1928 г.

3-е ИЗДАНИЕ
Издат-во Всероссийского Союза Поэтов

Д. Бурлюк.   С. Третьяков.
Т. Толстая.   С. Рафалович.

БУКА
РУССКОЙ
ЛИТЕРАТУРЫ

МОСКВА, 1923 г.

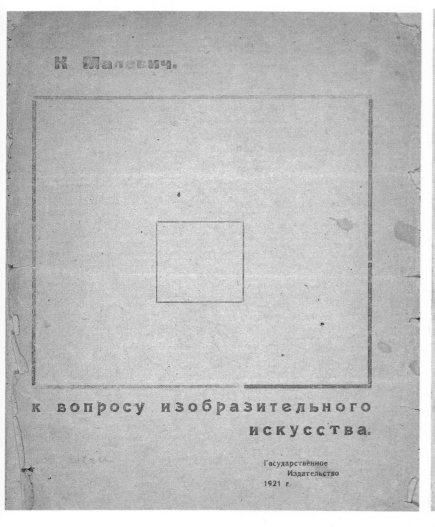

K. MALEVITCH, bookcover and text, *Questions Concerning the Visual Arts,* 1921.
EL LISSITSKY, illustrated book, 9 x 11″ (22.7 x 27.8 cm), *Concerning Two Squares,* Vitebsk, 1920, printed in Berlin in 1922. Left-hand page: A. RODCHENKO, bookcover, 5 x 6 1/2″ (13 x 17 cm), of the *Catalogue of the Soviet Section,* Exhibition of Decorative Arts, Paris, 1925. EL LISSITSKY, bookcover, 8 x 10 1/4″ (20.4 x 26 cm), *The Isms of Art* by El Lissitsky and Hans Arp, 1925. G. KLUCIS, bookcover, *The Processes of Lenin's Oratory Art* by A. Krutchonykh, 5 1/4 x 7″ (13.3 x 17.4 cm), Moscow, 1928. Cover art by N. NAGORSKAYA, *The Bogeyman of Russian Literature,* drawing by Kliun, Moscow, 1923.

Postage stamps: I. DUBASSOV, *Commemorating the Jubilee*, 1922. *Portrait of V. Lenin*, 1924. *The Children's Committee of the V.T.S.I.K.* (Central Executive Committee of Russia), circa 1920. *For the Civil War Wounded*, Georgia, circa 1920. *Ukrkymvozdukh*, aid to the airforce flottila, circa 1920. G. PACHKOV, *Exhibition of Agriculture and Traditional Handicrafts*, 1923.

A. RODCHENKO, bookcover, 8 x 10 1/2″ (20 x 27 cm), of the collective work,
Decorative and Industrial Art in the USSR, published during the
Exhibition of Decorative Arts, Paris, 1925.

S. TELINGATER, bookcover for *Loud and Strong* by
Mayakovsky, 4 3/4 x 7 1/4″ (12.2 x 18.7 cm), Moscow-Leningrad,
1931. A. RODCHENKO, bookcover for the magazine *Lef, The Left Front*,
6 x 9 1/4″ (15.5 x 23.5 cm), Moscow, 1923-1925.

Mayakovsky's Youth, book by P. Kamensky, Constructivist bookcover, anonymous, 1931.

A. RODCHENKO, cover, 5 x 7″ (13 x 17.5 cm), of a poetry collection by S.
Tretyako, *The Wordary*, Moscow, 1929.

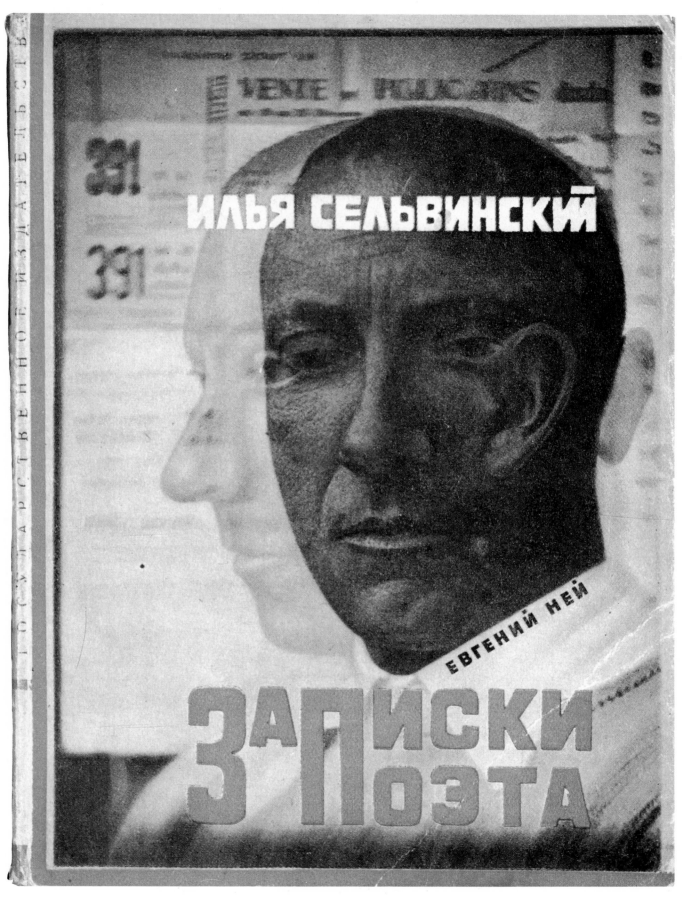

EL LISSITSKY, bookcover, 5 x 6 3/4″ (12.5 x 17.4 cm) *Notes by a Poet,* by I.
Selvinsky, Moscow-Leningrad, 1928.

A. RODCHENKO, cover, 6 x 10 3/4″ (15.5 x 27.5 cm), of the review *New Lef,*
1927-1928. A. LAVINSKY, cover, 6 x 8 3/4″ (15.2 x 22.4 cm), of the book by
O. Brik, *She's Not a Fellow Traveler,* Moscow-Petrograd, 1923.

V. KULAGUINA-KLUCIS, cover, 5 1/2 x 7″ (13.9 x 18 cm), of the book by
A. Krutchonykh, *Transrational Language*, Moscow, 1925.

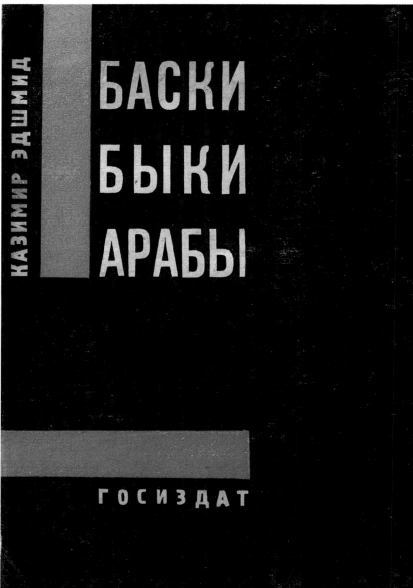

F. TAGUIROVA, cover of the book by K. Edchmidt,
Basques, Arab Bulls, Government Publications,
Moscow-Leningrad, 1929. V. and G. STENBERG,
cover 5 1/4 x 6 3/4″ (13.4 x 17.3 cm) of the book by
A. Pushkin, *The Kamerny Theater,* Government
Publications, Moscow-Leningrad, 1927.

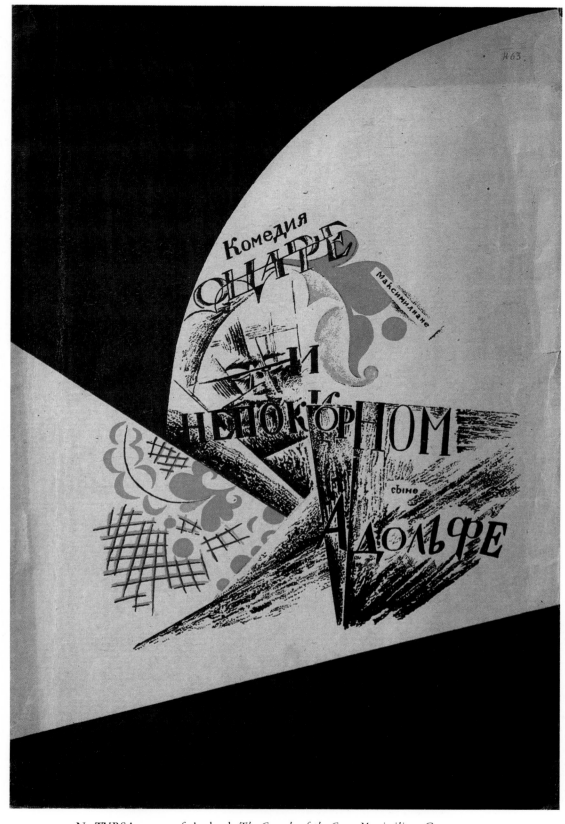

N. TYRSA, cover of the book *The Comedy of the Czar Maximilian*, Government
Publications, Moscow, 1921.

A. EXTER, cover of the book *Picasso and Surroundings*, Moscow, 1917.

I. POPOVA, cover of the exhibition catalogue *5 x 5 = 25*. Cardboard, paper, and collage, 8 1/4 x 6 1/2″ (21 x 16.5 cm) Moscow, 1921. A. VESNIN, cover of the exhibition catalogue *5 x 5 = 25*. Paper, India ink, tempera paints, 8 1/2 x 5″ (22 x 12.5 cm) Moscow, 1921.

A. RODCHENKO, poster for the film by Eisenstein, *The Battleship Potemkin*, 1927.

ART
AND
INDUSTRY

K. MELNIKOV, plate design bearing the emblem of
Makhorka, the Tobacco Union. Gouache on paper, 1923.

Porcelain

Whether in the USSR or in Western Europe, porcelain art was, in the 1920s, a revelation.

In June 1918, by a decree handed down by the Council of People's Commissars, ceramic and glass factories were nationalized. Production suffered from the difficult conditions of the period: there was a shortage of manpower, fuel, raw materials, and means of transportation. In 1918, there were only sixty-eighty glassworks, ten faïence factories, ten factories of oven-proof tableware, and a handful of pottery-works.

At the fourth Congress of Glass and Porcelain Workers, several steps were taken to encourage and develop this art. These included improvement of the artistic training of professionals and skilled workers, the introduction of planning, and the organization of competitions. The first competitions for low-cost decorated tableware were held in 1919 and 1920. In the years 1918-1922, the most productive factory was the National Porcelain Factory. Formerly the Imperial Factory, it became in 1925 the Lomonossov Factory. At the end of the nineteenth century and the beginning of the twentieth, the leading faïence factories were, from a technical point of view, far in advance of their epoch. The porcelain produced at the Imperial Factory and at the Kornilov and Kuznetsov factories was distinguished by its purity and whiteness and by the richness of its colors. Artists invented new techniques; for example, they revived the glazing methods used in Danish porcelain. Another specialty was the reproduction of paintings. In 1913, Lanceray, aided by the sculptors Kuznetsov and N. Danko, was named artistic director of the Imperial Factory. After the Revolution, the workers put into action Lenin's directives concerning art: art was to be used as a medium for propaganda. Lanceray was replaced in 1918 by the designer, ceramist, and enamellist Tchekhonin. As early as September 1918, the Council of the Economy commissioned a large order of dinner services with revolutionary themes from the National Porcelain Factory. Such commissions produced pieces like Tchekhonin's dish *The First Anniversary of the Revolution* and the plate by Altman, *Earth to the Workers*, whose vivid and contrasted colors, design, and calligraphy remind one of posters. The style used for propaganda porcelain was not substantially different from that used for celebration decorations, posters, monumental sculptures created for purposes of propaganda, or the decoration of propaganda trains and boats.

M. LEBEDEVA, serving dish entitled *The International*, with a border design depicting the inhabitants of the republics of the USSR, 1920.

R. WILDE, serving dish entitled *May 1, 1921*, with a central design bearing the hammer and the sickle, 1921.

The team of ceramists and sculptors working at the National Porcelain Factory included Tchekhonin, Kuznetsov, N. and E. Danko, Kobyletskaya, Adamovitch, Wilde, Lebedeva, and Shchekotikhina-Pototskaya. Tchekhonin was able to bring to porcelain a skilled blend of graphism and decoration, touching up the white with strokes of color. Monochrome compositions were rare; on the contrary, Tchekhonin's preference went to thematic ornamentations outlined in gold, the somber colors contrasting with the white background. His ornamentation was often floral in inspiration. Stylized plants and flowers emerged from baskets or bowls to unfurl around the edges of dishes or plates or to merge into inscriptions or human figures. Fantastical and symbolical figures often merged with revolutionary emblems and the realist depiction of true-life events. The best example is undoubtedly the plate in a style reminiscent of Russian icons, depicting a starving woman and her two children *(Famine)*.

Tchekhonin and the other artists at the Factory were also inspired by the new art of revolutionary posters. An excellent example is a set of dishes and plates designed by Tchekhonin, entitled *The Struggle Engenders Its Heroes, Reason Cannot Tolerate Slavery, The Reign of the Workers and Peasants is Unending.*

Tchekhonin was also attentive to calligraphy, which became increasingly decorative; sometimes each letter of a word or of a slogan had its own graphic design. The techniques used by the pottery-makers of Gjel and their large brushstrokes *(agachka)* also served as a source of inspiration.

It is important to remember that during the 1920s, artists worked on undecorated stock dating from before the Revolution. New forms appeared subsequently. Tchekhonin was the first to propose a new form for a tea service dubbed *Narkompros,* one that remained in use until 1953.

Tchekhonin worked side by side with Shchekotikhina-Pototskaya, who excelled in stylized, often grotesque designs, original color schemes, and irregular forms. She was also a skilled set designer. Her classical style, superficially imitative of folk art, contrasted radically with that of Tchekhonin. For Shchekotikhina-Pototskaya, folk art was both the base and the stimulus for her work. From 1918 to 1928, she painted scenes of peasant life and fantastical images in the Russian *lubok* style. In the plate called *The Bell-Ringer,* the old and the revolutionary coexist within the inscription, "Long live the Eighth Soviet Congress," juxtaposed to a human figure directly inspired from the work of Kustodiev.

As for Adamovitch, his preference went to realistic miniatures of landscapes and the old quarters of Petrograd. Subsequently, he worked on depictions of the life of Red Army soldiers and battle scenes. During the 1920s, he opted for propaganda themes, with the result that his style began to resemble that of revolutionary posters. Kobyletskaya and Lebedeva were chiefly interested in revolutionary themes: slogans, the struggle against famine, themes concerning the Cheka and the sixth anniversary of the Revolution.

An amateur of Asiatic miniatures, Vorobievsky's output from 1926 to 1929 depicted true-life events in a precise and original style, dominated by purples, blues, and greens. *The Star* dish and *Persian Flowers* service are good examples of his style.

The work of Chachnik and Suetin drew a certain amount of criticism. Always interested in new techniques, Suetin was particularly attentive to geometric forms and lines, to primary colors and to contrasts between light and dark tones. Geometrical motifs were at times in contradiction with the form of the objects, or the forms themselves were unusual: cubes, spheres, prisms, etc. Suetin's inkwell and Malevitch's teapots, for example, were never mass-produced.

On Gorky's initiative, propaganda porcelain was exhibited for the first time in 1920, in Riga. The genre was also presented at the Helsinki, Berlin, and London fairs in 1922, and Tallin, Lyons, and Stockholm in 1923. It received the gold medal in Paris (1925) and in Monza (1927) and was greeted with enthusiasm by foreign critics. As Lunatcharsky noted, the National Porcelain Factory was always mentioned first when the handicrafts industry was being discussed.

In the early twenties, the Dulev, Dmitrov, and Tver factories were also extremely innovative, but their output was small. Their production did not keep pace with the massive needs of the time. At the Dulev factory, revolutionary motifs were common, as were abstract and sober geometrical motifs, such as the tea service by Kolossov decorated with vertical orange stripes, the hammer and the sickle, and the inscription in black and gold, "USSR-1925."

In 1920, the People's Commissariat for Education decided to found a public College of Arts and Crafts which included a ceramics workshop. This was the first and only professional school of ceramics in the Soviet Union. Its goal was to prepare artists in the fields of production technology and management. The program of studies lasted four years (subsequently, five years). Artistic rather than technical disciplines were emphasized. In 1921, the ceramics students received an important commission: the gifts to be given to the participants of the Third Congress of the Komintern. The group in charge of the commission, led by Tatevossian at the Dulev factory, had 1500 dishes made in forty days, each marked with a seal depicting a potter at his wheel, with the inscription "School of Ceramics - Vhutemas College of Arts and Crafts." Of the fifty-one projects submitted, three received prizes and twelve were selected for production, among which was the plate by Tatevossian, with its stylized design in black, red and green symbolizing the liberation of the Orient, and its inscription in Arabic, "Workers of the World, Unite!" The School of Ceramics closed its doors in 1930; in all, it trained fourteen master ceramists.

A. SHCHEKOTIKHINA-POTOTSKAYA, plate entitled *The Commissioner*, 1921.

A. SHCHEKOTIKHINA-POTOTSKAYA, plate entitled *The Russian and the German*, bearing the slogan *Workers of the World, Unite!* 1921.

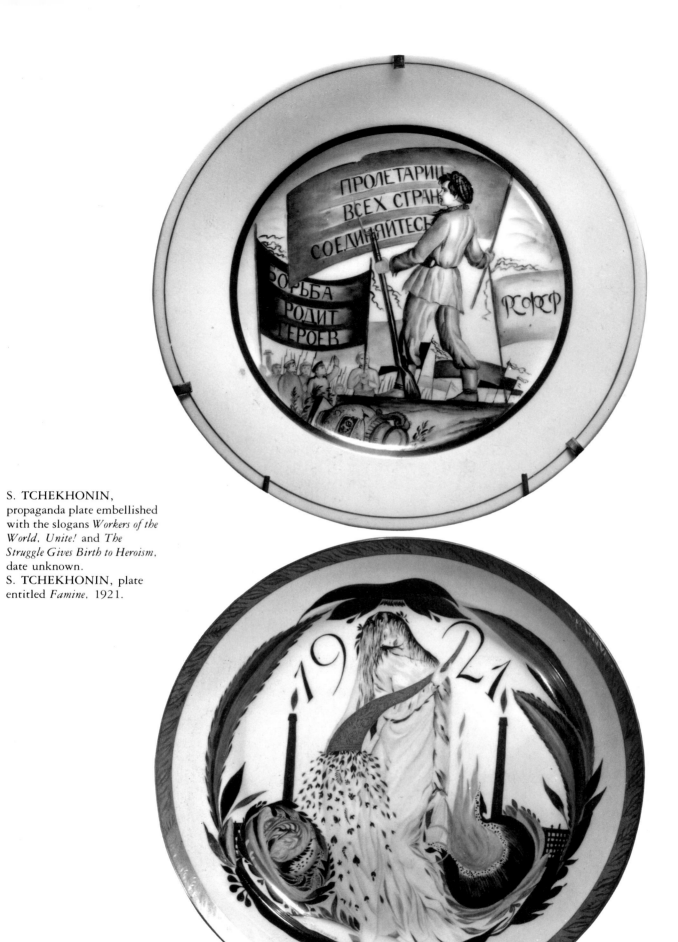

S. TCHEKHONIN,
propaganda plate embellished
with the slogans *Workers of the
World, Unite!* and *The
Struggle Gives Birth to Heroism*,
date unknown.
S. TCHEKHONIN, plate
entitled *Famine*, 1921.

Mention should be made of the Lomonossov factory, particularly distinguished at the Moscow exhibition of 1926, an event which marked an important milestone in the evolution of Soviet porcelain.

At the end of the 1920s and at the beginning of the 1930s, following the policy of industrialization of the Soviet Union, the faïence and porcelain industries had to face restructuring, increasing specialization, and production standardization. The isolation of the porcelain industry slowed down its production; a reorganization was imperative.

In 1927, three large trusts were founded: the Tsentrofarfortrust (the factories of Leningrad and Novgorod, including the Dulev, Tver, and Lomonossov factories), the Siberian trust (the Khaitin and Krasnoyarsk factories), and the Ukrfarfortrust (a dozen factories in the Ukraine). This division allowed for specialization of production. The factories of Russia (Dulev, Dmitrov, etc.), of Khaitin, and of the Ukraine produced porcelain dishes, the factories in the northeast and southwest of the country specialized in faïence, and the Leningrad factory kept its status as a center for artistic experimentation.

It was now necessary for the various types of production to attain an equilibrium. Until then, too many factories produced high quality tableware and neglected cheaper items intended for the rural market. As a consequence, the urban market was the most developed.

The porcelain industry offered a vast and original range of dishes, especially those produced by the Dulev factory: tea services, tableware for urban and rural use, porcelain for export to Persia and other Oriental countries. The most popular tea services were N· 39 *(Cylindrical)* and N· 3 *(Kiev),* while the most requested butter-dishes were *The Sheep, The Duck, The Raspberry, The Strawberry, The Radish, The Tomato, The Dove* and *The Admiralty.* The Dmitrov factory manufactured por-

Two Ukrainian plates from the Mezhigorye factory, circa 1925.

A. SHCHEKOTIKHINA-POTOTSKAYA, plate entitled *The Hunchback*, 1918.

A. SHCHEKOTIKHINA-POTOTSKAYA, dish, *Suffering Russia*, 1921.
M. ADAMOVITCH, cup and saucer, *The Red Army*, with decoration
symbolizing fraternization between the army and peasants, 1921.

L. RUDNEV, plate, *Parade ground*, 1921.
P. VITCHELJANIN, plate with a floral decoration, embellished in the center
with the emblem of the Republic of Russia, 1921.

V. TIMOREV, plate, *The Liberation of the Orient*, 1921.

A. PODOGOV, F. BEDIN, plate and teacup with a floral pattern.
S. TCHEKHONIN, tea service with a floral pattern, 1928.

celain tea sets, producing models from before the Revolution: *The Lily, Moscow, Limoges, Bavaria.* The Proletariat and Red Pottery factories produced simple, low-cost dishes, similar to traditional folk pieces, for the rural market. The range of items in faïence was less extensive. Less costly than porcelain, it was employed as everyday ware. The forms used were generally the same as before the Revolution, less decorative and with unified motifs. Majolica, on the other hand, offered a range of forms that was so vast as to attain the level of the absurd.

Tableware was henceforth mass-produced. The keynote was "standardization"—of forms and ornamentation, as well as of raw materials, size, whiteness, and thickness of the potsherd. Incidentally, this new phenomenon was introduced simultaneously in Germany and in the United States.

N. SUETIN, circa 1920.

Standardization created a certain number of problems. 200 types of tableware had been eliminated from production and less than 100 types maintained, while at the same time, the demand for new forms of tableware increased. As early as 1921, the artistic bureau of the Institute of Silicates, directed by Filippov, was involved in researching new forms. Without a doubt, Filippov was the most eminent historian concerned with the role of ceramics in the period before the war, and he played an active role in the restructuring of the porcelain and faïence industries.

It soon became apparent that neither life-styles nor the utilization of the objects in question had been taken into account. Chance or arbitrary decisions were often the only criteria. In addition, the way of life of the Soviet people was itself being transformed. For example, samovars were used less and less, thus creating the need for changes to be made within teapot forms.

Teapot forms, too small and badly proportioned, created difficulties in packing and transport. One exception was pieces whose forms were inspired by Russian porcelain from the early nineteenth century, low-cost dishware which had preserved the simplicity of Gjel porcelain. In most cases, however, typical weaknesses were an absence of style and a lack of formal and decorative unity. The results of research helped to simplify forms and to create an inner logic. Artistic qualities were based on functional, technological and economic conditions. Three forms were retained to serve as standard models: the semicircle, the cylinder, and the parabola. Each form was the basis for a type of tea service, designed to meet the needs of specific groups of consumers. The semi-spherical teapot, having a "large liquid capacity" and giving off more aroma, had been conceived in terms of its "Oriental aspect" as well as its appeal to the "aesthete" among consumers. The creators of this type of tea service were aiming at the Middle Eastern clientele and the "European consumer with traditional tastes." Cylindrical services, on the other hand, boasted a "severity, deliberately researched, which was a reflection of modernity."[1] These projects never reached the manufacturing stage. Standardization proved to be a long and complicated process. The diversity of the public's

needs conflicted with the extreme rationalism governing the design and production of such articles.

The fashion at the time was for an "economical" as well as a utilitarian style, in comparison to former "styles of luxury." Thus saucers were now given a more compact and homogeneous design. Handles, spouts, and knobs were no longer visually differentiated from the rest of the object, but were part of a whole which

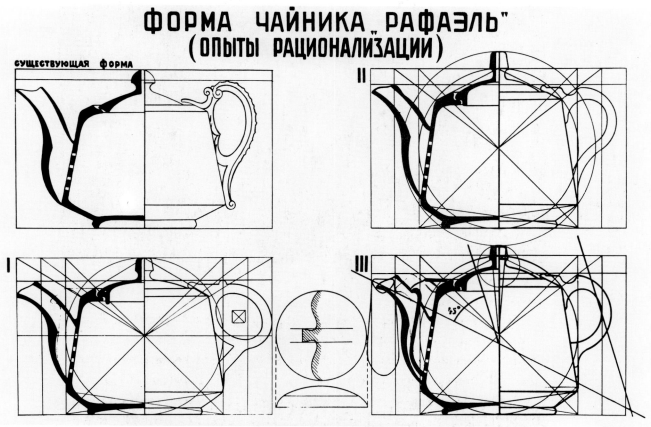

ФОРМА ЧАЙНИКА „РАФАЭЛЬ"
(ОПЫТЫ РАЦИОНАЛИЗАЦИИ)

A. FILIPPOV, sketch for a teapot, 1926-1928.
A. FILIPPOV, teapot, 1926-1928.

N. SUETIN, teacup and saucer, *Suprematism*, 1923.
N. SUETIN, tea service, *Suprematism*, 1920.

K. MALEVICH, Suprematist tea service, 1918.

gave the somewhat misleading appearance of being shaped from a single mass. The only tea service created along such functional lines was designed by Dorofev, a student at the Arts and Trades College workshops (1928, Dulev Factory); the service was mass-produced and exported to the United States. It was octagonal and had a cylindrical base and top. Coral tones brought out the whiteness of the porcelain and the eight edges of the body. This tea service is one of the rare successful examples of a strictly utilitarian design. In 1930, the experimentation with new forms was interrupted by the closing down of the Institute of Silicates, whose work was taken over by the Academy for Understanding of the Arts. The Academy was primarily interested in creating tableware for the masses within the context of a socialist reconstruction of everyday life. In the same year, under the aegis of the Academy, the first national conference of glass and porcelain artists was held in Moscow. During the various lectures, there was much talk of "proletarian thematics" combating the "eclecticism and supremacy" of forms that were "ideologically foreign to the proletariat." It was imperative to "urgently replace anti-artistic and ideologically harmful forms with new ones." The idea of creating experimental laboratories within the factories was aired. There was also mention of basing production standards on practice rather than theory.

I. TCHACHNIK, circa 1920.

In June 1930, the artistic advisory committee of the Rossteklofarfor took a series of concrete measures. Designs which alluded to Western culture or which dated from before the Revolution were removed from production; ideological and artistic directives were given; and a group of artists was picked to design cups and saucers. These artists were Kobyletskaya, Lebedeva, Frentz, Pakhomov, and Tsivchinsky. The difficulties caused by such restructuring were reflected in the production of the largest factory, the Dulev. In 1930, five young artists were named to this factory. Thus began the struggle for the new Soviet project of mass production of tableware. This highly active team of artists organized debates, lectures, and exhibitions (in particular, the "Class Struggle in Art" exhibition which presented tableware "for the rich" and "for the poor"). Most of the factory workers were hostile to this project, with the exception of younger workers or older porcelain masters. The artists explained that mechanization had more of a future because it was more economical and that mass-production would not affect decoration. The new themes were electrification, industrialization, collectivization, the Red Army, the defense of the USSR, sports, and the pioneer movement. Floral motifs were discarded, being considered a "heritage of the bourgeois past." Artistic elements borrowed from poster art, monumental drawings, and graphic art were used. However, while the politics of the civil war period remained in favor, there was a radical change in style. "Revolutionary romanticism" was no longer the order of the day, but rather sobriety and rationalism. Brush strokes and colors were

E. LENEVA, tea and coffee cups with decoration symbolizing the rise of
industry, 1930-1931.
N. PACHTCHINSKAYA, mugs with stylized designs bearing the inscriptions
Generation After Generation (pioneers) and *Brush Your Teeth*. 1930-1931.

S. TCHEKHONIN,
propaganda plate bearing the
slogan *The Reign of the Workers
and Peasants is Unending*,
1920.
A. SHCHEKOTIKHINA-
POTOTSKAYA, *Grossizdat*
(government publications)
plate bearing an advertising
slogan encouraging the
public to read government
publications, 1921.

162

Z. KOBYLETSKAYA, teacup and saucer, *The Red Army of the Workers and Peasants*. The center of the saucer bears the number 10 and the letters RKKA symbolizing the tenth anniversary of the RKKA (The Red Army of the Workers and Peasants).
A. DOROFEV, octagonal tea service, *Coral*, 1928.

more restrained. Examples of this work can be seen in Leneva's designs, *We Shall Rebuild the Turksib, Petroleum for the Nation, To Reach and Go Beyond, Reinforce Military Defense* (pilaf dish, goblets, glasses). Pashtinskaya's designs were similar to propaganda posters: *For a General Line! Here, and There, Carrying On, Listen to the Radio, Brush Your Teeth, In a Canoe.*

The talented designer Smirnov understood the thematic material better than anyone else. His designs depicting the navy (dancing sailors) and the Red cavalry (rows of horsemen, with the silhouette of the Petropavlosk fortress in the background) were decorative, almost ornamental in spirit.

Artists from the older generation undertook to produce new designs, without, however, escaping from the contradictions inherent in the use of new themes and traditional artistic techniques. On cups by Tikhonov, for example, the symbol of the new campaign—a tractor—was enclosed in medallions and encircled by complex friezes. Elsewhere, work symbols were shown against bucolic backgrounds. On plates and cups by Adamovitch, kolkhoz workers were depicted in a traditional and sentimental fashion.

In 1930, at the Dmitrov factory, Podriabinnikov began to militate for mass designs, as the Dulev group had done earlier. He made improvements in the stencil technique and tried to lower the price of china by using industrial decorations (*Toothed Wheel* service, *Woman Tractor-Driver* cup, *I'm on My Way to the Kolkhoz* tray). Like the Dulev group, he believed that restructuring was incompatible with compromise. The artists at Dulev believed in breaking with the past and simplifying forms and colors. But this was to the detriment of the tradition of china, the materials used, and the people for whom these objects were intended. The new procedures were not able to make headway in the porcelain industry. The Dulev group worked for only two years at the factory: Podriabinnikov, four years. Mechanization, shoddy decorative work, and simplification had failed to win over either the factory workers or the consumers. It was obvious that tableware could not be renewed in so radical a fashion.

In May 1931, the Second Conference of Porcelain and Faïence Manufacturers was held at Dulev. The entire production for that period received enthusiastic support from the representatives of the arts section of the Institute of Literature and Languages of the Communist Academy. This was true not only for "modern style" dishware and Soviet production but for more traditional models as well. Among the pieces dating from before the Revolution were four designs by Tchekhonin, Suetin, Malevitch, and Chachnik, and three designs by Dulev artists (Ilovayskazya and Kolossov). In 1932, the Plenum of the Central Committee took the decision to expand the production of vitally needed items. Although the projects concerning china and faïence were never carried out, the expansion policies were contin-

A. VOROBIEVSKY, coffee cup and saucer, *The City and the Country*. The decoration on the border of the saucer symbolizes the perfect harmony between the two worlds.

ued, including intensified exportation to Persia, Turkey, Manchuria, eastern China, South America, etc., by the May First and Dmitrov factories.

In 1931, in view of massive production of vitally needed objects, the first porcelain laboratory was set up in Leningrad. When a second laboratory was built at Dulev, the Leningrad specialists turned their attention to the creation of unique pieces. By the end of 1932, the Leningrad laboratory was run by Suetin and Lapchin. Their goals were quality, mastery, and refinement. These pieces were easily recognizable with their blend of professionalism and traditional techniques. Suetin's work, which used pure, geometrical forms, was composed of "severe ar-

L. KAYA, tea service, *The Blockade of Leningrad,* 1943. Each piece is decorated with a single design depicting the different poignant episodes of the historical siege.
L. PROTOPOPOVA, tea service *From the Taiga to Construction,* 1933. Each piece relates a different stage of the evolution.

M. LEBEDEVA, plate
bearing the slogan *Who Does
Not Work, Does Not Eat*.
1920.
S. TCHEKHONIN, floral
patterned plate with a central
decoration consisting of the
emblem of the Republic of
Russia, 1920.

chitectural constructions," as Danko observed. This can be seen in the oval and cylindrical vases, and the *Lensoviet* and *Crocus* tea services produced during the 1930s. The artist E. Strikker was invited to the Leningrad factory. She designed the *Intourist* tea service, produced in 1932, and the *Standard* service (1933). In 1934, she went to work at Dulev, where she designed tea and coffee sets, a large dinner set, liqueur and water services, smoking articles, and dishes for restaurants and nursery schools.

Some time later, Iakovleva arrived in Leningrad. Under Danko's influence, she designed the famous tea service *Tulip* in 1936.

In the mid-thirties, color took on importance. Suetin, for example, was attentive to the relationship between design and background, as well as to the proportions of color.

In Vorobievsky's work, diaphanous landscapes were interwoven with exotic colors and webs of lace. Mysterious castles were hidden behind pale pink gardens; a sailboat floated on infinite blue waters. His work was essentially decorative; it included vases (*Southern Spring, Fantastical Venice*); tea services (*Winter Pleasures,* 1933, *Gingerbread, Blue Evening,* 1935, *Fruit and Flowers*); serving-dishes (*The Blue Lake,* 1935, *Arctic Fantasy,* 1936, *Arabesques, Floral Patterns,* 1937, *Oriental Ornament,* 1939), etc. Vorobievsky generally grouped his motifs, separating them from the background which he kept white, as in the plaque *Fantastical City* (1935) or the *Yellow* tea service (1938). Mokh's work was also of significance during the 1930s. From the decorative and multicolored floral motifs executed with heavy brush-strokes of his earlier work, he went on to graphic compositions. Schematic forms (the *Metal* and *The Orient Awakens* tea services, 1930) evolved into affirmative lines (*The Old Park* tea service, 1933). On *The Bakhchissaraya Fountain* tea service, an ensemble of astonishing beauty dating from 1936, the miniatures were arranged with an almost geometric severity, as if on the pages of a book.

As for Riznich, he exploited a single theme, animals; his work from the late 1920s consists of numerous dark blue panthers, mauve tigers, lilac-colored wolves, and golden foxes. In his later work, the color contrasts and dynamism of the lines were underplayed, and the brush strokes delimiting the animals' forms adapted their movements to the porcelain surface (the *Panther* dish, 1936). In his most beautiful tea service (*Samolovy,* 1934), the representation was more concrete, while the color and general outline of the forms preserved a necessary measure of "decorativeness."

Many artists were drawn to thematic subjects, the most difficult to achieve in porcelain. Consequently, a great number of mediocre designs saw the light of day, such as *The World's First Subway* (1937) *From the Taiga to Construction,* and *Animals of the Far North,* whose weaknesses, thanks to ornamental and emblematic elements, went largely unnoticed.

GOLUBKOVY, opaline vase celebrating the rise of industry and the October Revolution, 1927.

On her *Kirovsk* tea service, Bespalova-Mikhaleva depicted, in 1934-1935, an ore-enrichment factory, a rolling mill, a tourist camp, and a hydroelectric plant. The rich and heavy blue-green colors gave height and force to these everyday subjects, curiously enclosed in medallions. On the occasion of the hundredth anniversary of Pushkin's death, this same artist displayed her talent by illustrating a tea service with a tale by the famous poet, *The Tales of Czar Saltan.* Scenes from the tale were depicted on the porcelain, with no framework or borders. The drawings—traditional wooden houses and headdresses—stood out against the white background, or, on the contrary, were included within larger subjects. Bespalova-Mikhaleva's choice of colors was particularly daring. On another of her services, *Flowers and Plants,* dating from 1936, she used a dark cobalt blue to contrast with pale pink. Around the middle of the 1930s, responding to the demand for more traditional tableware, the Leningrad factory resumed production of standard decorative motifs—borders, medallions, and lattice-work. Flowers were once again popular, immense ones by Efimova, miniatures by Vorobievsky.

Lebedinskaya remained the specialist of decorative motifs based on floral compositions. At first, she produced small bouquets and wildflowers (*Daisies,* 1934, *Snow-Drop,* 1935, *The Golden Dandelion,* 1936), followed by large garden flowers (*Peonies, Hortensias, Double Poppy,* 1938, *Camellias,* 1940). Concurrently, a new tendency appeared, reflecting the traditions of the Moscow school, a sudden return to decorative folklore, to fine brushwork, and to the naïvety and richness of colors. The Dulev laboratory under Leonev's direction began immediately to produce popular motifs (the *Black Eyes, Little Brothers, The Gossips of Riazan, Moscow Spring* tea services) with their simplified range of two or three uniform, flat colors. This was the so-called "textile" type of design.

That same year, the artists Kuznetsov and Konchalovsky were invited to the Moscow factories. Konchalovsky was the author of some twenty designs, few of which were reproduced on porcelain, as the form of porcelain dishes did not lend itself to still-life motifs (with the exceptions of the *Rowan Tree* tea service and the *Vegetables* serving dish). The Dulev factory once again occupied the place of honor at the Moscow Porcelain Exhibition in 1934. It received an important order from the American ambassador in Moscow: a thousand-piece service for Roosevelt. The off-white porcelain was gilded and then decorated with red and black designs reminiscent of the folk art of Khokhloma. It reproduced line for line a model manufactured before the Revolution by the Kuznetsvo factory.

In Moscow in 1935 and in Paris in 1937, Leonov exhibited his best work, characterized by pale blue and gilded lines, traditional colors, and carpets of flowers. The Dulev factory received the Grand Prize and Gold Medal at the Paris exhibition.

GOLUBKOVY, opaline case celebrating the rise of industry and the October Revolution, 1927.

Z. KOBYLETSKAYA, tea cup and saucer, 1920.
S. TCHEKHONIN, tea cup and saucer, *The Rose and the Carnation*, 1923.
Right-hand page: VILTSE, plate, *Victory to the Workers of January 25*, 1919.

In 1934, a laboratory for artistic research was opened at the Dmitrov factory as well, with the artists A. Kalochin, Fedulov, Chekulina, and Smirnov. Influenced by Tikhonov's traditional Russian style of decoration and composition, these young artists produced stylized floral miniatures with continuous lines and arabesques.

This style was continued at the Verbilsky factory when Smirnov, Fedulov, and Tikhonov went to work there. Fedulov and Tikhonov concentrated on glazing, with designs that covered the entire surface of the china. Gold threads, like sewing stitches, created the motif against a cobalt background under glaze, or else in transparent halftones. Smirnov revived the principles of figurative and decorative art with his tea services (*Tea*, 1938, *The Gardens of our Country*, *The Red Army Is the People's Army*, 1939), while Chekulina created designs from photographic portraits.

Prototypes continued to be produced at the Leningrad factory. The manufacturing of sculptures expanded, with busts in unglazed porcelain, curios, and statuettes. In 1936, a time when there was a rising demand for porcelain in the domain of architecture, the Leningrad factory received a commission for forty-six porcelain capitals for the "Kiev" subway station and for ten-meter-long bas-reliefs and plaques for the "Dynamo" station. The factory also manufactured the facade ornamentation for the river terminal at Khimkin in 1937.

The Dulev factory was also given commissions for the architectural sector, with fountains for the National Agricultural Fair, for a sanatorium in Kislovodsk, both designed by A. Sotnikov, and for the Aragvi restaurant in Moscow (*Doe and Tigers* by S. Kojin). Enormous vases were produced at the Leningrad factory, with titles like *The Maritime Route Via the Far North* by Riznitch, *The Moscow-Volga Canal* by Protopova, and *The Red Cotton Convoy* by L. Black.

Toward the mid-thirties, master-craftsmen were often invited to participate in the artistic creation of pieces. For the 1937 Paris Exhibition, the Dmitrov factory invited craftsmen from Kokhloma, Podogov, and Bedin, who received a Gold Medal in Paris, while the Dulev and Konakovo factories invited master artists from Palekh, Khrenov, Vassiliev, and Khikhyeva.

There were difficulties again in the years 1937 to 1940. Quality was poor; nearly three-hundred outmoded forms and designs were removed from production, and nine-hundred new ones were introduced.

Production in central Russia and in the Ukraine was abandoned during the war years. The Leningrad factory moved to the East. The Dulev and Dmitrov factories reduced the production of ordinary tableware and increased that of urgently needed industrial porcelain. In spite of this, artists continued to work during the

Leningrad blockade, as can be seen by the *Leningrad During the Blockade* tea service by Lebedinskaya, Shchekotikhina-Pototskaya's *Alexander Nevsky* vase, and Bespalova-Mikhaleva and Kubarskaya's vases celebrating the defense of the city.

NOTES

1. See *Projects for Porcelain Tea Service Models*, Moscow, 1929, pp. 3-4.

R. WILDE: Milk pitcher.
Milk pitcher bearing the
initials RSFSR, 1918-1919.
Oval plate from the tea
service *Altalena*, designed in
1921 and realized in 1926.
S. TCHEKHONIN, hot
water pitcher from the service
The Three Roses, 1923.
N. DANKO, figurines:
Woman Sewing a Flag, 1919,
and *Hunter*, 1919.
N. ALTMAN, tea cup and
saucer, *October 25, 1917*.
Right-hand page: L.
PROTOPOPOVA, milk
pitcher from the service
Industrialization, 1930.

A. FILIPPOV, soup tureen, 1926-1928.
Right-hand page: T. PODRIABINNIKOV, tea cup and saucer, *Construction*, proletarian factory, 1929.

PAGE 176: A. FILIPPOV, soup tureen, 1926-1928.
PAGE 177: T. PODRIABINNIKOV, tea cup and saucer, *Construction,
proletarian factory*, 1929.
PAGE 178: M. MOKH, tea service, *The Old Park*, 1933.
N. SUETIN, tea service, *Women or Peasant Women*, 1930.
PAGE 179: S. TCHEKHONIN, cup, *The Three Roses*, 1923.
PAGE 180: M. ADAMOVITCH, propaganda plate, *Who Does Not Work, Does Not
Eat*, with a portrait of V. Lenin, 1923.
PAGE 181: O. TATEVOSSIAN, plate commemorating the Third Komintern
Congress, bearing the Arab inscription *Workers of the World, Unite!* Vhutemas
College of Arts and Crafts, 1921.
PAGE 182: S. TCHEKHONIN, propaganda plate, *Reason Cannot Tolerate Slavery*,
1918.
PAGE 183: P. VITCHELZHANIN, propaganda plate bearing the inscription
Down with the Bourgeoisie and Capitalism, 1920.
PAGE: 184: S. TCHEKHONIN, plate, *The Red Ribbon*, with a central decoration
of the hammer, the sickle, and an ear of wheat, 1919.
PAGE 185: N. ALTMAN, propaganda plate, *Land for the Workers*, 1918.

FROM LEFT TO RIGHT AND FROM TOP TO BOTTOM:
R. WILDE, propaganda plate bearing the slogan *We Must Dare Today For Tomorrow*, 1921.
S. TCHEKHONIN, plate embellished with the hammer and sickle, 1918. Z. KOBYLETSKAYA, dish, *Newspapers, Petrograd*, 1921. A. SHCHEKOTIKHINA-POTOTSKAYA, plate, *Moonlight*, 1919. V. TIMOREV, plate bearing the inscription *The Reign of the Workers and Peasants is Unending*, 1920. S. TCHEKHONIN, dish bearing the hammer and sickle, 1918. S. TCHEKHONIN, dish bearing the initials *RSFSR*, 1918.

Z. KOBYLETSKAYA, propaganda plate with a
floral pattern, printed with the slogan *We'll
Change the World Into a Flowering Garden*, 1920.
S. TCHEKHONIN, plate bearing the inscription
*It Is Easier To See the Dawn of the New Morning from
the Peaks of Science Than from the Valley of Daily
Tumult*, 1919. M. ADAMOVITCH, plate, *The
Red Star*. The plate edge is embellished with a
decor symbolizing industry and agricultural
work.

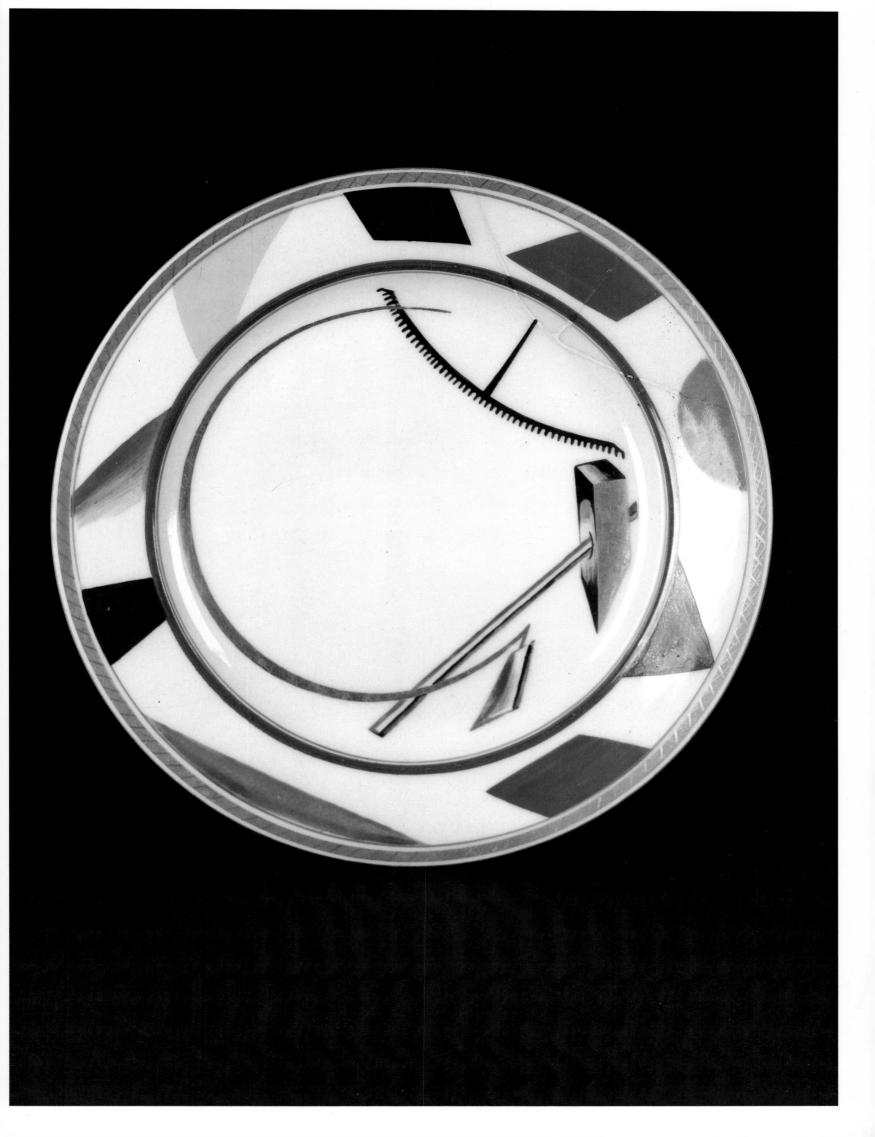

PAGE 188: S. TCHEKHONIN, plate bearing the inscription *The Struggle Gives Birth to Heroism*, 1918.

PAGE 189: S. TCHEKHONIN, plate with a Cubist-inspired motif, and hammer and sickle, 1922.

PAGE 190: O. TATEVOSSIAN, coffee cup and saucer commemorating the Third Komintern Congress, bearing the Arab inscription *Workers of the World, Unite!* Vuthemas College of Arts and Crafts, 1921.

PAGE 191: S. TCHEKHONIN, propaganda plate, 1920.

PAGE 192: Z. KOBYLETSKAYA, plate, *Long Live the Eighth Congress of the Soviets*, 1920.

PAGE 193: V. TIMOREV, propaganda plate bearing the inscription *Who Works, Eats* with, in the center, a food card designed by A. Lunatcharsky, 1920.

PAGE 194: Plate, *The Liberation of the Working Class Is Up to the Workers*, 1920.

PAGE 195: A. POLENSKINA, propaganda plate bearing the slogan *We'll Ignite the Whole World With the Flame of the Third International*, 1920.

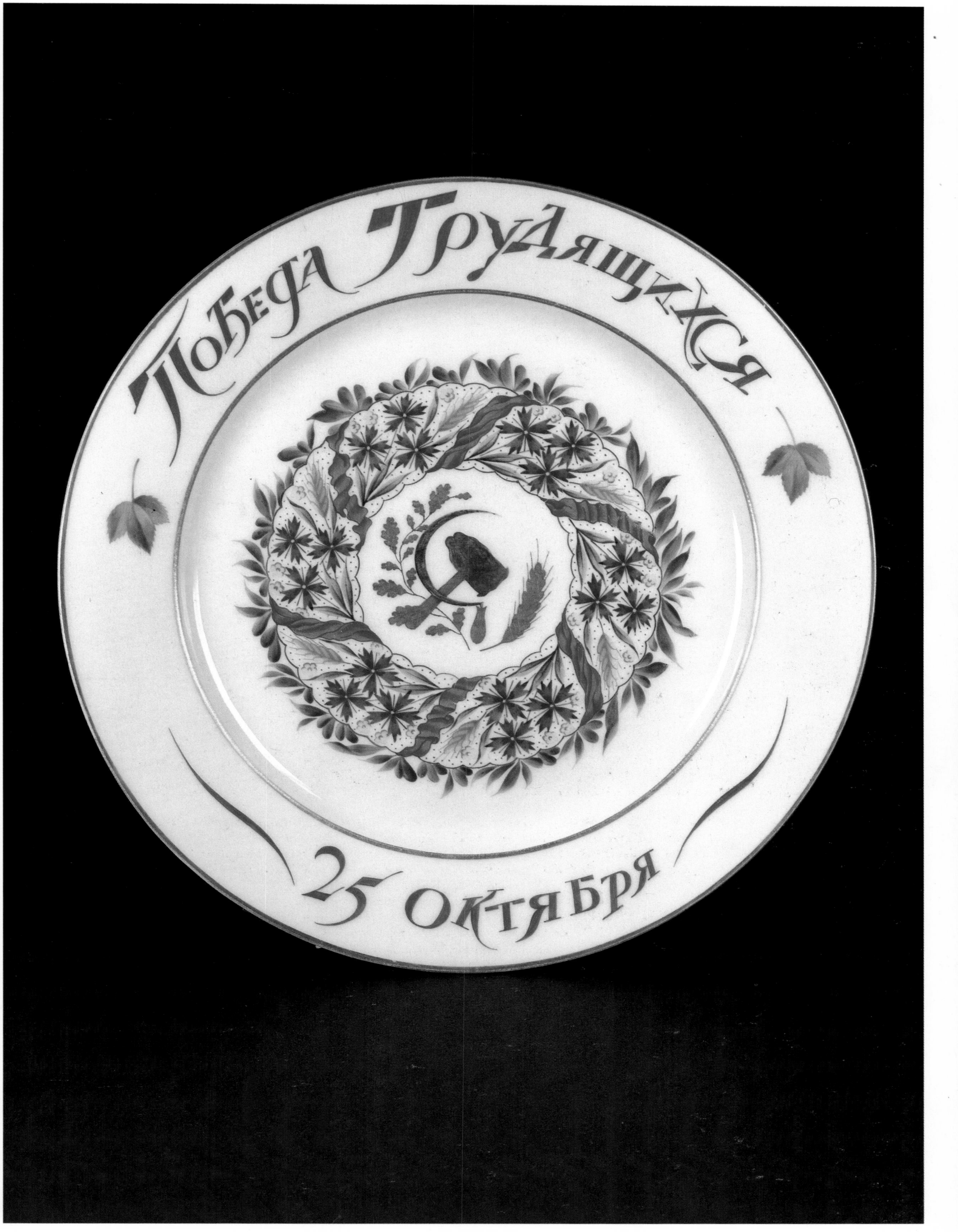
Победа Трудящихся
25 Октября

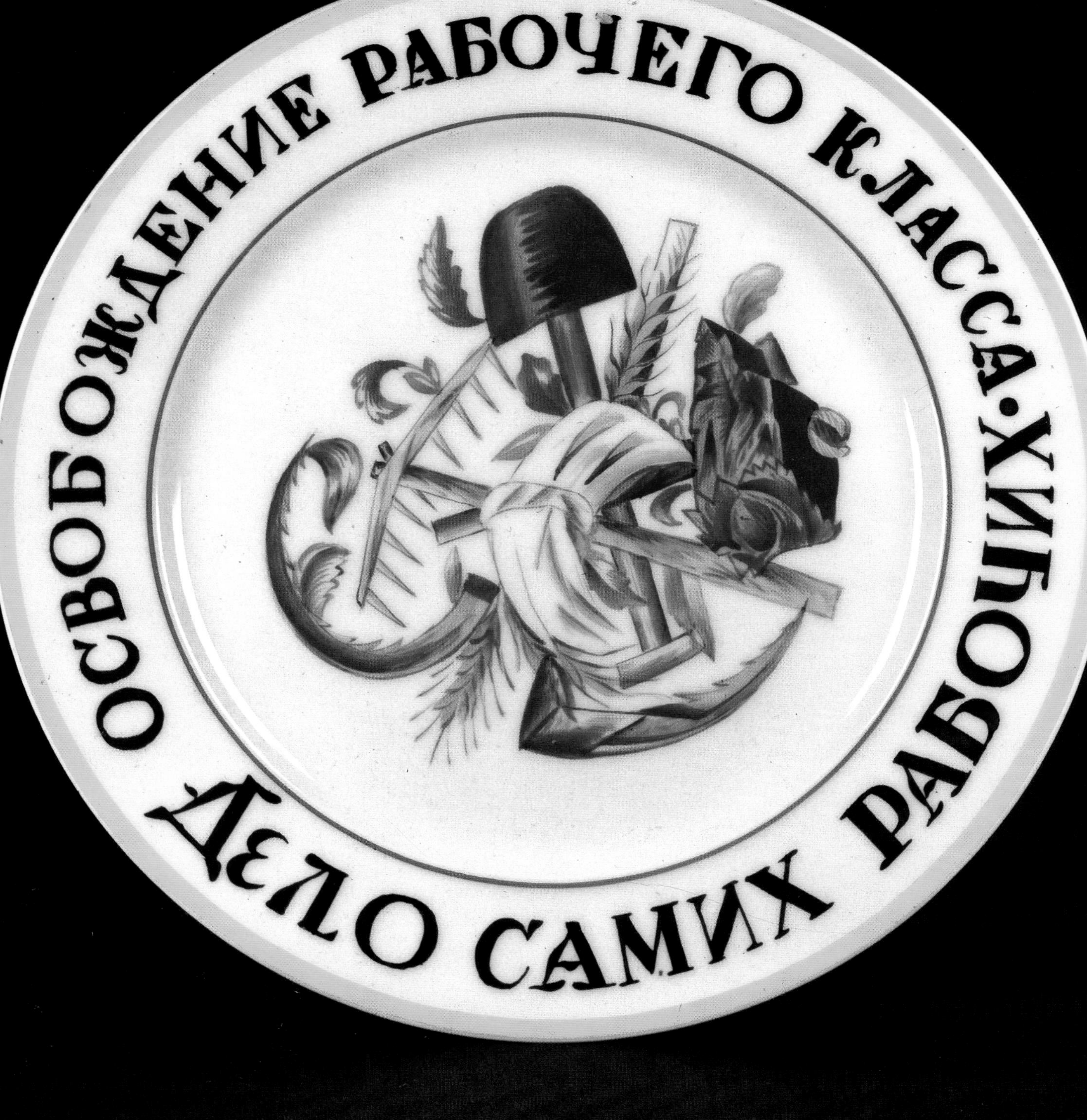
ОСВОБОЖДЕНИЕ РАБОЧЕГО КЛАССА·ХИЩОБ
ДЕЛО САМИХ РАБОЧИХ

V. KANDINSKY, tea cup and saucer, *The City*, 1923.
M. ADAMOVITCH, sauce boat and plate, *Industrialization and the Cultural
Revolution*, 1926. The plate edge is decorated with various hand implements to
mark the evolution of industrialization.

A. KOLOSSOV, tea service, *USSR 1925*, Dulev Porcelain Factory, 1925.

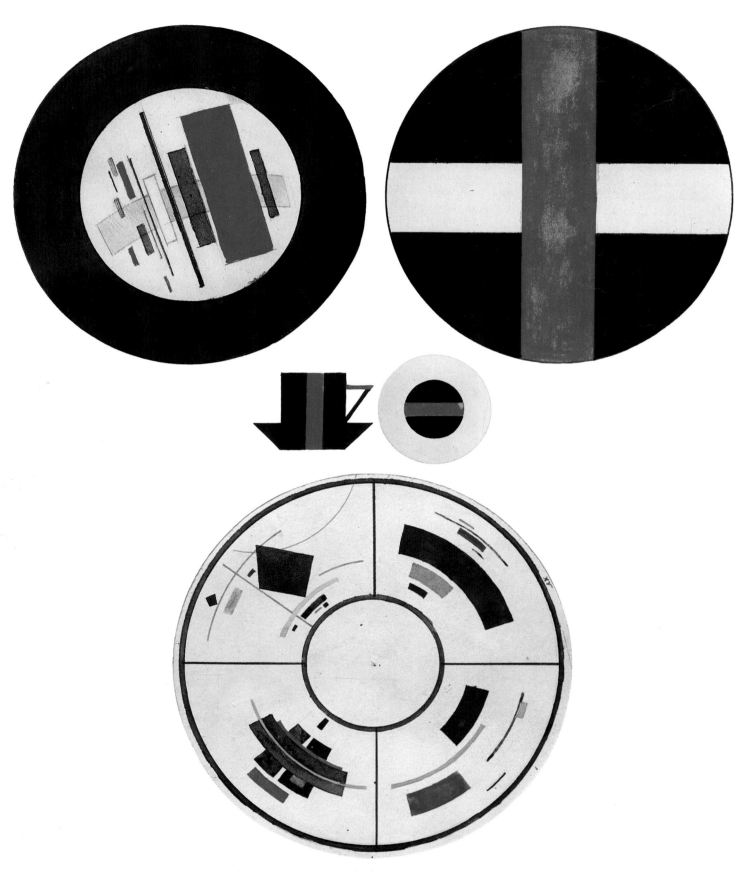

I. TCHACHNIK, plate designs, 1923-1925. Coffee
cup and saucer design, 1923.
L. KHIDEKEL, plate design, India ink, circa 1920.
Right-hand page: K. RODZHESTVENSKY, tea cup
and saucer with Suprematist motif, circa 1925.

I. TCHACHNIK, N. SUETIN, Suprematist dishes.
Right-hand page: A. SOTNIKOV, baby's drinking cup
with spout, after a design by V. Tatlin, 1929.
PAGE 202: N. DANKO, porcelain figurine, *The Sailor Carrying a Flag*, 1923.
PAGE 203: N. DANKO, porcelain figurine, *Woman Worker Sewing a Banner*, 1920.

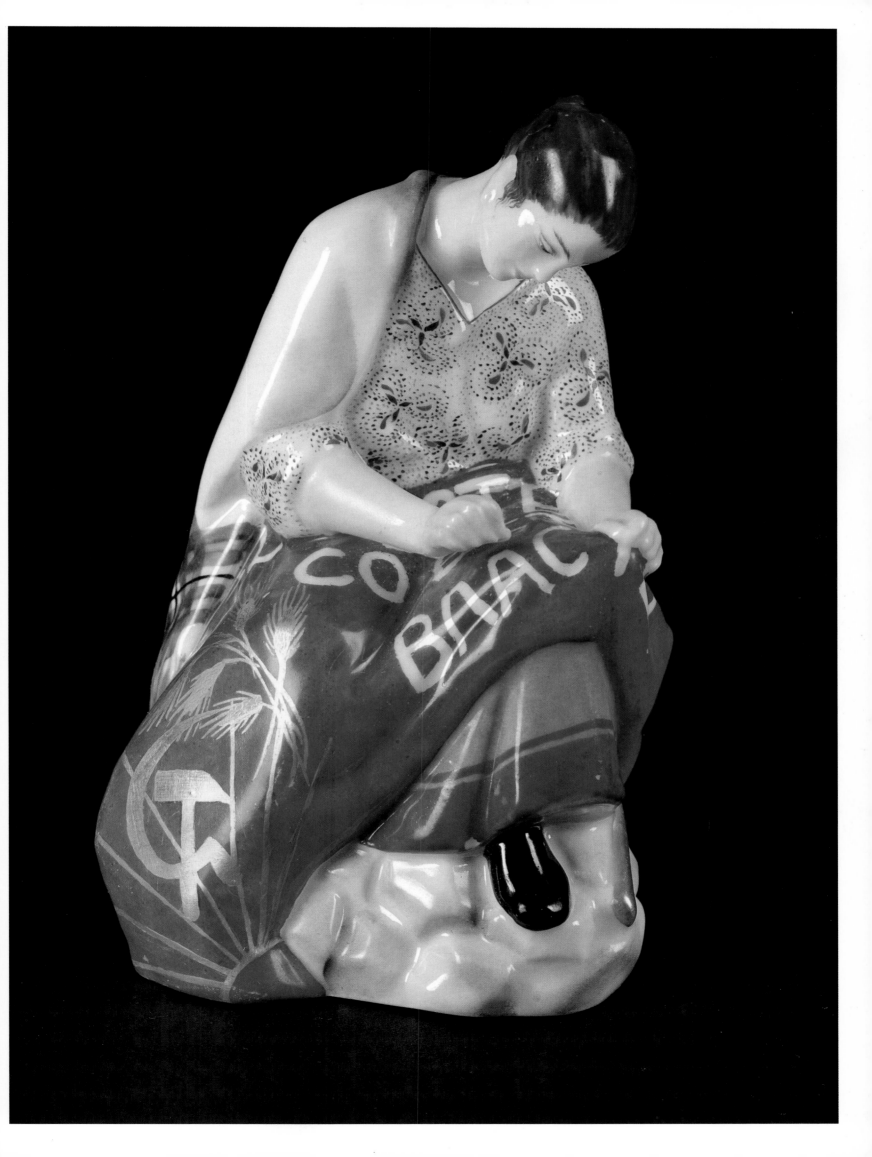

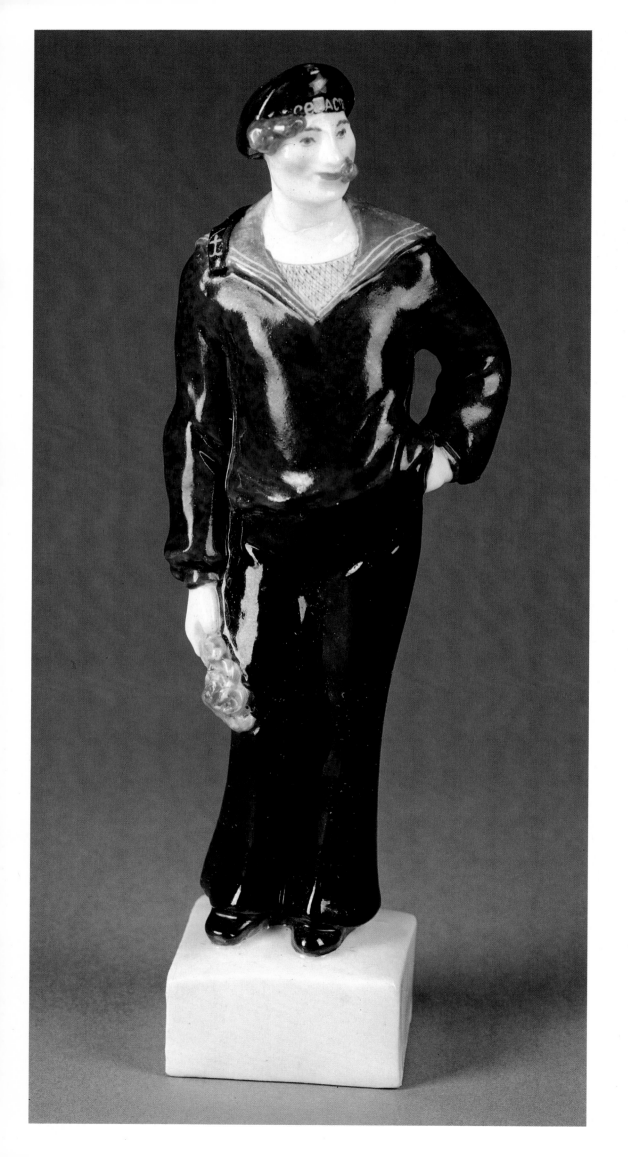

PAGE 204: N. DANKO,
porcelain figurine, *The Merry
Sailor*, 1919.

PAGE 205: B. KUSTODIEV,
porcelain figurine, *Village
Girl*, 1920.

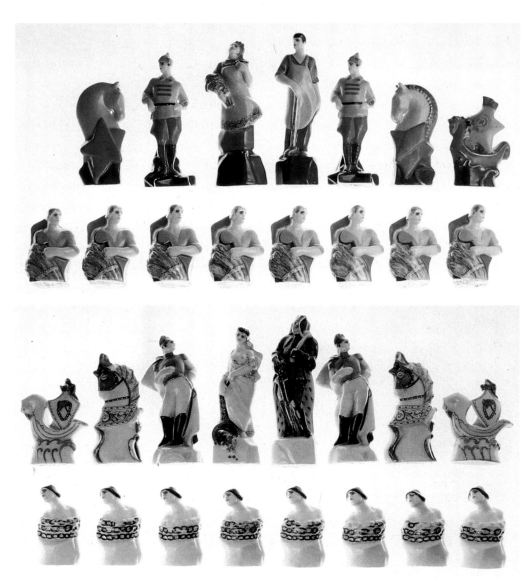

N. DANKO, porcelain chess pieces, *The Red and the White*, 1922.

Figurines

The figurine genre underwent considerable development during the 1920s, thanks to the efforts of talented artists. This original form of sculpture, at the border of applied decorative art, was produced in wood, porcelain, ivory or clay, and manufactured in porcelain factories or in the workshops of Bogorodskoye, Tobolsk, or Dymkovo. While retaining their status as living-room figurines, the porcelain figurines of the 1920s were able to reflect revolutionary realities as well as tendencies of propaganda art of the period. During the civil war, the stores of Petrograd displayed figurines representing Red Guard soldiers, sailors, partisans, and chess pieces *(The Reds and the Whites)*. Most of these items were produced at the National Porcelain Factory. The models used dated from before the Revolution: a series of figurines called *The Russian People* by Kamensky, *Woman Water-Carrier* and *Young Girl with Yoke* after originals from the early nineteenth century, the bust of Tolstoy by I. Ginzburg, *The Nursemaid* by Schpiss. Before the Revolution, the factory had already produced work by Sudbinin, Stelletsky, Kuznetsov, and Danko.

Kuznetsov worked at the factory from 1914 through 1919. As a sculptor of monumental pieces, he had some difficulty adapting to the creation of porcelain miniatures, but rapidly produced interesting pieces such as *The Months of the Year* series begun in 1914. In this poetic work praising the eternal strength of the common people, the months of the year were personified by tranquil peasants. Kuznetsov used porcelain as if it were a mass of hard and compact crystal, constructing large surfaces joined by sharp angles. The volumes were geometric, the forms organic and vibrant, Kuznetsov was fond of the rhythmical interplay of pleats and flaps, interrupted only by the roundness of hips and knees.

The most accomplished item in this series is the "Twins—month of May," known as *The Mowers*. Its movement is majestic and ample, its rhythm both harmonious and energetic. In Kuznetsov's best known piece of work, *The Red Guard*, produced in 1918, he used a style that was more concrete and down-to-earth, less poetic. Inspired by the popular *lubok* tradition, this figurine is remarkable for its classical sculptural clarity. The vertical rhythms and geometrical compositions give way to broken forms in which volumes are not so much constructed as suggested. The decorative aspect is subordinated to expression, and a certain psychological depth makes itself felt, reminiscent of portraiture. While the rhythms in *The Mowers* are vertical, horizontal, and diagonal, the frail silhouette of *The Red*

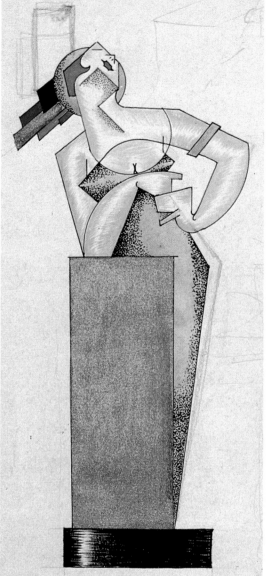

I. RUBINTCHIK, design for
propaganda chess pieces, gouache on
paper, 1925. GNIMA.

Guard is dominated by lines that are slightly oblique and not parallel—as if to emphasize the hesitation of the young guardsmen before entering into action.

One of Kuznetsov's students was N. Danko, who worked with her sister E. Danko. From 1919 to 1934, N. Danko directed the sculpture section of the National Porcelain Factory. Like Kuznetsov, she entered the factory in 1914. Her best work was done between 1919 and 1923: *Partisan in the Country, Woman Worker Sewing a Banner, Woman Agitator.* In contrast to Kuznetsov, all of N. Danko's human figures are shown in activity, seized in the midst of their everyday lives (*Militiawoman,* 1920). These were contemporary figures, ordinary revolutionaries. In later years, N. Danko's work lost its radiance, weighted down with trivial details and poor composition (*Sailor With Flag,* 1921).

The Danko sisters also created and decorated utilitarian objects such as beer mugs, pipes, umbrella handles, salt shakers, vases, butter dishes, and bottles. With the goal of embellishing everyday life, they combined the utilitarian with the decorative, reflecting the optimism and celebratory atmosphere of their era. Their inkwell *Sleeping Peasant Woman* (1919) and the figurine *Dancing Girl* (1921) are the best examples of this work.

Matveyev also worked at the National Porcelain Factory from 1923 to 1924. His work celebrated the beauty of the human body, but his nudes were severely criticized; he was accused of borrowing themes used by the Gardner Factory before the Revolution. In fact, his work could not have been more different, with soft, fresh forms. His quasi-luminescent whites were awarded a gold medal in Paris in 1925. Matveyev was commissioned to execute a series of delicate statuettes: *Young Girl Putting on a Shoe* (created in 1923 and produced to this very day) is the most well-known.

Kustodiev worked on and off at the factory, creating figurines in the nineteenth-century tradition, such as *The Accordionist* and *Woman Dancer.* At the end of the 1920s, the Dmitrov porcelain factory opened a sculpture section with a new team of artists: Ivanov, Bruschetti-Mitrokina, Sudeikina, Strakhovskaya, Trupiansky. In Leningrad, Kutchkina and Koltsov began collaborating with the Danko sisters. Inspiration for these artists came from models created by Ingal, Pinchuk, and Pakhomov. Following the production of unsuccessful pieces that were judged both too melodramatic and precious (*The Fountain at Bakhtchissarai,* 1932, *Kolkhoz Youth,* 1934), N. Danko retired to the countryside to renew her art and immerse herself in new rhythms. Her work for the Moscow Sverdlov Square subway station in 1937 and a series of portraits for the theater in 1939 showed remarkable mastery. Her human figures, however, lacked depth.

Kutchkina and Koltsov worked together; they had a profound knowledge of folk art as well as of the work of Kuznetsov and N. Danko. The arms, legs, and necks of their figurines are reminiscent of the "pretzel" shape of the old porcelain *luboks*. Rounded volumes and clothing enveloping bodies with soft pleats marked their work. One of Kutchkina's most successful pieces was the statuette *Mother Nursing her Child*, 1939.[1]

At the end of the 1920s and the beginning of the 1930s, the Komakovo faïence factory produced original pieces thanks, among others, to the work of Frich-Khar. He had already begun to use a variety of materials such as marble and faïence for different genres: living-room statuettes, monumental bas-reliefs, sculptures, and utilitarian objects. His statuettes were produced in faïence (*The Old City*, 1928, *Shish Kabob Seller*, 1934).

The Old City is a piece made in faïence whose colors and gilded edges dazzle against a white background. A few details stand out in relief—a man carrying a bundle on his head, a shish kebab seller, the joyous confusion of a marketplace. His style was naïve and popular. Similarly, the picturesque style of *Shish Kebab Seller* is reminiscent of the shop signs by the Georgian naïve painter Pirosmanichvily.

At the end of the 1930s, the Dmitrov factory owed its renown to the sculptor Orlov. His fairy-tale pieces were extravagantly colored and gilded (*Little Hump-Backed Horse*, 1938, *The Circus* series, *The Tale of the Fisherman and the Fish* group, 1939), but their overabundance of decoration bordered on the superficial. Without a solid visual base, this approach lacked perspective, although it did bring originality and freshness to small sculptures.

In the early 1940s, young sculptors came to join the work force of the Kanakovo faïence factory. Kholodnaya appears to have been the most interesting of the group, with *Young Girl with Sunflower*, 1939, and *Sleeping Boy*, 1941.

Simultaneously, unique pieces of work in wood, ivory, and stone were being developed. Evangulev was the master of this genre, with expressive use of color, polish, hard surface and the very texture of the material used. In the stark forms of a mammoth's or walrus's tusk or in pieces of stone or wood, Evangulov could already envision the finished piece of work; it was simply a question of eliminating what was superfluous. He was a connoisseur of Egyptian, Indian, and Japanese statuettes as well as of the ivory work produced in Kholmogory and Tobolsk. His specialty was animals; ivory allowed him to reproduce the suppleness of a sable or the heavy fur of an Eskimo dog.

Efimov and Vatagin, famous sculptors of animals, used all sorts of materials to produce small sculptures: wood, stone, bronze, porcelain, metal, ceramics, and glass.

During the war, some artists experimented with military and patriotic themes in these materials. The most well-known are Dobrinin, Sotnikov (who

N. DANKO, porcelain pipe,
La Fenice. 1921, porcelain
bottle, *The Sun and the Moon*.
1921; porcelain pipe, *La
Fenice*. 1921; porcelain pipe,
Two Faces. 1923.

N. DANKO, porcelain figurine, *Oriental Dancer, Afghanistan*, 1929. The figure is standing on the map of Afghanistan.
D. IVANOV, porcelain figurine, *The Dancer T. Karsavina* interpreting *Zobeida* in the ballet *Scheherazade*, 1923.
N. DANKO, porcelain figurine, *Woman with Chador*, 1929.

worked in porcelain), and Bazhenova. Most of these pieces were done in majolica with, mostly, green glazes (*Our Comrade's Funeral*, *Machine Gunner* by Dobrinin).

NOTES

1. Work by Kutchkina: *Girl with Chicken and Chicks* (1938), *Youth* (1938-39), *Girl with Rabbits*, *Girl with Geese* (1939).
   Work by Koltsov: *The Dog Laika* (1930), *Woman with Sheep* (1938), *Lomonossov, Young Man and Woman, The Reindeer, The Penguin*.

N. DANKO, porcelain figurine,
Turkish Woman, 1921.

D. IVANOV, porcelain figurine of the dancer *T. Karsavina* in the ballet *The Firebird* by Stravinsky, 1920.

N. DANKO, porcelain figurine, *Woman Worker Holding a Speech in Her Hand*, 1923.

B. KUSTODIEV, porcelain figurine, *Harmony*, National Porcelain Factory, 1929.

C. SOMOV, porcelain figurine, *The Lovers*, created in 1905 and reissued by the
National Porcelain Factory in 1928.
PAGE 218: V. KUZNETSOV, porcelain figurine, *Red Guard*, 1918.
N. DANKO, porcelain figurine, *The Militiawoman*, 1920.
PAGE 219: N. DANKO, porcelain figurine, *Partisan in the Country*, 1919.

M. ANUFRIEVA, cotton with an Oriental-style motif, entitled *Turksib*, 1928.

Textiles
Clothing Fabrics

Textile production was one of the most active branches of industry. In 1913, there were 873 textile factories employing over one-and-a-half-million people. The most important factories—Morozov and Sons, the Brothers Nossov, the Tsindel Company, the Moussy–Gougeon silk factory, and the Prokhorov factory—were equipped with the most updated and sophisticated English machinery. For decades, Russia had exported high quality sateens and calicos to Asia. Strong competition incited the Russian factories continually to expand their choice of fabrics and to pursue research and experimentation. Two out of ten presses at the Kouvaiev calico factory in Ivanovo-Vossnessensk were employed to this end. The motifs were either imitations of foreign designs or typically Russian motifs inspired by folklore: large flowers and bouquets on sateens and calicos from Ivanovo and delicate arabesques on printed kerchiefs from Staropavlovsk.

Until the end of the 1920s, the factories that produced clothing fabric (Three Mountains Factory, the first calico factory in Moscow, and the factories of the Ivanovo trust) created furnishing fabrics as well. Only the delicacy of the motifs differentiated the cloth that was intended to be made into clothing.

For the rural populations of Central Asia and the Caucasus, designs consisted generally of bright roses against a colored background or else multicolored garlands of flowers. Oriental elements appeared in certain fabrics, as did cashmere motifs and stripes on silk produced in Central Asia. Motifs were sometimes rather eclectic; cloth with motifs of clocks and chandeliers, produced in the cities and factories, was particularly appreciated by the peasants of the North Caucasus.

The Russian Textile Union was created in 1921 to reorganize and direct the global textile industry. The Union's task was to encourage each factory to diversify its production, to create a national pool of raw materials, to study internal and foreign markets, and to train specialists.

The Union organized trusts by grouping together several factories: the Orekhovo-Zouiev trust, the Ivanovo-Vossnessensk trust, the Serpukhov trust, the Tver trust, the Pietrotextile trust, the Mossukno trust, etc. Artistic guidelines were provided by the People's Commissariat for Education, and in 1918, a research workshop was founded at the Three Mountains Factory.

It was only after the middle of the 1920s that artistically valid creations began to be produced. In the preceding years, dozens of factories had been forced to close

Cotton with a stylized palm tree motif, Prokhorovsky Factory, 1915-1916.

223

S. BURYLIN, *The Farm*, printed cotton based on a design by I. Bilibin, circa 1920.

S. AGAYAN, shawl with an Armenian motif, 1938.

their doors due to the scarcity of raw materials, fuel, manpower, and organized means of transportation. The shortage of textile products, their poor quality, and the lack of choice were felt until the end of the 1930s.

Until 1923, solid-colored fabrics were the most numerous, in broadcloth, canvas, military cloth, common wool, yarn, cotton, and calico. The first truly Soviet designs were extremely low-key: the hammer and the sickle and the five-branched star were included within traditional floral compositions. Such cloth tended to be lackluster, with solid backgrounds. Artists, too concerned with being modern, neglected the practical aspects of textile design. Furnishing fabrics, in contrast, were more easily adapted to the use of new emblems. Grün, an elderly artist at the Three Mountains Factory, created a calico of some interest: intended to be used as curtain fabric for a club, the cloth was decorated with sickles, hammers, and ears of wheat against a background consisting of the world and the rising sun. The hammer and the sickle appeared to be clamped around the world itself. The highly contrasted graphic style was suggestive of porcelain dishes of the era. This cloth dating from the early 1920s was a forerunner of the monumental character of the furnishing fabrics of the 1930s, designed for public buildings whose decorative elements had to be visible from a great distance.

Grün was the first to conceive industrial motifs—shuttles, bobbins, and other implements of the textile industry—and realistic human figures. During this era, furnishing fabrics, kerchiefs, and handkerchiefs commemorated important anniversaries, often in a rather inartistic manner, and always along the same lines: a portrait in the center, and a thematic scene in each corner.

Maslov, of the Teikovskaya factory (Ivanovo trust), created in 1924 a calico motif with agricultural scenes intertwined with garlands of leaves and fruit. Landscapes, tractors, and horses appeared to stand out in relief. The motif as a whole was reminiscent of French carpet or textile design.

During the 1920s, led by the artists Popova and Stepanova, a concerted effort was made to improve the artistic development of the textile industry. New geometrical forms and methods of dealing with floral decors were imagined, intended to imitate painting and bring about a closer relationship between artistic and industrial milieus.

These easily recognizable motifs included bands, circles, squares, and stripes of contrasting colors. Popova and Stepanova's one weakness, however, was a lack of concern for the type of cloth to be used for the motif; no modifications were made between the design on paper and the printed motif. On the other hand, special attention was paid to motif rhythms in zig-zags or jagged lines, to proportions, and to colors, which were generally enclosed in squares or circles.

In 1924, Stepanova created one of her most beautiful motifs. The basic ele-

L. MAYAKOVSKAYA, *The Roses*, velvet painted with an airbrush, circa 1926.

L. MAYAKOVSKAYA, silk painted with an airbrush, geometrical motifs, circa 1926.

V. STEPANOVA (on the left) and L. POPOVA, photo by A. Rodchenko, 1924.

ment was a finely-traced semicircle whose repetition suggested a floral motif. For a motif entitled *The Building of a Bridge,* on the contrary, she used a pattern of irregularly broken lines. Popova's designs were simpler and more expressively colored, more in keeping with the clothing for which they were intended.

The mathematical strictness of Popova's and Stepanova's work was subject to criticism. In her notebook, entitled "Register of Textile Models for 1924," Stepanova noted the criticism of the Artistic Council of the First Printed Calico Factory, whose members reproached her for her use of geometrical motifs which, according to them, lacked emotion and fantasy. Such designs, in short, were not considered to be "artistic."

These fabrics entered the history of textiles in the USSR as the "first Soviet fashion," but their Constructivist extravagance rapidly became tiresome. In 1925, the Artistic Council directed its artists to reintroduce floral themes.

During this period, artists like Iuon, Vesnin, Exter, and Mukhina, were interested in designing calico motifs. Some worked with new emblems, while others experimented with geometrical forms.

Mayakovskaya, who worked at the Three Mountains Factory, played an important role in the art of textiles during the 1920s. In addition to her work as an artist, she was also a technologist. It was thus that she was able to improve airbrush techniques, enabling her to realize an infinite number of geometrical motifs. In contrast to Stepanova and Popova, her colors were more nuanced, the contrasts less sharp, and the contours softer.

In the middle of the decade, Soviet industry began to master the techniques of synthetic silk (for underclothing and shirts) and jersey (in silk and in wool) which

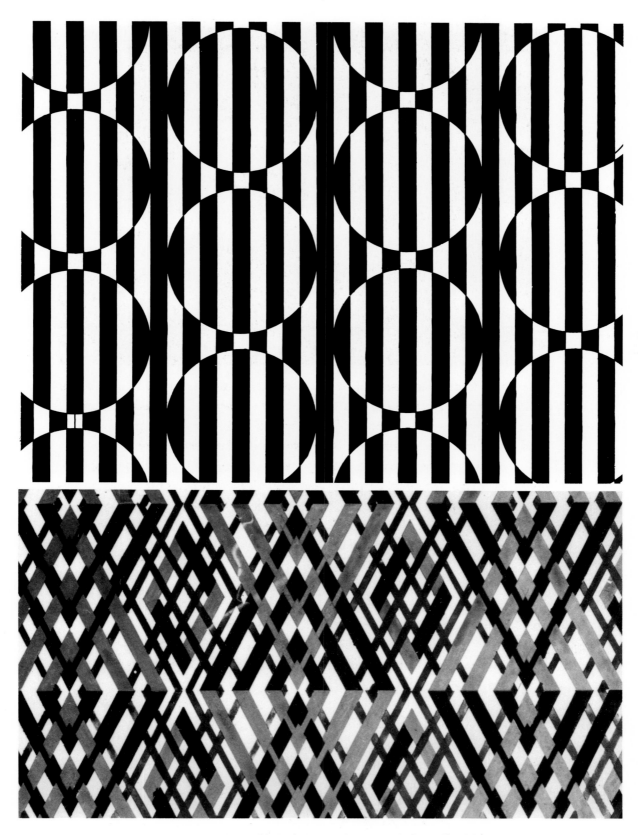

V. STEPANOVA, fabric design with geometrical motif, 1924.
L. POPOVA, fabric with a geometrical motif, 1920.

229

Roses, crêpe de Chine, c. 1930.
LEFT: printed calico with a stylized floral motif, Ivanovo Factory, 1932.
V. GURKOVSKAYA, printed calico with a stylized floral motif, 1930.

L. POPOVA, cotton printed with a geometrical motif, 1921-1923.
M. KHVOSTENKO, *The Milky Way,* 1934.

particularly appealed to certain designers. Their designs attempted to imitate the textures of these new materials.

Artistic problems and outdated structures persisted in the textile industry, and it was not until 1926–1927 that the total production was able to exceed that of 1913. This result was obtained thanks to the construction of new factories in Leningrad, Ivanovo, and in the Vladimir region. The lack of specialists was increasingly felt, and to this end schools and classes were created within the existing textile institutes and at the Arts and Trades College.

The future of Soviet decorative art was discussed in the press; critics stated that Soviet art had to eliminate, once and for all, the bad influence of "petit bourgeois" taste. There was also debate about the textile industry, with its obvious lack of well-trained and innovative artists.

In 1928, the students at the Arts and Trade College attempted to find a solution by organizing an exhibition entitled "Soviet Textiles for Everyday Use." The young artists Poluektova, Nazarevskaya, and Raitzer campaigned for a renewal of textile designs in order to elevate them to the level of pictorial art. Their goal was to transform textile art into a means of propaganda. Designs thus became thematic: illustrations of the building of Socialism and the organization of industry, and depictions of kolkhozes, komsomols, and pioneers.

V. STEPANOVA working on fabric design, photo A. Rodchenko.

Grouped under the initials AKhR (Association of Artists of the Revolution), such designers admitted only contemporary themes and Marxist ideology, rejecting all work which deviated from this line. Artists of the previous generation and of the LEF (Artists' Left Front) were particularly singled out for reprobation.

In 1930, the Vhutein Arts Council decided that it was necessary to "eliminate designs that are neutral, negative, and foreign to our class, and to replace them with new designs that are socially effective, intended for our class, and which support the building of Socialism."[1] In four months, more than five thousand motifs among the 18,775 existing motifs were destroyed.

The problem of motifs was complex. Could one be certain that the motif would fit the cloth, where the pattern was repeated and the material was mobile? It must be remembered that the designs were intended not for static furnishing fabrics but for clothing.

The graphic style used in furnishing fabrics was often inspired from posters: skiers, for example, saluting sailors on their ship (fabric designed by Lotonina, *The Navy*), or gymnasts (*The Parade,* a printed carpet, by Poliakova). The critic Arkin saw a real danger in the use of such themes for textiles: "A poster is never intended for long usage—it is this that gives it its force, its bite. It meets today's vigorous

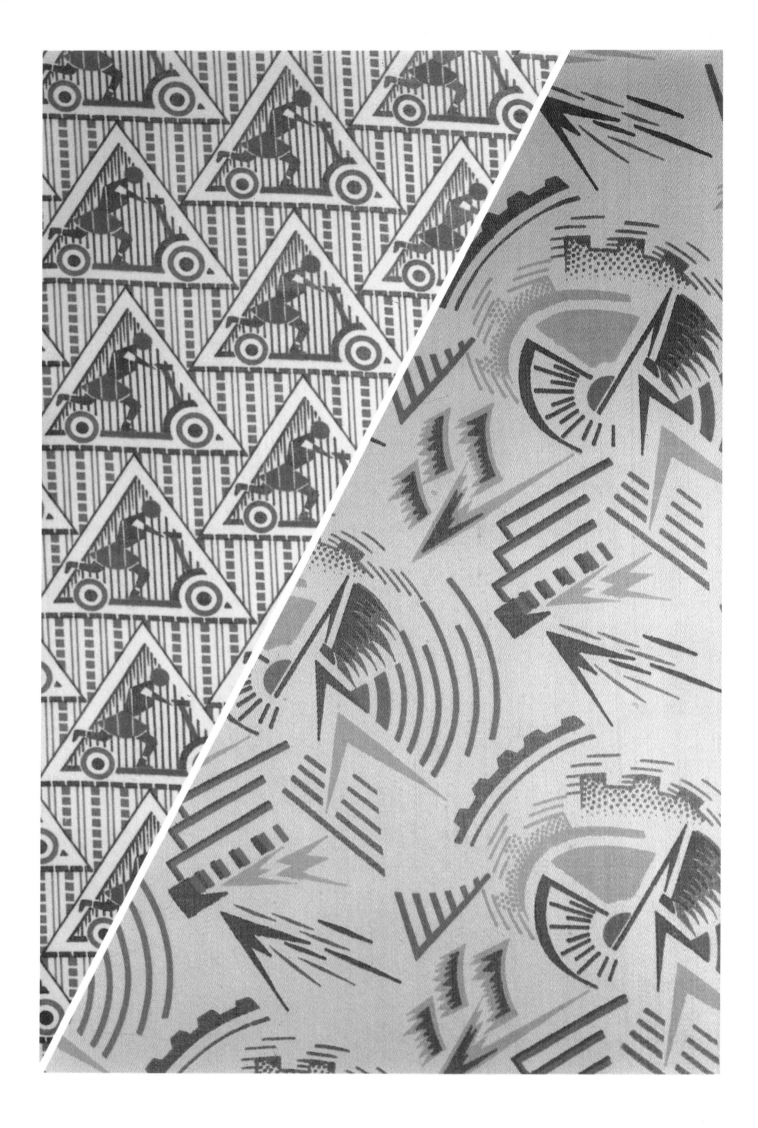

L. POPOVA, cotton print with a stylized geometrical motif, 1924.
Crêpe de Chine with a motif of striped circles, circa 1930.
PAGE 234: Cotton print with a stylized motif of girls on scooters, Moscow.
Cotton print with a geometrical motif suggesting
movement, Alekseyev Factory, Leningrad.

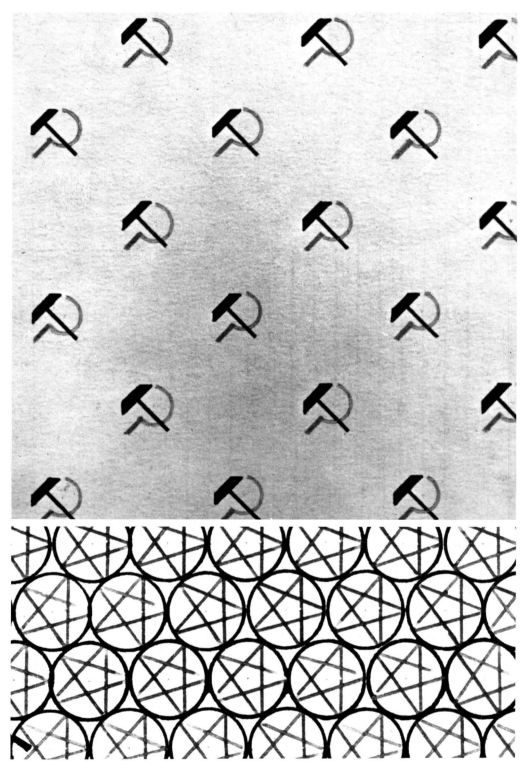

Printed calico with USSR emblems, 1921-1923.

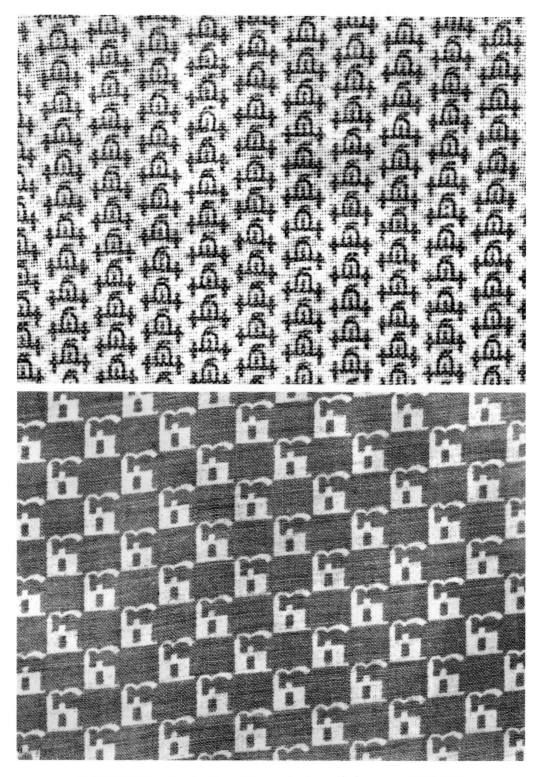

S. BURYLIN, printed calico with a stylized motif of tractors, 1930-1931.
S. BURYLIN, printed calico with a stylized motif of factories, 1930-1931.

M. NAZAREVSKAYA, *Likbez or Literacy Project*, 1920-1930.

themes head on. Textiles, on the other hand, are conceived for a long life. One would soon tire of a poster design."[2] Within this category, mention should be made of the work of Burilin at Ivanovo and in particular of *The Factory*, Nazarevskaya's calicos with ornamental motifs *(Literacy Projects, Electrification)*, *Winter Sports* by Anufrieva, *Industrial Motif* by Gurkovskaya, and calicos with motifs of toys by Bogoslovskaya.

Portraits were particularly ill-received on cloth; this was true even of Raitzer's design, *Young Komsomol Women Laughing*. Since the artists did not take into account the needs of the clothing for which the cloth was intended, thematic motifs often turned out to be ridiculous on articles of clothing and created problems for cutting. A compromise was attempted with the use of symbols and stylization, setting off a better debate between the critics Arkin and Fedorov-Davidov and the ideologists of the Association of Artists of the Revolution who considered that recourse to stylization was "socially detrimental." The partisans of thematic designs believed it was necessary to reflect "the dynamics of life": speeding locomotives, skiers and bicyclists in motion. They conceived of their work as realistic canvases. Thematic fabrics, however, were not popular, and in 1932, numbers of artists and consumers wrote articles in the press protesting against their preponderance.

In 1933, an article by Ryklin appeared in *Pravda*, entitled "In Front of a Tractor, Behind a Combine Harvester." With great sarcasm, Ryklin pointed out how ridiculous the thematic designs were: "Dresses and suits should remain dresses and suits. There is no reason to transform Soviet men and women into a gallery of ambulatory paintings."[3] The same year, the Soviet of People's Commissars published a decree concerning "the inadmissible characteristics of a certain type of fabric production of ugly and incongruous motifs."[4] From this point onward and until the end of the 1950s, thematic motifs disappeared almost entirely from fabric design, with the exception of fabrics for children which continued to use toy and animal motifs. On a practical level, this marked a return to the past: artists, lacking imagination, simply reworked floral designs. During the early thirties, the most striking realizations were produced by artists studying folk traditions in textile art. Leonov, Khokhlytchev, Burylin, and Russian were thus able to hand down their knowledge and create cloth designs in the traditional Russian floral style.

The most interesting work produced during the second half of the thirties was by Khvostenko, Chumiatskaya, and Chapovalova of the Three Mountains Factory, Russin and Butorlin of the First Printed Calico Factory, Agayan, Lugovskaya, and Skliarova of The Red Rose Silk Factory, and Gurkovskaya, Khokhlytchev, Bogoslovskaya, and Provorova of Ivanovo.

During this period, designs were fresh and light, cloth more refined and orig-

Printed cotton with a stylized ship motif suggesting working on cargoes, circa 1920.
Printed cotton with a stylized floral motif, circa 1920.
LEFT: cotton printed with a stylized repetitive motif of gear wheels. Serpukov
Factory. *Physical Education*, printed cotton. Serpukov Factory.

inal (cotton voile). Motifs generally depicted branches and leaves, with small spots of color suggesting bunches of flowers (for example, Nazarevskaya's *Birch Branch* design).

Among the printed fabrics in crêpe de Chine produced at The Red Rose Silk Factory, much of the work was primitive in execution, no doubt as a result of the new technique of photographic printing introduced in 1936. Floral motifs became miniaturized, with poppies, carnations, daisies, cornflowers, and ears of wheat in the work of Skliarova and Gurkovskaya, whose *Meadow Flowers* was singled out for praise at the 1937 International Exhibition of Art and Techniques in Paris.

Geometrical forms reappeared toward the end of the thirties. They were both simple and classical: checks, stripes, polka-dots, and circles. The first fabric in this style had appeared in 1934, *The Milky Way,* a cotton voile by Khvostenko executed at the Three Mountains Factory. The fabrics dating from this period were generally well-made—the print corresponded to the finished piece of clothing and even enhanced it.

A new trend emerged around this time, consisting of more voluminous designs on such fabrics as crêpe de Chine and cotton voile. Sumptuous lilacs and mimosas were depicted in motifs that resembled still-life paintings. At the same time, artists who had hitherto concentrated only on clothing fabric now began to create designs for furnishing, carpets, and kerchiefs, as well as for unique fabrics created exclusively for exhibitions. Soviet art became more complex not only in the domain of textiles but also in architecture, the visual arts, and fashion design. Opulent motifs with myriad details seemed at times to stifle the very structure of the clothing they were designed for. This new style was inspired from traditional motifs, very much in fashion in the late 1930s. Artists borrowed the colors and motifs of the Caucasus, the Ukraine, and the Far North (for example, a calico by V. Gukovskaya, *Ukrainian Motifs,* 1939). These fabrics, shawls, and kerchiefs with Oriental motifs, despite their curious blend of the modern and the traditional, were magnificent. They were a great success with the public as well as with artists.

NOTES

1. See N. Polovektova, "The Struggle for Soviet textiles," in *For a Proletarian Art,* 1931, n· 1, p. 20.
2. *The Voice of Textiles,* March 25, 1931.
3. *Pravda,* October 6, 1933.
4. *Izvestia,* December 18, 1933.

Anniversary of the October Revolution of 1917, commemorative shawl.

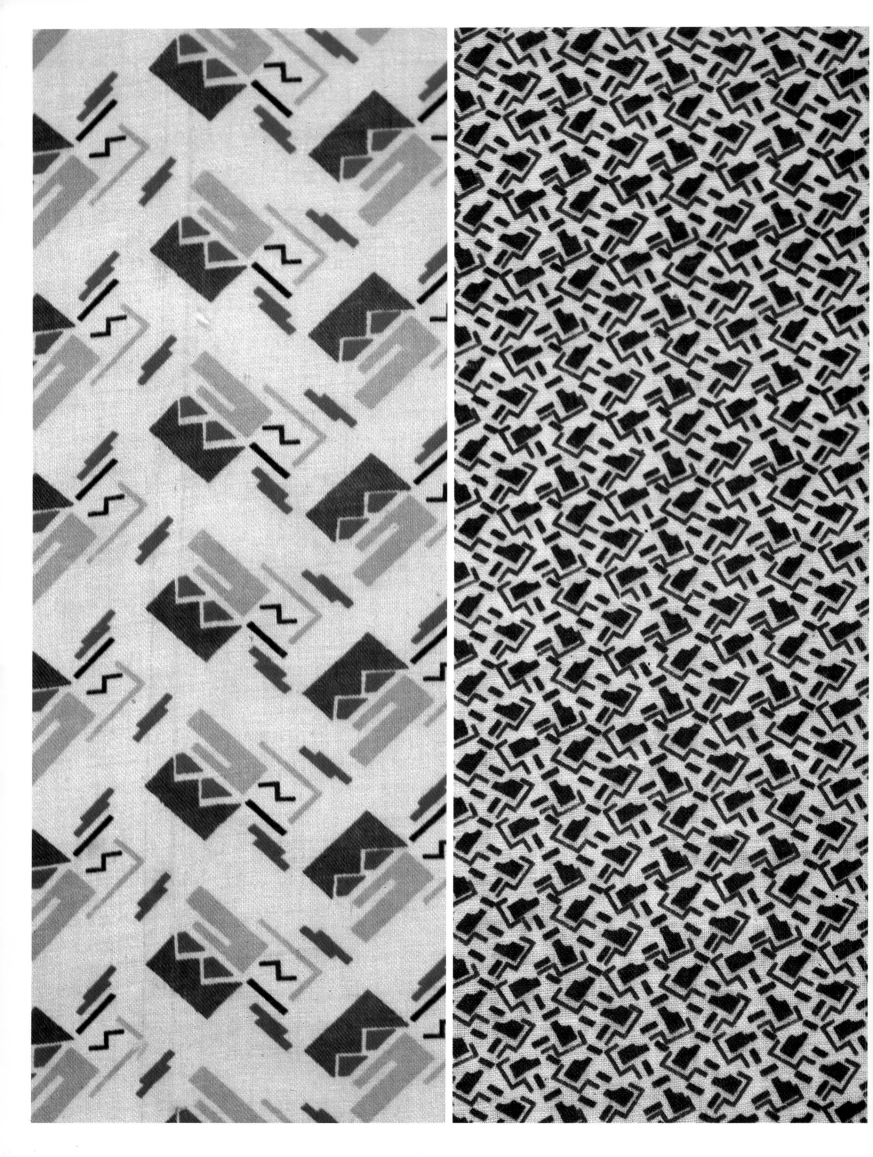

The Harvest, printed cotton. Sverdlov Factory, Moscow.
LEFT: O. BOGOSLOVSKAYA, cotton with a stylized industrial motif, 1927.
Cotton with a stylized industrial motif, Ivanovo, circa 1930.

S. AGAYAN, *Primroses*, crêpe de Chine, 1928.
S. AGAYAN, *Almond Trees in Flower*, crêpe de Chine, 1939.

Furnishing Fabrics

urnishing fabrics had suffered for a long time from a total absence of creativity. The first jacquard patterns, produced around 1930 by the Muscovite Furnishing Fabrics factory, were manufactured according to old methods, with few new designs. Upholstery fabrics, literally covered with fruit and flowers, were inspired by French classical art and traditional Russian decoration. The manufacturing of these fabrics, however, was at a high technological level. The fabrics were used to upholster sofas and door hangings, their solid texture serving both the practical and aesthetic needs of the consumers.

There had been a serious shortage of raw materials and dyes since the Revolution. Furnishing fabrics were dark in color—predominantly black. It was not until 1930 that a variety of fabrics began to be successfully manufactured—solid cottons in assorted colors, cloth with grainy textures such as shagreen, repp, toile, striped cloth. Certain types of heavy cloth, because of their texture and colors—heavy black and orange threads—resembled the handmade colorful cloths of popular tradition. Some of the new fabrics, such as shagreen, had to be abandoned for technical reasons. The artists who were involved in the creation of these fabrics were Moisseva, Chatchkiany, Lechtman, Voyekova, Bergner, and Bohrman.

During the 1930s, the choice of fabrics for furnishing increased substantially. Upholstery fabrics with reproductions of old floral designs from the seventeenth, eighteenth, and nineteenth centuries continued to be manufactured, but classical geometrical motifs were also produced—checks, stripes, and various shapes with toothed and irregular outlines. The texture of these fabrics precluded the use of rounded forms. A famous fabric from the years 1930–1932, *The Tiger*, by Tikhonov, was realized by interweaving blue, gray, and black threads in a hatched, laddered motif.

Other fabrics drew their inspiration from the carpets, embroidery, and printed cloth of the Ukraine, Moldavia, and Asia, although the colors and designs by Voyekova, Moisseva, and Lechtman did not equal the craftsmanship of popular weavers. Around the middle of the 1930s, a considerable effort began to be made to improve the quality and diversity of fabrics and wallpaper. Outdated motifs were abandoned, and the collaboration of new designers was sought. Particular attention was given to the interior architecture, and although the designers often had to make do with what was offered, nevertheless the accent was on a closer rela-

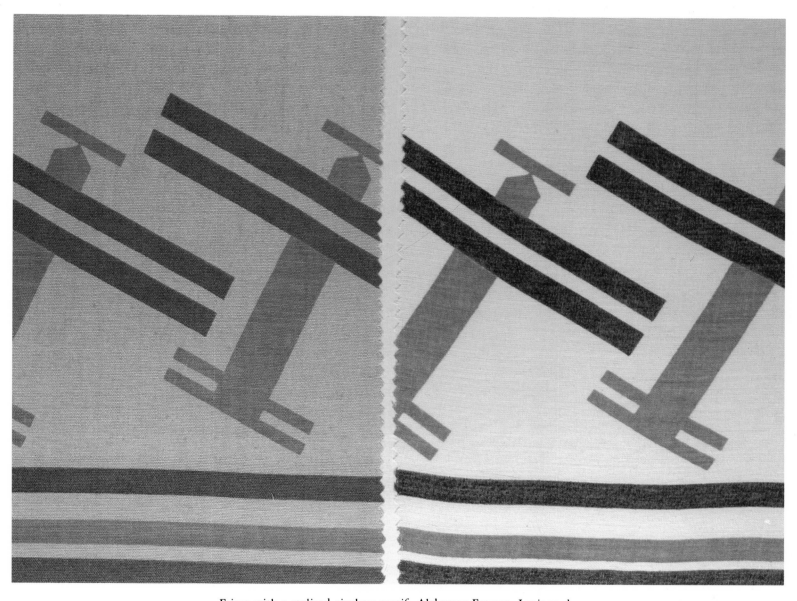

Frieze with a stylized airplane motif. Alekseyev Factory, Leningrad.
LEFT: cotton printed with stylized geometrical megaphones. Serpukov Factory. Cotton
printed with wheat, flag and sickle motifs forming C.C.C.P., the acronym for
the Soviet state. Alekseyev Factory, Leningrad.

tionship between the utilitarian and the artistic. Psychological reactions to decors and colors were studied, and several fabric projects were specially conceived for clubs, reading rooms, and children's sanatoriums.[1] Such research, however, was marginal. Most fabrics, carpets, and curtains remained uniform and unappealing; the most widespread motif consisted of asymmetrical stripes and checks.

The same problems arose concerning wallpaper, which was of consistently poor quality. Modern-style themes were repeated endlessly as were imitations of Chichkin's *Morning in a Pine Forest*.

During this same period, the Furnishing Fabrics factory was producing unique fabrics intended for public buildings or as commemorative fabrics. The curtain of the Bolshoi Theater and fabric for the Palace of the Soviets were examples of this kind of production. Motifs were usually monumental and solemn, in accordance with the architecture of the building for which they were designed.

Designed in 1929 by Fedorovsky, the curtain of the Bolshoi Theater is sumptuous. Gold threads glitter against a red and gold background, in perfect harmony with the red velvet and gilded wood of the seats and the reflections of the huge crystal chandelier. In brocade, natural silk, and gold brocade, the curtain is embellished with immense Soviet emblems—the hammer and the sickle, sheaves of wheat, the letters CCCP (USSR), and the important dates of the international workers' movement.

Important work was undertaken at the Palace of the Soviets in 1939 and continued after the end of the war, with the creation of an experimental weaving workshop. The Palace required the manufacturing of many different types of fabric: for furniture covers, wall-hangings, draperies for windows and doors, and insulation. These fabrics needed to be resistant and easily washable. Lastly, their aspect, size, and proportions had to be in keeping with the building's interior architecture. For example, silk and upholstery fabrics were too heavy, their designs too intricate. Even the best patterns were rather conventional.

One of the most beautiful fabrics created for the Palace, *October* (1940–1946), designed for the civil war room, was the work of Nazarevskaya. This was a blend of traditional Russian ornamental motifs of the eighteenth and nineteenth centuries and modern decorative elements: an oak and laurels, and arabesques of machine-gun belts against a background of bayonets.

The products of the experimental workshop subsequently gave rise to other fruitful projects, including the restoration of old Russian fabrics preserved in the museums of Kuskovo, Ostankino, Tsarskoye Selo, and Pavlovsk, during the years 1948–1952.

However, the domain of furnishing fabrics did not greatly progress after the 1930s. Upholstery fabric, plush, repp, and cretonne were uniform and outmoded, and artist-weavers were loath to make any innovations. In 1939, at the First National Congress of Textile Artists (designers, colorists, engravers), an important problem was discussed, that of the discrepancy between the quality of the fabric, the type of clothing it was intended for, and the initial design. Another issue was the use of traditional motifs. It was decided that these were to be recreated rather than copied, but no analysis was made of the trends to be followed in the future. The leitmotif of the meeting was the depiction of Soviet reality and the heritage of the folk tradition.

During the years preceding the war, the results of the evolution in the Soviet textile industry were published in the magazine *Light Industry*. In comparison to 1913, the amount of cotton had increased by 70% and represented, in 1939, nearly four billion meters. Textile factories had been established in Central Asia and in the Caucasus, and institutes and research laboratories had been opened.

During the war, many factories were evacuated to the East, and their production was restricted to fabrics intended for the army. Other factories were destroyed. In Tashkent and Ivanovo, ordinary motifs continued to be designed. After 1944, the production of furnishing fabrics began again, using pre-war motifs.

NOTES

1. See Z. Miliavskaya, "Furnishing Fabrics" in *Architecture in the USSR*, 1940, n· 7, p. 20.

The Gift, printed cotton, circa 1930.

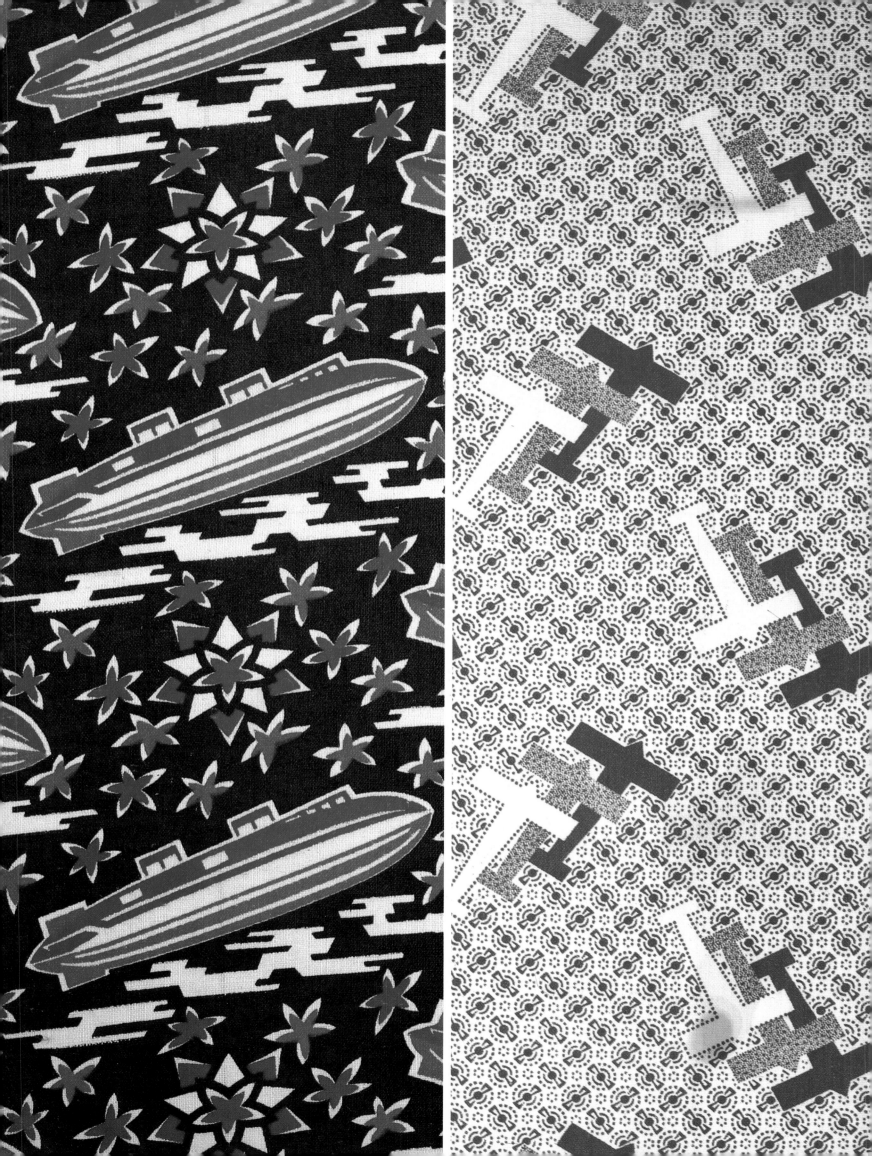

L. RAITZER, *The Mechanization of the Red Army*, printed fabric, 1933.
M. BOBYCHOV, *Agriculture*, printed fabric, circa 1930.
LEFT: cotton printed with a stylized dirigible motif against a background representing
a starry sky. Trechgornaya Factory, Moscow.
Cotton printed with a stylized airplane motif. Ivanovo Factory.

M. BOBYCHOV, costume for the play *The Beautiful Brook*, 1935.

V. STEPANOVA, sports outfits, circa 1920.

The Balloons, printed calico with a motif suggesting playtime, intended for
children's clothes, circa 1935. V. GURKOVSKAYA, *The Harvest,* printed calico
with a stylized argricultural motif, 1931.

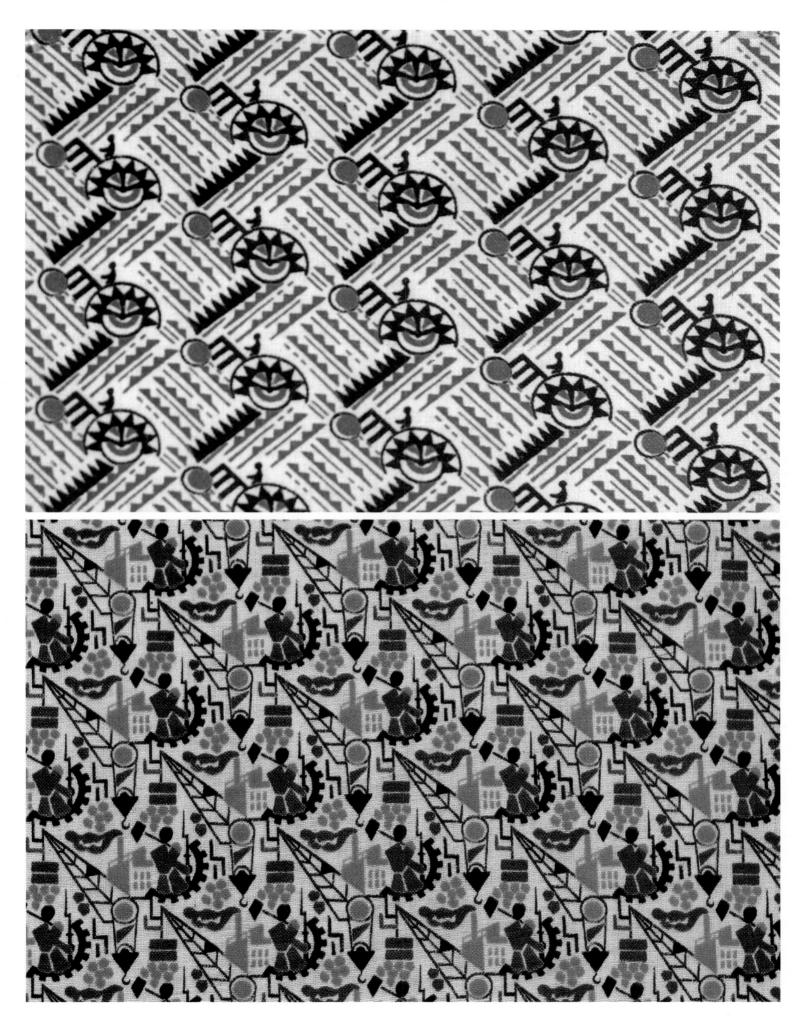

S. BURYLIN, *The Tractor*, printed cotton, 1930. *Building*, printed cotton, circa 1930.

S. BURYLIN, *Building,* printed calico, 1928-1930. S. BURYLIN, printed
calico with an industrial motif suggestive of mechanization.
LEFT: printed cotton with a stylized motif of fishermen. Trechgornaya Factory, Moscow.
In the Hollow of the Wave, cotton printed with a stylized motif of ships. Alekseyev Factory, Leningrad.

L. SILITCH, fabric with a stylized geometrical motif, entitled *The Harvesters*.
Printed cotton with a motif of stylized airplanes evoking the Soviet Air Force.

PAGE 261: Cotton printed with a motif of stylized pylons. Alekseyev Factory, Leningrad.
Printed cotton with a Futurist motif suggesting speed and movement. Serpukov Factory.

O. ANISSIMOVA, cover for the magazine *The Art of Dressing*.

The Clothing Industry

At the beginning of the century, two important events altered clothing fashions. Women's clothes became shorter, simpler, and more masculine. The second event was the change within the textile industry itself. Since the industrial production of textiles now took precedence over cloth produced by traditional workshops, the garment industry was increasingly intended for an urban population. The First World War and the important requirements of the army were the reasons behind the growth of large clothing factories in Moscow and Petrograd. At the same time, small traditional workshops continued to produce clothing. Tailors were both fashion designers and cloth cutters.

The Revolution brought about other changes within the structure of the garment industry. In 1921, there were 279 firms employing over forty thousand people. Division of labor had already been introduced into some of these. During the Civil War, the handful of functioning textile factories produced only military cotton, canvas, calico, and unbleached linen. All were of poor quality. Clothing was made from blankets, tablecloths, curtains, and sheets.

In 1918, a competition was organized to create new uniform designs for the Red Army. The participants included, among others, Kustodiev and Vasnetsov. Kustodiev's project for head-gear and greatcoat was selected (1918-1919): this was the birth of the famous Red Army uniform, the "Budenny" style cap with the red star, and the gray greatcoat with scarlet facings and frogged fastenings. The cap and greatcoat drew their inspiration from ancient Russian helmets and caftans. The whole uniform was bordered in red, the color symbolizing the Revolution. Its symbolic value was of greater importance to Kustodiev than its practical and functional aspects.

In 1918, one modern workshop did exist which produced clothing for the civilian population. It was run by the talented fashion designer, Natalia Lamanova. Other artists of renown also worked there, including Mukhina, Exter, and Pribylskaya. Their work was both theoretical and experimental. The articles they created were intended for the entire population, but in fact they received only private commissions, since existing clothing factories were both technically and economically unsuited for such production.

At this time, a heated debate sprang up between partisans of the old and of the "new." The detractors of traditional bourgeois fashion did not argue for new

E. SAVKOVA, dress with a traditional embroidery motif, 1939.

V. and G. STENBERG, costume designs for the Lecoq operetta, *Day and Night*,
14 1/2 x 6 1/4″ (36.5 x 16 cm) paper, India ink, gouache, 1926. A. Bashrushin,
Museum of Theater History, Moscow.

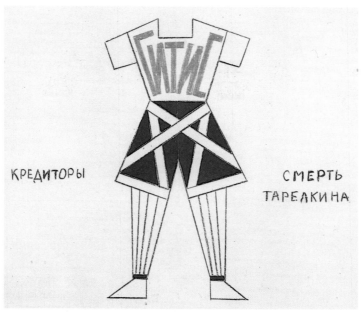

КРЕДИТОРЫ СМЕРТЬ ТАРЕЛКИНА

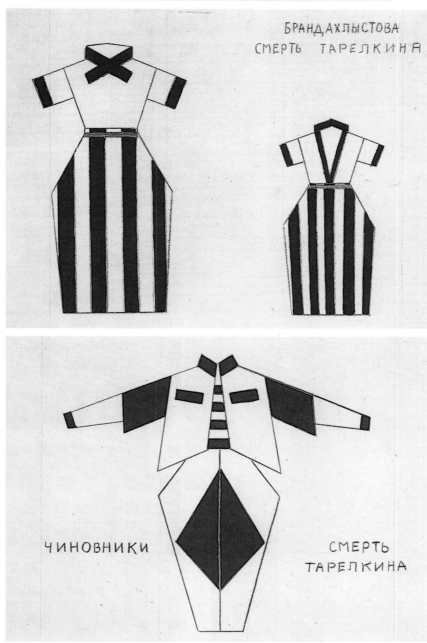

БРАНДАХЛЫСТОВА
СМЕРТЬ ТАРЕЛКИНА

ЧИНОВНИКИ СМЕРТЬ ТАРЕЛКИНА

V. STEPANOVA, costume designs for the satirical comedy *The Death of Tarelkin*. India ink on paper, 13 1/2 x 14″ (34.5 x 35.5 cm), V. Rodchenko collection, 1922.

V. STEPANOVA, sports outfits, circa 1920.

EL LISSITSKY, *Sportsmen,* lithograph, 21 x 18″ (53.3 x 45.5 cm), from the book
Victory Over the Sun, 1923.

Soviet type fashion, but rather they denied the very existence of fashion which they believed to be prejudicial to the Communist way of life. Nevertheless, unaffected by these polemics, new forms, simple and austere, came into being: "Proletarian fashion."

The debate nevertheless resulted in the birth of all sorts of original associations. The Futurists created harlequin costumes; the Down with Shame group wanted to eliminate clothing altogether; the Body Organization maintained that "physical culture can and should go beyond the limits of a sports terrain, and indeed it has already begun to do so. Last summer, comrades in shorts walked around the city, not only in organized groups, but individually as well."[1] New styles of sports and professional clothes were studied. They were to be rational, hygienic, and capable of meeting modern needs and new economic conditions.[2]

Among the most common articles of clothing of the 1920s was the Tolstoy blouse or Tolstovka which combined the lines of a military tunic with a Russian peasant blouse. The attire of the German "Jungsturm" organization was also popular. In addition, women activists were very appreciative of red scarves.

In 1923, the Moskvochvey trust founded a fashion house. It also published a fashion magazine, *Atelier,* but only one number appeared. This fashion house was considered to be the ideological and theoretical authority for everyday wear. Its objective was to attain the same level as European fashion, while maintaining aspects of the national character of Russian art.[3] The house created models intended for mass production as well as for individual orders. Also in 1923, during the First Russian Agricultural, Industrial, and Crafts Exhibition of Russia, articles of clothing designed by Lamanova, Mukhina, Exter, and Pribylskaya were displayed.

Lamanova had opened her own workshop in 1885. During the 1890s, she had begun collaborating with the Moscow Theater, and continued to do so until the time of her death in 1941. She worked with Stanislavsky, among others, and designed the costumes for *Aelita, Alexander Nevsky,* and *The Circus.* As Russia's first clothing theorist, she was particularly interested in professional wear and attached to the ideas of logic, rationality, and simplicity in clothing design. The basis of all her designs was the rectangle, with variations in the form of tunics, jackets, or caftans worn over a dress. The rectangular cut economized fabric and allowed for large-scale manufacturing of clothes even with the limited material of the era. In addition, her consistent commitment to mass production was able to reduce the amount of time needed for manufacturing. The very texture of low-cost fabrics (canvas, linen, unbleached linen), both stiff and easily wrinkled, called for a straight and severe cut. In other words, the material defined the shape. This elementary law was a true discovery. Before Lamanova, designers tended to neglect the characteristics of a particular cloth by attempting to disguise it behind a com-

E. YAKUMINA, women's work outfit in cotton, 1928.

A. **EXTER**, fancy dresswear, 1923.

E. PRIBYLSKAYA, shift, 1920.

plicated cut. Lamanova, on the contrary, accentuated the texture of each type of cloth by the form of the article of clothing.

Fabrics with large, smooth surfaces required a specific type of decoration—embroidery. Lamanova's embroideries were either traditional borders salvaged from old linen, or modernized decorations. Her designs are timeless; they never go out of style. Her ideas (rationality, severity, simplicity, economy of material, freedom of movement) were revived, moreover, at the end of the 1950s.

In 1925, to compete with French fashion magazines, the magazine *The Red Field* published a special number, *Art in Daily Life,* with simple and practical models and patterns by Lamanova and Mukhina. Intended for private use, these patterns offered both fashionable styles and typically Russian clothing: summer dresses, city ensembles, coats, sports clothes, and pioneer uniforms. The two artists, for example, who had often collaborated with each other, designed a simple, shirt-waist cut for an elegant dress based on a black scarf by Pavlovsk decorated with traditional small flowers. In general, they offered clothes made in inexpensive fabrics (toile, unbleached linen), ornamented with ribbons or bands of color sewn onto the garment.

For the Decorative Arts Exhibition in Paris in 1925, Lamanova and Mukhina prepared a series of dresses, matching skirts and blouses, hats, handbags, and jewelry. They used simple materials: string, rope, straw or embroidered linen for hats; wood, stones, or dough for jewelry. Their efforts were rewarded with a Grand Prize.

ABOVE: dresses realized at Lamanova's workshop. M. ORLOVA, woolen blouse with traditional embroidered motif, 1928.

A. EXTER, costume in a Far East style.
A. EXTER, coat dress with a geometrical motif.

N. LAMANOVA, costume designed for the actress A. Khokhlova, her favorite model.

TOP: K. BOZHNEVA, M.
VYCHESLAVTSEVA,
woolen blouse with a
traditional motif, 1939.
BOTTOM: M. ORLOVA,
white cashmere blouse with a
traditional embroidered
motif, 1928.

In 1928, an exhibition of Handmade Cloth and Embroidery in modern women's clothes was held. Lamanova and Pribylskaya exhibited an assortment of linen garments that won the critics' approval. Arkin was enthusiastic about the fact that the designers had subordinated design to fabric and the decorative elements to the cut of the clothes.[4] Lamanova's name became known in Europe and even in America. In Russia, the "Lamanova style" was popular among the NEP (New Economic Policy) bourgeoisie.

Pribylskaya also worked at the Moskvochvey fashion house, but her main activities were with handmade textile organizations. Her work maintained a number of crafts methods within industrial production. The coarse and poorly-dyed linens of the period were improved by embroidery, but in spite of this, Pribylskaya's designs were not suitable for mass production.

Exter was another designer who worked at the fashion house, where she was already known as a theater designer. She, too, adhered wholeheartedly to the idea of simple and functional clothing which, however, she thought should be adapted to each type of individual: "The different categories of people should be studied in relationship with the character, form, and color of the garment."[5] Exter's best creations were her dresses for little girls, her professional women's clothing, and a man's coat in coarse linen. Her raincoats in contemporary fabrics are still worn today. But her work was characterized above all by elegant and extravagant gowns, unique garments that were variations of theater costumes. Here, she deliberately side-stepped the rules of common dressmaking, leaving behind proportion, logic, and the relationship of the style to the fabric. Instead, diagonal lines sectioned the dress in unusual places, creating seductive geometrical figures. Exter liked to combine fine fabrics of different textures—satin, fur, silk, and brocade. Such extravagance was further emphasized by intense color contrasts—violet, orange, and black, or raspberry and black. She also introduced Egyptian motifs, accentuating the "theatrical" aspect of the garment.

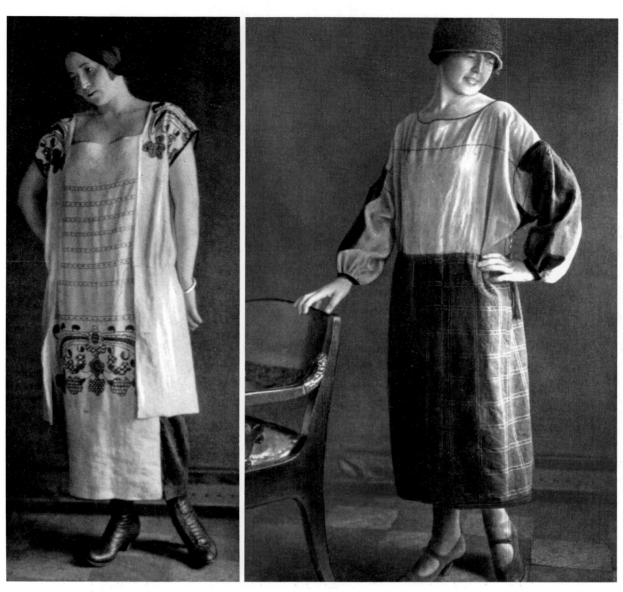

N. LAMANOVA, lightweight dress in hand-embroidered fabric using a
traditional motif, circa 1920.
N. LAMANOVA, lightweight dress in hand-embroidered fabric, circa 1920.

A. EXTER, evening dresses, 1923.

V. MUKHINA, evening dress, 1923.

TOP: dress designs from the 1920s.
BOTTOM: E. YAKUMINA, cocktail dress, 1928.

V. KHODASSEVITCH, covers of the magazine *The Art of Dressing*, 1923.

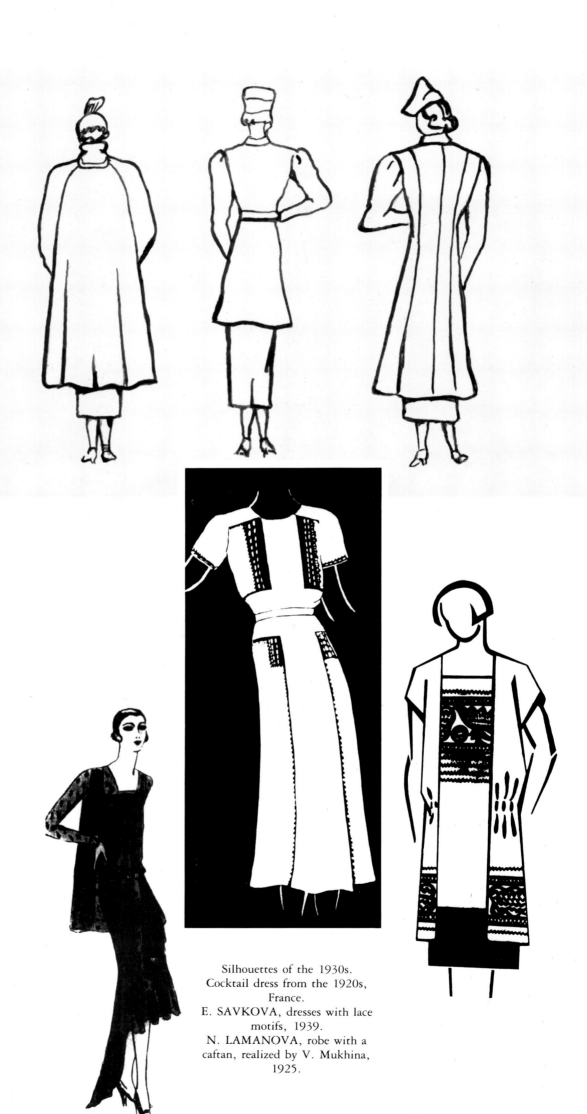

Silhouettes of the 1930s.
Cocktail dress from the 1920s,
France.
E. SAVKOVA, dresses with lace
motifs, 1939.
N. LAMANOVA, robe with a
caftan, realized by V. Mukhina,
1925.

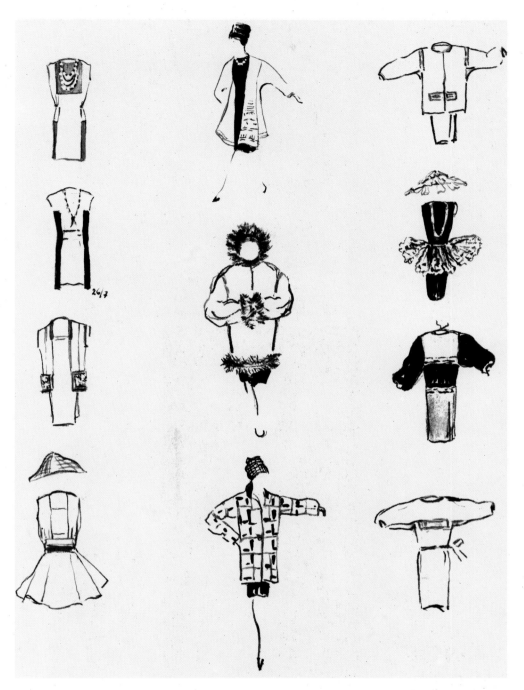

N. MAKAROVA, sketches, 1925–1928.
Cocktail dress from the 1920s, France.

K. BOZHNEVA, M. VYCHESLAVTSEVA, woolen pullover, 1939.
Girl's dress, 1920–1930.
Boy's short coat, with fur officer's collar and matching cap, 1920–1930.
Girl's short cape and cloche hat, 1920–1930.

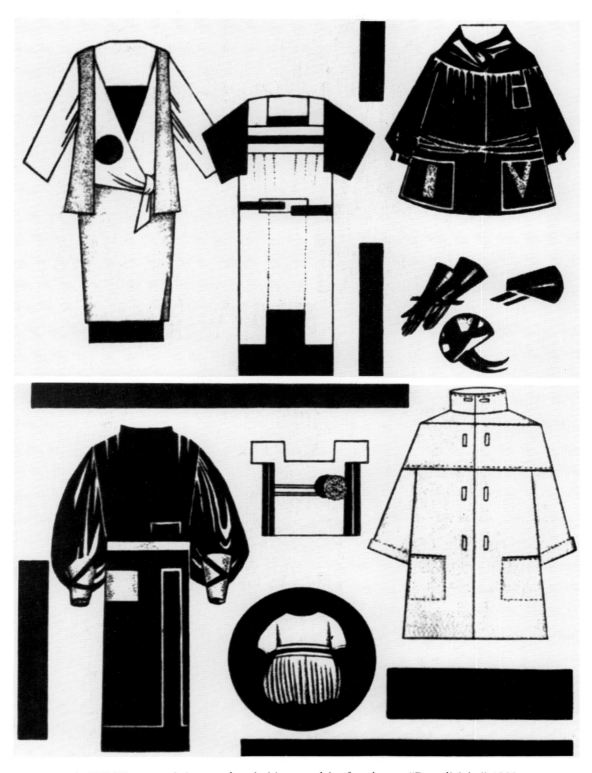

A. **EXTER**, research in everyday clothing, model referred to as "Prosodiejola," 1923.

TOP: V. and G. STENBERG, costume designs for the Lecoq operetta *Day and Night*, 14 1/2 x 6 1/4" (36.5 x 16 cm), India ink and gouache on paper, 1926. A. Bakhrushin, Museum of Theater History, Moscow.
BOTTOM: V. and G. STENBERG, costume designs for *The Kulirol* by P. Antokolsky, 14 x 6 1/2" (35.5 x 16.5 cm), India ink and gouache on paper, 1925. A. Bakhrushin, Museum of Theater History, Moscow.

In 1923, a number of artists like Rodchenko, Tatlin, Stepanova, Popova, the Vesnin brothers, and Lavinsky proposed a variety of theories and experimental models. All these artists were interested in everyday clothes, declaring the coverall "today's outfit."[6] Stepanova designed uniforms for surgeons, firemen, and pilots, while Rodchenko borrowed certain details of professional outfits (overalls, zippers, patch pockets, etc.). Sportsclothes were also a source of inspiration because of their simplicity and colorful effects. Stepanova and Popova created both sportsclothes and sports-inspired clothes in printed fabrics with geometrical motifs.

In 1920 the Kustexport organization was founded for the clothing industry. This craftsmen's association worked in collaboration with the Department of Foreign Trade. Although the final product was to be mass-produced, the artists created only models for private customers. Peasant cooperatives in Tula, Kaluga, Novgorod, and Riazan provided the cloth, embroidery models, lace, and printed calico. With great profit to the State, this organization also helped to support folk crafts. The models were often modernized; to this end, Stepanova, Rodchenko, Lamanova, Davidova, and Pribylskaya were invited to work at Kustexport.

In 1928, the publication of the first number of the magazine *The Art of Dressing* was a major event. The magazine carried articles on the history of cloth and costumes, on fashion and on hygiene, as well as illustrations and clothing patterns. Most of the styles were French, but certain models created by Orchanskaya, Orlova, and Anissimova used traditional Russian motifs. Pravossudovitch and Iakumina designed clothing in modern styles. The magazine existed for two years and was then abandoned, as certain articles were entirely devoted to foreign clothing models.

N. MAKAROVA, fur coat, circa 1930.

At the end of the 1920s, thanks to the policy of industrialization, huge clothing factories were built in Moscow, Kiev, and Baku. In 1928–1930, professional high schools were opened in Moscow and Leningrad, and specialized training departments were created within textile firms. A number of technical problems remained concerning the basting and assembling of garments. A solution was found in 1930 with the opening of the Institute of Research for the Clothing Industry. As of 1929, with the appearance of the monthly review *Technique and Economy in the Clothing Industry,* the various steps in the making of a piece of clothing were outlined in detail. For ten years, this magazine was the unique source of research in the clothing industry. The 1930s were rich in debates and discussions, in particular on the necessary link between textile design and types of garment (articles by D. Arkin and A. Fyodorova-Davidova).

While the 1920s had been involved in researching new forms, the 1930s were concerned with the diversification of styles in view of mass production. An article

N. LAMANOVA,
broadcloth lumber-jacket,
1921–1922. Ski outfit, circa
1930.

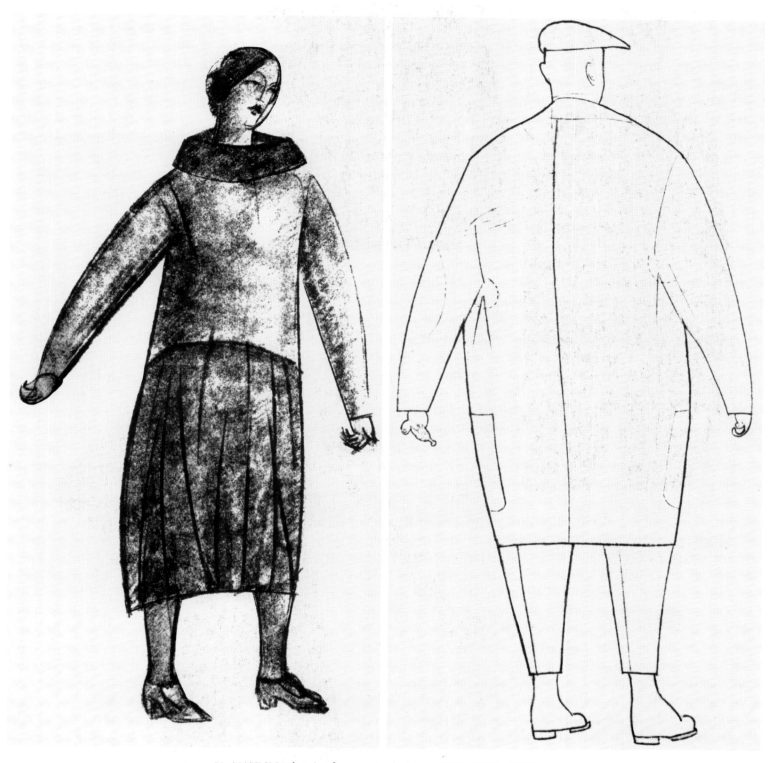

V. TATLIN, sketch of women's clothing, 1922–1924, GNIMA.
V. TATLIN, sketch of men's clothing, 1922–1924, GNIMA.

ПЛАТЬЕ из СУРОВОГО ПОЛОТНА

Платье из сурового фабричного или любого кустарного полотна с отделкой из кумача. Оно состоит из двух полотнищ: на переднем (рис. 1) делаются надрезы по линиям аб и вг; получившийся от надреза кусок материи абвг или отрезывается или завертывается как это показано на рис. пунктиром. На заднем полотнище такие же надрезы делаются по линиям а1, б1 и в1, г1. Верхняя часть полотнища выкраивается, как показано на чертежах. Так как перед у платья шире спины, то его излишняя ширина от боковых швов стягивается на резинке на высоте бедра и у воротника, как это показано на рисунке. Излишек ширины нижней части платья образует глубокую складку, закладывающуюся от бокового шва на переднее полотнище.

Рис. 1 переднее полотнище. Рис. 2—заднее полотнище.

N. LAMANOVA, unbleached linen dress, drawing executed by V. Mukhina, circa 1920.

N. LAMANOVA, elegant dress worn with a cashmere shawl, drawing executed
by V. Mukhina, circa 1920.
N. LAMANOVA, woman's coat in military broadcloth, drawing executed by V.
Mukhina, circa 1920.

L. POPOVA, sketch for the cover of a fashion magazine, summer 1924, gouache and collage on paper. Tetryakov Gallery, Moscow.

L. POPOVA, sketch for the cover of a fashion magazine, summer 1924, gouache and collage on paper. Tetryakov Gallery, Moscow.

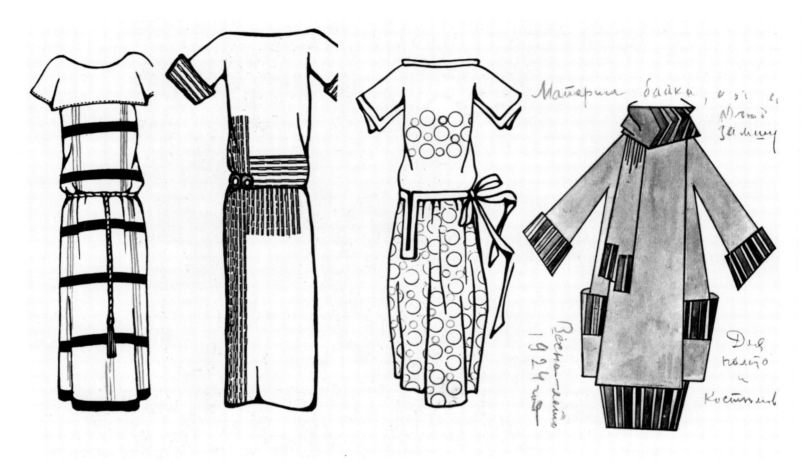

Материл байка, ...
... ...
заму...

Весна—лето
1924 ...

Для
пальто
и
Костюм...

L. POPOVA, sketch of calico dresses, 1924.

L. POPOVA, fabric design project and dress designs in the same fabric, circa 1920.

Parade procession of Soviet athletes on Red Square in 1932, photograph taken by A. Rodchenko.

by E. Eichenholtz, "The Problems of Mass Produced Clothing," is still valid to-day. The author maintained that the dress designer should no longer work with a handmade pattern, but rather that the pattern should be adapted to the conditions necessary for mechanized production. Only the lines of the garment and the color should be expressive; aside from that, the article of clothing should not be depen-dent on any kind of added decoration. The opposite point of view was held by the "sociologists." They wanted the uniform to be introduced as the basic form of clothing. Lamanova's work and the idea according to which "the material defined the form" was violently criticized. Passionate discussions on the form of garments took place. Critical articles and features appeared daily in the newspapers, like Ilf and Petrov's series *The Bowknot Directive* and Nilin's study *A Life of Luxury* (1934).

An exhibition of mass-produced clothing was organized in Moscow in 1932. The most flagrant shortcomings were in evidence: lack of technical and artistic savoir-faire, insufficient knowledge of fabrics. Calico dresses were cut as if they were made in silk, with ruffles and pleats; elegant dresses were made in either broadcloth or silk, as if there were no difference between the two. Professional out-fits were the most successful. On the other hand, the garments designed for kol-khoz workers were pitiful; none of the existing theories had been applied. Skirts and blouses were overburdened with colors, puffed-up in the traditional style; men's coats were long and heavy. The specific aspects of life and work on the kol-khoz farms had not been taken into account at all.

As of 1931, new research centers were established, in particular the Moscow pattern studio which opened in 1934. Its first directress was Makarova, a talented student of Lamanova. She drew inspiration from nature, utilizing forms and colors of flowers, birds, and animals. The form of petals was the basis of a dress; birds' heads were used as inspiration for children's caps. The distribution of color on the fabric was suggestive of traditional Russian costumes: Turkish red for collars, sleeve cuffs, and hem borders, and combinations of white and red or blue and gray. During the 1930s, Makarova used motifs from the Far North, the Caucasus, and the Ukraine.

N. MAKAROVA, summer dress, 1925.

The fashion bureau headed by F.A. Gorelenkova, another student of Lama-nova (as well as of Liamina and the theater costume designers Topleninov and Su-dakevitch), was given the task of supervising the work of the garment industry and designing models suitable for mass production. Its artistic committee included not only dress designers but also famous artists: Pimenov, Goncharov, Mukhina, Arkin, and Favorsky. The bureau also filled private orders, but before being of-fered to the buyer, the patterns had to be approved by the artistic committee, a system which kept a check on individual taste.

In 1939, a fashion show was held in Leningrad, with, for the first time, the

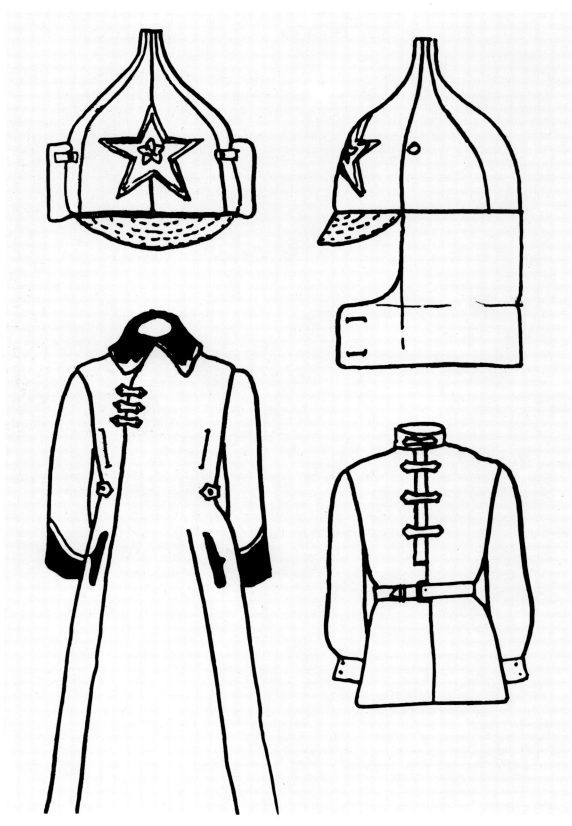

B. KUSTODIEV, Red Army uniform, circa 1918.

participation of other Republics (the designer Lozovsky from the Ukraine; Khassanov, from the Uzbekistan).

The Ukrainian designers were extremely traditionalist; they had even preserved the puffed embroidered blouse. The Uzbekistan, on the other hand, was the first Asiatic republic to introduce European styles. From 1936 on, two exceptional artists worked at the Kossino hosiery factory, Bozhneva and Vycheslavtseva. Their work was innovative in the domains of jersey and knitted goods. They introduced alternating stripes of color in jersey where, until then, only small motifs had been used. On modern cuts and styles, they revived traditional Russian motifs, stripes, and arabesques.

At the end of the 1930s, the following topic was debated: should the USSR follow European fashion or create a national style of clothing? The strictest artists believed that while Western technology and principles should be adopted, it was out of the question to produce carbon copies of their styles. Chekhman, a fashion theorist, defined the ideal Soviet clothing as being discreet but not drab, simple but not simplistic.

Meanwhile, since the beginning of the 1930s, both the cut and the decoration of clothes had become increasingly complex. A style accentuating the silhouette had replaced shirtwaist dresses. Waistline and shoulders were emphasized, dress fronts contained a myriad of pleats and darts, sleeves were puffed, and collars, ruffles, pleats, and belts were larger than before. Ready-to-wear clothes were, however, simpler than the articles created for fashion shows.

During the war, clothing factories were shut down, evacuated, or requisitioned for manufacturing clothes for the military. Laboratories concentrated on research on practical and inexpensive synthetic fabrics and fake leather for army uniforms and shoes. Fatigue jackets, gray, hooded cloaks, boots and overalls were the most predominant articles of clothing, even for the civilian population. Soldiers' and officers' uniforms were more practical and lighter in weight. At the end of the war, a full-dress officers' uniform was designed, with gilded belt, dagger, long pants. From 1943 on, civilian clothing began to be produced again in the factories.

B. KUSTODIEV, Red Army uniform, 1921.

NOTES

1. *Revolution in Thought*, 1924, n· 2, p. 61.
2. See the magazine *The life of Art*, 1919, May 21.
3. See P.R. Trifonov, "Industry and Artistic Production" in *Atelier*, 1923, n· 1, pp. 44–45.
4. Arkin, "The Art of the Object" in *Annual Review of Art and Literature*, Moscow, 1929.
5. See the following articles: A.A. Exter, "In Constructive Clothing" in *Atelier*, 1923, n· 1, pp. 4–5, and "Simplicity and Practical Aspects of Clothing" in *The Red Field*, 1923, n· 21, p. 31.
6. See Varst (V. Stepanova) in *Lef*, 1923, n· 2, pp. 65–66.

Page from the album *The Soviet Blue Blouse*, Muscovite Editions, *Work and Books*, 1927.

N. LAMANOVA, men's Tolstoy blouse, drawing executed by V. Mukhina, 1925.

ERMILOV, silver filigree
bracelet with a floral design
embellished with
aquamarines, circa 1930.
ERMILOV, silver filigree
bracelet embellished with
amethysts, circa 1930.

Jewelry

From the time the Soviet government first came to power, the art of jewelry was taken very seriously. In August 1919, the Plastic Arts section of the People's Commissariat for Education organized a congress in Moscow which assembled the workshops of the free states. Aside from the difficulties of the art industry, the problems of the development of jewelry, enamelware, artistic ironwork, gem cutting, and work in bronze were discussed. The Academic Committee of Productive Industry had decided in 1918 to continue the former Imperial Gem Cutting Factory at Peterhof and to transform it into a workshop-school in order to train master gem cutters and jewelers, as well as to create a research institute and museum. This factory was the only production center for gem cutting in the 1920s. Its production was limited to technical articles, including agate compasses and crystal components for navigation instruments. Nevertheless, the first director of the Peterhof factory, Transeyev, insisted on obtaining a larger market for stones and consequently on lowering prices, but without lowering quality.

S. KURBANOV, pepper mill with a stylized "Kubak" floral motif, 1936.

Organizing this type of production was still extremely difficult, since all jewelry items were made for export. There was a great need for foreign currency. After 1923, the manufacturing of colored stone articles in "Russian shapes" was again authorized. The production of pieces inspired by the work of famous sculptors—Konenkov, Golubkina, and Alechin—had already been permitted in 1918. Mukhina designed a brooch in the form of an oval medallion encircled by two female nudes.

Whether such projects were actually manufactured remains to be seen. Russian jewelry was undergoing a difficult period, having lost its habitual clientele: the Church, the upper middle classes, and the wealthy ruling class. The Soviet Union, a country abounding in precious stones and metals, was in search of a market.

To combat speculation and smuggling, mining and setting gold had been declared a State monopoly in January, 1918. The State was represented by the Russian Precious Stones and Aldan Gold trusts. Before the Revolution, renowned private jewelry firms existed in Moscow and St. Petersburg—Fabergé, Ovchinnikov, Grachev, Chapochnikov. Their articles in gold, silver, platinum, and precious stones were unique pieces, internationally famous for their quality. These firms

N. KARASSEV, small box decorated with emblems of the Soviet Republic,
Rostov-Yaroslavsky, 1938.
Powder box with a peasant motif, Rostov-Yaroslavsky, circa 1920.

Brooch depicting Lenin's Tomb, Veliki-Ustiug, 1936.
Brooch with hammer and sickle, Veliki-Ustiug, 1930.

Cigarette case in a stylized floral motif, Kubatchy, circa 1930.
V. OKUNEVA, cigarette case, 1936.

Perfume bottle, Kubatchy, 1930.

were shut down after the Revolution and their material requisitioned. Most of their proprietors fled to foreign countries. As for the jewelers, they found other jobs or filled orders for *Nepmans* by procuring raw material on the black market. Some of them worked for the State restoring unique pieces of jewelry; others began to design the first Soviet decoration and medals.

During the 1930s, with the increase in the number of jewelry workshops, production expanded, though its main output was intended for exhibitions. Jewelry production was concentrated in workshops in Moscow, Leningrad, and Sverdlovsk. Qualified workers were hard to come by, and all commissions were executed by elderly jewelers. Only a handful of professional schools were able to train high-level artisans, but the models used were still those from before the Revolution.

One of the most important pre-war commissions was realized after a design by Fedorovsky, a series of stars in gilded bronze with precious stones from the Urals, which surmounted the Kremlin towers. Completed in 1935, these stars replaced the imperial eagles, and were themselves replaced in 1937 by stars made of rubies and illuminated from within.

The master-jewelers of Sverdlovsk and of the Peterhof factory produced in 1937, on Ordzhonikidze's initiative, an enormous map, "The Industry of Socialism." Twenty-seven square meters in surface, the map was composed of 45,000 fragments of lapis-lazuli, rhodonite, jasper, opal, and ruby, representing the administrative divisions of the USSR, the 450 largest cities, the rivers, the lakes, and even the topography. It was exhibited in New York and in Paris, and is presently located in the St. George room of the Hermitage.

During the war, jewelers created new decorations: the Order of Suvorov, the Order of Alexander Nevsky, the Order of Nakhimov, and the Victory Medal.

V. MUKHINA, opaline glass, 1939–1940.

Glassmaking

The glassmaking industry was already underdeveloped in Russia and became even more so after the First World War and the Civil War. Of the 180 glassworks which had existed under the Czar, only sixty remained in 1921. All glassworks were nationalized in December 1918, and a year later, the Central Bureau for the Glass Industry was founded. This in turn gave birth in 1922 to one of the most active research centers—the experimental Institute of Silicates (split in 1930 into two sections, one for glass and the other for ceramics). Thanks to the glassmakers' persistence, glassworks continued to function despite the lack of material and fuel and various attempts at sabotage. Production was limited, of course, to only the most essential hollow glassware (glasses, saucers, jars) and lamp glass. To remedy the lack of ordinary dishes, a competition on the theme of "Tableware for All" in porcelain and glass was organized in 1919. The intention was to create simple forms of tableware for peasants and workers, but from 1921 on, interest also developed in glassmaking as an art. Few pieces from the 1920s have come down to us. We can still admire a fruit bowl and carved light green vase in Urano glass, which already bore the Soviet emblem of the hammer and the sickle.

The First Russian Congress of the Porcelain and Glassmaking Industries in 1922 decided to upgrade the quality and quantity of glassware production. Four experimental factories were designated: Bakhmetiev in Nikolskoye, Gussev, Diatkovo and Chudovo. The production of green pressed glass was banned so as to economize costly material and skilled glass blowers. In the 1930s, the choice of articles expanded to include some thirty types of glassware, but the artistic level remained mediocre. At best, pre-Revolution styles from the Maltsev factory were copied, under traditional names: "Water-green," "Rococo," "Marseille" for decanters; "Turkey" for vases, and so on. Lotus flowers, irises, poppies, and landscapes, executed according to etching techniques, and Art Deco vase designs were subsequently reintroduced for the decoration of milk glass. Glassware tended to be somewhat overdone in decoration so as to hide its poor quality, especially in the case of pressed glass.

During this same period, new techniques were used in a way that was contrary to the artistic possibilities of industrial glass. For example, pressed glass was made to resemble cut glass. Similarly, diverse subterfuges were invented to imitate the technique of painting on glass. White was replaced by frosted crystal, red by ruby glass.

Violently criticizing the "falsification of an object's inherent richness," the artist A. Guretsky experimented with a technique that had not previously been used for glassmaking. At the crystal glassworks of Diatkovo, he tried out the airbrush technique to decorate frosted glass. In this way, he created a series of vases with illustrations of human figures, suggestive of porcelain statuettes of the nineteenth century.

Crystal production in the 1930s was even less successful. Colorless crystal was almost nonexistent. However, crystal cobalt and manganese could be heated and then polished or engraved. On heavy or opaque articles, cut glass lost its effect. Worse, colored crystal was covered with designs and gilt.

How are we to account for the weakness of the artistic level of hollow glassware? During this entire period (the twenties and thirties), the industry's stated goal was to increase production of household glass (the nation was lacking in tableware) as well as to cast glass for building and technical glass. Technical progress and improvements in the heating of glass caused traditional glassware to be neglected. Priority was given to the construction of sheet glass and technical glass factories. Hollow glassworks for tableware were reconstructed only between 1933 and 1937 (the Diatkovo and Gussev factories, the Red Giant factory). Glass and bottle production was automated around this time. The engineer Blagobrazov perfected a new blowing-iron which no longer required workers to breathe into the glassblower, thus liberating them from an unhealthy task.

The mediocrity of the artistic level can also be explained by a lack of professional guidance. Before the 1930s, no center for artistic research in glassmaking had existed, nor were there more than a handful of master-glassmakers (A. Jakobson, who worked at the Red Giant before the Revolution, G. Egorov at Gussev, A. Lipskaya and N. Rostovseva at Gussev and Diatkovo), most of whom were self-taught. The development of glassmaking was also hindered, in design as well as in production, by the stranglehold maintained by the partisans of industrialization and standardization. In their view, artistic creativity was unnecessary. Guretsky also felt that mediocrity was a consequence of economic policies. It was only in 1939, when his post as artistic director of the glassmaking section of the People's Commissariat for Light Industry was reaffirmed, that new forms and decoration began to be introduced.

In 1927-1928, the situation had come close to being catastrophic, with limited choice, poor quality, a scarcity of certain articles and an overabundance of others. Glass was thick ($\frac{1}{4}''$ to $\frac{3}{8}''$ instead of the standard $\frac{1}{8}''$), heavy, green, and nearly opaque. Until the middle of the 1930s, no transparent and colorless glass tableware existed.

Nevertheless, from 1918 to 1928, a real effort had been made in the technical area: mechanization, gas ovens, and automation had been introduced; factories had been granted improved access to national raw materials. As of 1934, a number of decrees were enacted in favor of artistic glassmaking. In 1938, the Arts Committee of the People's Commissariat for Light Industry was founded, and Mukhina, Kachalov, Jakobson, Chaikov, and Kovalsky were nominated to it. Lipskaya and Rostovseva headed the laboratory founded in 1940. Jakobson organized a professional training course and classes in the history of glassmaking.

In 1939, articles which were deemed to be anti-artistic were removed from production: etched vases with lotus and iris motifs, opalines with colored designs, old models of pressed glass, etc.

During the second half of the 1930s, decoration became more contemporary, using Soviet aesthetics and events: themes concerning the conquest of the North Pole (a vase by Porokhov, a pitcher by Makarov), folk tales (Porokhov's *Ruslan and Ludmilla* vase, Romadin's *The Tale of the Fisherman and the Fish* wine glass set).

On the occasion of the agricultural exhibition of 1939, Lipskaya and Rostovseva designed a series of blown vases with folklore motifs from each republic of the USSR. The artistic quality of these vases, with decorations influenced by textile and embroidery motifs, was far from perfect. In 1938-1939, a series of vases was decorated with the pavilions of the National Agricultural Exhibition. The glass was colored by the etching method.

The most memorable souvenir objects from the end of the 1930s were a tumbler decorated with sheaves (Rostovseva and Mecheriakov), a glass entitled *Sheaves of Wheat* by Lvov and Kulechov, a stem glass entitled *VSKhV* (National Agricultural Exhibition) by Egorov, and paperweights in colored glass, bearing the VSKhV emblem (Jakobson). During the 1930s, variations on "Maltsov" (pre-Revolution) cut-glass articles were fashionable for all types of tableware, from glasses to serving dishes. Floral motifs were generally popular, with ears of corn, sheaves of wheat, and plants by Lipskaya, Jakobson, Porokhov, Travkin, and Kurtsayev done in a variety of techniques. Travkin, trained by the master-glassmakers of the Gussev crystal works, created the most brilliant models. His taste went to plant, wildflower, leaf and bird motifs. Although his naïve and poetical designs were executed on old-style everyday objects, he was nevertheless a worthy descendant of the Russian school of glass engraving.

Kurtsayev excelled in the cut-glass technique. At the Red Giant Factory, he created a vase, *The Branches,* in the late thirties which reflected his research in cut glass. The innovations he introduced became widespread in the years 1950-1960. But the greatest artist of all was Jakobson, the master of Vertuzayev, Prokhorov,

N. TYRSA, opaline bottle, *The Countess*, 1940.

V. MUKHINA, vase, *Aster*, 1941.

Kurtsayev, and Kalagin, among others. He used smooth and bright backgrounds, with lightly-drawn motifs of stars and snowflakes. A pair of his vases in cobalt glass, dating from 1937–1938, are preserved at the Russian Museum. Other items of interest from this period are articles decorated in "Venetian filigree." This ancient technique of filigreed arabesques was reintroduced by the master-glassmaker Vertuzayev, of the Red Giant factory, who created in collaboration with Jakobson a series of everyday dishes decorated in Venetian filigree. The People's Commissariat for Light Industry then decided that this technique should be extended to other factories.

Before organizing an experimental workshop, Mukhina had worked as a glassblower. In 1938, at the Red Giant factory, she conceived a round table and crystal service (*The Kremlin*) for the Presidium of the Supreme Soviet. (Later, her taste went to flat vertical facets). The service, based on spherical forms, was decor-

V. MUKHINA, vase, *Repka*,
1940–1941.

ated with floral motifs. One of the pieces, a vase referred to as *The Aster* vase, is
preserved at the Russian Museum in Leningrad. Lines engraved directly onto the
vase represent the stems of a bouquet of flowers with jagged petals. Mukhina used
this same motif for a service in dark gray crystal. Subsequent vases, *The Little Radish, The Bluebell,* and *The Lotus* (1940–1941), bear witness to the artist's concern
with combining function and decoration.

Mukhina's work methods were sometimes based on improvisation. The form
of the object was found in the few minutes it took for the molten glass to cool in
the vat. Kachalov remembers Mukhina's way of standing near the vat, in close
contact with the glassblower, without so much as a sketch or a design. She herself
described the process: "What the glass wanted and what the artist wanted came
together and gave birth to a form."[1]

Mukhina's accomplishment in the domain of glass figurines was equally productive and innovative. The tradition of glass figurines, widespread since the seventeenth century, had been neglected since the early 1900s.

At the end of the 1930s, the Chemeco-Technological Institute of Leningrad perfected a new casting process. The funnel and mould, both in porcelain, were maintained at a high temperature. The funnel was filled with glass debris. Then the melted glass poured out of the funnel and into the mould, which was broken in order to remove the object. In this way, a unique cast was obtained. This technique had been used for sculptures with other materials, such as a bronze bust of Pushkin by Vitali and porcelain statuettes by Terebenev (*Young Girl with Yoke*). Mukhina and N. Danko as well as the animal sculptor Sylova pursued research in this area over many years.

Two other artists, Uspensky and Tyrsa, pursued parallel research during the same period. Uspensky, a skilled draftsman, had begun to work with glass in 1940. He was particularly interested in refining blown forms. His pieces were so perfect that they required no decoration.

Tyrsa, another draftsman interested in the possibilities of blown glass, used instruments—tongs and forks—to work the exterior forms, obtaining tortuous shapes, particularly in his series of wine carafes with bulging necks, produced in 1940–1941.

The war interrupted the research work conducted at the Leningrad glass works. The other glassmaking factories concentrated on producing war articles, while tableware production was almost completely stopped. Lipskaya's drinking cups and stemware, designed as gifts for war heroes, received military medals in 1942 and 1945, but were never mass-produced. For this project, Lipskaya had drawn inspiration from nineteenth-century banquet cups (*The Order of Uchakov* cup) or Empire style (*For the Defenders of Leningrad* glass). She invented original forms, such as that of a lighthouse (*The Order of Nakhimov*) or of a grenade (*For the Partisans*).

NOTES

1. Speech by Mukhina: Conference on decorative applied arts at the USSR Academy of Art, 1952.

V. VERTUZAYEV, crystal cruet with a long spout, 1939.

S. KONENKOV, wall decoration, 1918.

FURNITURE

S. LISSAGOR, M. GINZBURG, E. POPOV, design for workers' housing in Saratov, circa 1930.

Interior Architecture

Pertaining at once to the organization of space and its fitting out, interior architecture, practically a synthesis of all art forms, was a concept that was generally misunderstood by Soviet architects. Realized independently of architectural projects, decorative elements—furniture and lighting—were rarely in harmony with the interior designs of private or public buildings.

After the Revolution, palaces and large private estates housed businesses, schools, clubs, hospitals, and rest homes. Until 1920, their decoration consisted of propaganda art: banners, posters, portraits of revolutionary heroes. In addition, the policy of confiscating private homes could not meet the needs of the new society, and the construction of interiors which corresponded to the new demands and innovative aesthetic requirements was imperative.

As of 1918–1919, the architectural sections of the Soviet of the Economy and the People's Commissariat for Education inaugurated a policy of constructing residences and interiors for cultural puposes, with an emphasis on the following criteria: economy, hygiene, rationality, and aesthetic qualities. (It was allowed, for instance, to preserve local features.) This was an era of daring projects which, for lack of means of production, often remained unrealized. Cabinetmaking workshops had ceased to operate. The factories which had produced Art Nouveau furniture for the bourgeoisie were in trouble. Such problems needed to be remedied without delay.

The objectives of a society in transition no longer made it possible, for instance, to design a workers' center according to principles dating from before the Revolution. Pursuing the dream of a future Communist society, the new principles aimed at a restructuring which would imply the creation of canteens, daycare, nursery schools, etc. One of the consequences of these objectives was the appearance of "communal" apartments which included collective rooms to create closer relationships among the inhabitants.

In 1919, in Moscow, requisitioned houses were renovated into 300 communal residences with lodgings for 45,000 workers. Dining rooms, laundry rooms, and rooms reserved for propaganda purposes were collective. At this time, a number of projects came under consideration: workers' centers (1919–1920), collective residences for Petrograd (projects by Burychkin, Tverskoy, and Ol), apartment buildings (Vesnin's project), and club houses (Ivanov's project, 1924). In addition to private lodgings, canteens, reading rooms, and storage rooms were conceived as centers for collective activities. These projects, often inspired by the industrial cities, workers' cottages, and low-income housing developments of the West, were not realized until the second half of the 1920s. Hygiene and aesthetics were the two major obstacles which had first to be overcome.

In 1923, a number of interesting projects were proposed for a competition organized to design workers' housing in Moscow. Chernichev's proposal had bedrooms and secondary rooms located at the far end of the apartment, while Vesnin created larger living spaces by combining the kitchen and dining room. Melnikov designed an apartment on two levels, an idea that was adopted by the Constructivists.

Housing development projects were particularly successful. This type of construction corresponded to the economy of the years 1917 to 1925—for example, The Falcon village designed by Morkovnikov in 1923 and the Dukstroy village by Venderov in 1924–1925. The development consisted of small individual houses or cottages with collective facilities. It was difficult, however, to locate such developments in large cities.

From 1917 to 1925, the students and teachers of The College of Arts and Crafts designed ingenious styles of furniture: combination beds-and-wardrobes, folding shelves, bed-sofas, etc. Many members of the college teaching staff believed that functional pieces of furniture were necessarily beautiful. But excessive utilitarianism was ultimately detrimental to the aesthetic aspect of the object. Only Lissitsky and Rodchenko were able to soften the severity of purely functional objects by playing on colors and proportions.

Tatlin was at the time director of the wood and metal department at the college. His chief concerns were aestheticism and economy. In 1925 he designed a series of simple and elegant chairs. The seat was round, an iron bar served both as chair leg and support, and a second bar formed the back and the elbow-rests. The armchairs in airports designed in the 1960s drew their inspiration from these chairs.

Artistic transformations were more radical in public buildings than in houses. Such changes chiefly concerned buildings with new social functions such as workers' clubs and halls. Large halls were designed to accommodate rallies, meetings, and theater performances, while other rooms were reserved for studying or cultural activities, in addition to reading rooms, museums, amphitheaters for adult education, gymnasiums, canteens, etc. This type of collective interior was the basis for all interior architecture projects of the 1920s. The guiding lines concerning the Workers' Hall of Petrograd were (1) social life, (2) science and art, (3)

Z. BYKOV, bookshelf designs, 1923.

Entrance hall to the Proletariat Club in Moscow, 1927–1929.

A. RODCHENKO, interior architecture and design of a workers' club presented
at the Exhibition of Decorative Arts in Paris, 1925.

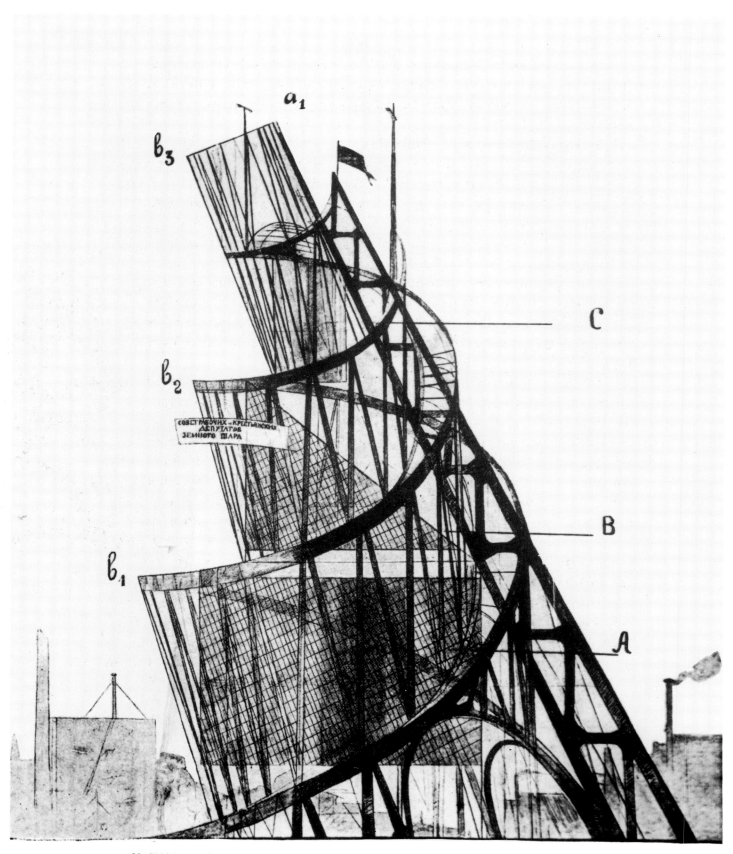

V. TATLIN, design for the monument celebrating the Third International, 1919–1920.

rest areas, and (4) sports. The construction of the Palace of the Soviets and the Hall of Work also gave rise to new interior structures which tended to combine social, administrative, and cultural functions (meetings, theater performances, and club activities).

In honor of the Revolution, interior architecture was to "surprise by [its] size, lighting, and space."[1] Accordingly, meeting halls for "mass activities" were bright and spacious. Project designs for large halls, public baths, and crematoriums drew their inspiration from diverse sources—the columns of Russian classicism, the luxury of Florentine palaces, medieval castles, Roman baths, Egyptian temples, and so on. These styles were modernized and simplified so as to obtain, in Fomin's words, a "Red Doric" style.

Other architects worked towards the creation of a new aesthetic vocabulary, using modern materials and techniques—tall buildings in glass and steel. The "Tatlin Tower" is the best example of this type of construction. A monument to the Third International (1919), it also housed the conference rooms of the Third International.

In 1923, a competition was organized for the construction of the Hall of Work in Moscow. The symbolic character of the new architectural tendencies gave way in this circumstance to more concrete priorities. The guidelines for the competition stated that both exterior and interior should be at once luxurious, simply designed, and modern in feeling, without historical influences. Only the Vesnin brothers respected these conditions: their proposal was selected as the foundation of the project. The core of their composition was an immense oval amphitheater, surrounded by a circular hall. Intended for rallies, it had a seating capacity of 10,000. A partition made of folding metal slats separated the amphitheater from a rectangular conference room to be used for meetings of the Moscow Soviet. The two spaces could thus be transformed into one even more immense space. This was one of the first attempts at creating a transformable space. The building itself was built along the plans of a tower, and was to house a work and social sciences museum, a library, a news agency, a radio station, an observatory, and a weather station. The project was compact, logical, and practical.

The principles proposed by the Vesnin brothers inspired an innovative tendency in Soviet architecture—Constructivism. The first realizations were exhibited in Paris in 1925. The Soviet pavilion, built by Melnikov, was deliberately conceived to confront the marble and gold of the Western pavilions with a new style that was pure and daring. The materials used were glass and wood. The rectangular interior was divided diagonally by a stairway leading to the first floor. The walls in glass, with partitions to delimit the exhibition halls. An opening above

G. KLUCIS, kiosk model for a radio tower, India ink on paper, 1922.

the stairway and a mast with fretwork accentuated the open, luminous, and dynamic character of the pavilion.

The workers' club by Rodchenko was the booth that drew the most attention. It was composed of several different spaces, including a reading room with a "Lenin corner" and a conference room. This last was equipped with a folding partition for film projections, a rostrum, and a wall panel with sliding shelves for newspapers. The center of the reading room was occupied by a desk-table and simply-designed chairs. On the left was a display case for books and magazines and a cupboard for storing them. The ideological center was the "Lenin corner" which exhibited the leader's portrait and a movable display case for documents and photographs. Surfaces were emphasized by a harmonious composition of red, gray, white, and black. The furniture was geometric in form. The chairs consisted of rectangular planes with the back and armrests continuing the oval form of the seat. At the end of the exhibition, the club was presented as a gift to French workers.

During the second half of the 1920s, Soviet architecture shifted its orientation toward mass construction. There was a great deal of discussion about what type of habitat should be constructed. The Constructivists offered a series of dy-

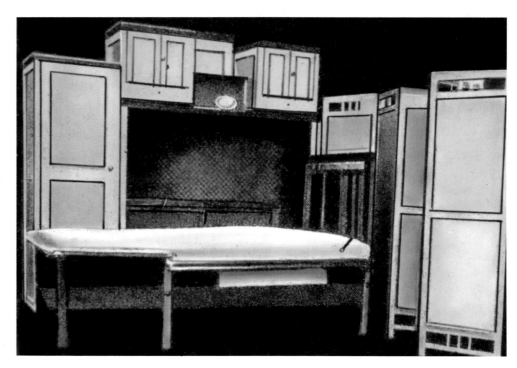

Design of a transformable cupboard-bed-folding screen module, 1932.

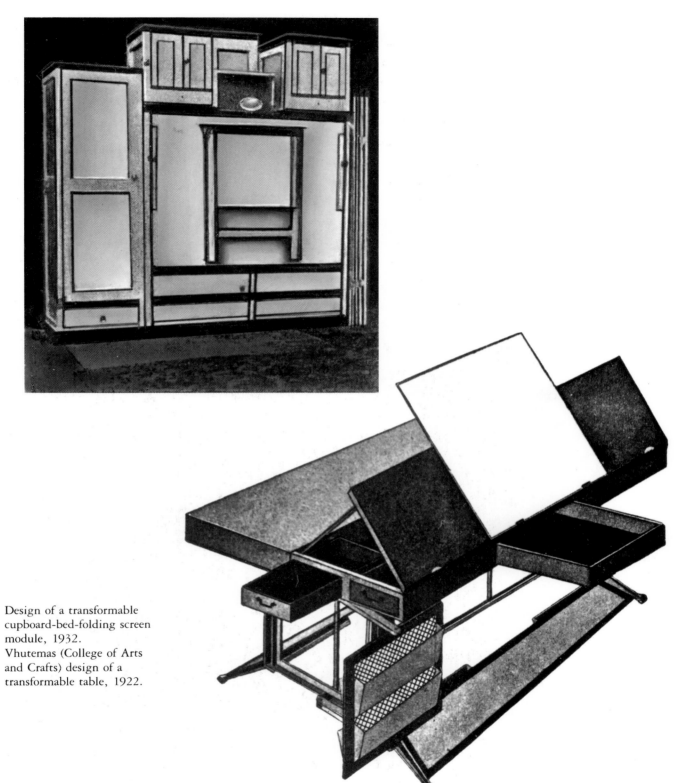

Design of a transformable
cupboard-bed-folding screen
module, 1932.
Vhutemas (College of Arts
and Crafts) design of a
transformable table, 1922.

S. LISSAGOR, M. GINZBURG, interior architecture and design of a worker's
apartment in Saratov, circa 1930.

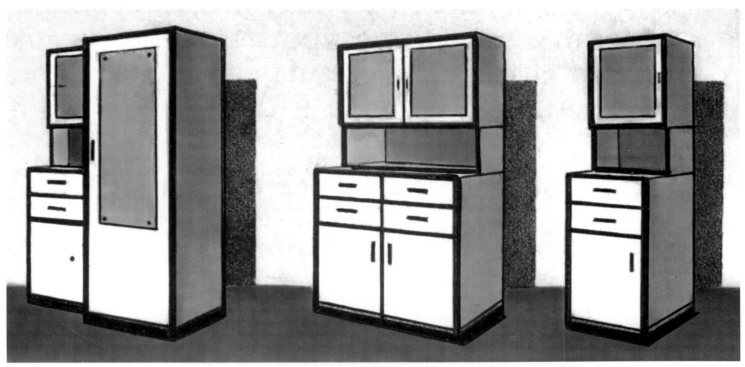

Modular cupboards, 1932.
G. GLUCHTCHENKO, interior design of a kitchen, 1927.

GUEGUELLO, housing complex for workers.

namic solutions. Most architects were unable to imagine modern urban housing that did not include traditional apartments. The Constructivists invented "communal housing." In projects from the years 1926 to 1928, private apartments (including bathroom and kitchen) and collective facilities (clubs, day-care centers, reading rooms, etc.) were included within the same building complex. Ginzburg, Ol, Ivanov, and Ladovsky designed duplex apartments; Vorotynseva and Poliak imagined a network of arcades which joined living areas; Sobolev counted one room per person; Vladimirov juxtaposed six apartments per floor.

At the end of the 1920s, the Stroikom group headed by Ginzburg designed interiors that were quite original. The building at 25 Novinsky Boulevard in Moscow is a typical example. It was divided into one residential section and one section which served as a community center. The residential section was raised on round pillars and consisted of duplex apartments whose upper level, consisting of the living room and dining room, also served as an air reservoir for the rest of the apartment. The living room was open to the lower level but could be closed off by means of folding partitions. Vast hallways were lighted by large windows, and the terrace roof included a solarium and flowerbeds. The community center was joined to the lower arcade of the residential section by a covered walk, a sort of one-story high cube with one side completely in glass. There was a sports center with showers and dressing rooms on the ground floor, and a canteen, reading room, and rest area on the second floor. An open stairway linked the two levels. Concrete, glass and metal were used as building materials, with great attention to detail (doors and windows, plumbing). Two color scales were freely intermingled, one of warm colors, used to delimit volumes (ochre, pale yellow, pink, brown) and one of cold colors to give depth to volumes (blue, gray, verdigris, white). The ceiling, usually more vivid than the walls, controlled the color scales. Contrasting colors for the doors distinguished the entrances for the two different levels. The hallways and landings were particularly decorative.

The apartment interiors were organized into several different areas. There was a living room, a sleeping area, an eating area, and a work area. Special types of furniture were conceived specifically for each space. A desk, an armchair, and a low, long shelf were designed for the work area and placed close to the window. In the rest area or living room, in addition to a round table, three poufs were lined up

N. BOROV, G. ZAMSKY, I. JANG, project for the interior design of the office
of the Editor-in-Chief of *Pravda*, Moscow, 1934.
N. BOROV, G. ZAMSKY, I. JANG, office of a *Pravda* journalist.

Moscow subway station.

N. BOROV, G. ZAMSKY, I. JANG, project for the interior architecture of the
conference room of *Pravda*, Moscow, 1934.
I. FOMIN, theater foyer, Dinamo, Moscow, 1928–1930.

G. LUDWIG, design for a Hall of Work.

along one wall, creating a right angle with the sofa. This angle had the function of marking off this section of the room. On the upper level, the bedroom consisted of two beds and a folding console placed near the window. Each area had its specific source of light. In this type of apartment, in Moscow and in Saratov, ceiling-high niches served as bookshelves or wardrobes. Lissagor and Popov designed furniture intended for this type of housing which could be industrially produced; tables and chairs were in wood, leather, and metal. The metal legs were narrow and slightly curved, and the seats were thick, with curved metal fretwork supports.

Communal housing was also conceived for single adults and small families. Small apartments without kitchens or lavatories were located along a hallway which measured the length of the building, while a vast structure of collective facilities completed this hotel-type complex. One of its advantages was that it simplified domestic tasks.

In Moscow, Leningrad, and Sverdlovsk, this type of communal housing was not altogether faithful to the initial plan. Often it consisted of simple habitats reduced to mere bedrooms, or else of entirely independent apartments. In Moscow, a building located on Khavsko-Chablovsky Street, designed by the architects Wolfenson and Volkov in 1928–1930, had the particularity of presenting both types of habitats. Individual apartments and sleeping areas with communal lavatories and kitchens were located in the wings of the building. The central part of the building held the canteen, club room, reading room, day-care center, and nursery school. However, the system of hallways and the insufficient number of lavatories, showers, and stoves was a source of daily conflict between the families who were forced to share these facilities.

Hotel-type communal housing designed by Ol was also found in Leningrad, on Rubinstein Street. The individual bedrooms were small in size.[2] On Donskaya Street in Moscow, a student dormitory was designed along the same lines by the architect N.S. Nikolayev. The rooms, intended for two, were the size of cabins (twenty square feet). Such communal housing was generally cold and ascetic in feeling, with naked and monotonous geometrical surfaces. The lack of comfort was due more to poor utilization than to faulty construction. To make matters worse, since population density requirements were not respected, facilities were over-crowded. In short, the result was the exact opposite of the project's initial objective.

At the end of the 1920s, the program of "building a Soviet way of life" began to attain absurd proportions, imposing its regulations on individuals and their lives.[3] For extreme Constructivists, transforming the way of life meant the complete destructuring of the nuclear family, considered to be a residue of the bourgeois past. Separate rooms were considered tantamount to individualism. Instead, the Constructivists proposed a collectivized way of life in seven parts: 1) Rest, sleep, and recuperation; 2) Nutrition; 3) Sexual activity; 4) Education of children; 5) Physical and cultural development; 6) Domestic, sanitary, and hygienic services; 7) Health services.

The internal structure of this type of super-collectivized housing was astonishing—"sleeping cabins" of 5 to 8 square meters, endlessly long hallways, communal lavatories and kitchens. Children, grouped according to age, lived separately from their parents in specially adapted living quarters. The center of the building was reserved for the canteen, library, conference rooms, etc.

Bartch and Vladimirov designed a building project capable of housing one thousand adults and 680 children. Referred to as a "housing combine," its objective was to impose a strict way of life and use of time on its inhabitants. More moderately inclined Constructivists, like Ginzburg, made ironical jokes about being taken in hand "from birth to the crematorium." Such "housing combine" projects were never erected, thanks in particular to a decree of the Central Committee in 1930 which condemned their "harmfulness."

An opposite tendency then appeared in reaction to communal housing. The "anti-urbanizers," architects like Okhitovich, believed that cities were capitalist creations and should thus be done away with. The Socialist form of habitation, they believed, should be structured within "green cities": ground-floor houses built on piles along highways or railroad lines. A single room in each house combined all facilities. The interior was arranged according to the needs and taste of the inhabitants and was designed to put them in closer contact with nature. To this end, the exterior walls were in glass and could be folded back like screens to join the exterior and interior space. Le Corbusier thought that these "huts... were habitable only on the weekend."

In the late 1920s and early 1930s, the ASNOVA (New Architects' Association) group began to design habitats in the form of spheres, circles, and parabolas. Taranov, in 1929, conceived an apartment complex located within the exterior perimeter of a circular building. Slightly concave walls allowed for all sorts of interior decoration and furniture arrangements. Round buildings created interiors that were compact, free, and original. Such projects, however, were never carried out.

There was one single exception. This was the cylindrical house designed by Melnikov, located on Krivoarbart Street in Moscow (1929). The central axis was a spiral staircase, around which partitions were placed to define the interior space. The bottom floor consisted of two joined cylinders which, on the upper floor, became two spacious, well-lighted rooms.

The debate concerning Soviet forms of habitat resulted in a return to the individual apartment. This return was officially put on the record by the Plenum of the Central Committee of the Party in 1931. In 1932, the Moscow Soviet prescribed apartments of two, three, or four rooms for a single family. But the housing problem was actually resolved, more or less, by the organization of communal apartments within new buildings. Interiors became progressively more spacious with more light and better facilities (central heating, gas, garbage chutes and sometimes even built-in furniture). The house of the National Insurance Workers, designed by Ginzburg in 1926–1927, is one particularly successful example.

K. MELNIKOV. The architect's house, interior with hexagonal windows, Moscow, 1927.

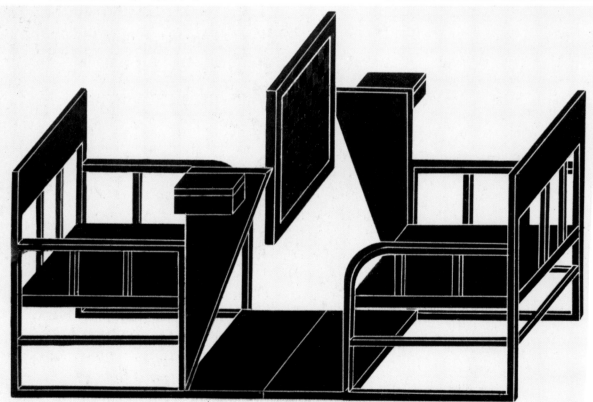

A. LAVINSKY, design for the interior architecture of a reading room.
A. RODCHENKO, design of chess table and chairs for a workers' club,
presented at the Exhibition of Decorative and Industrial Arts, Paris, 1925.

The building of the Leningrad Soviet on Karpovka Street, designed by Levinson and Fomin in 1931–1934, is also of interest. The composition of the apartments varied greatly, from two to six rooms (with a maximum of 330 to 360 square feet) which included some duplex apartments. Those apartments located on the top floor were given terraces, while the lower floors had loggia-type balconies. Much care was given to details (doors, built-in furniture, and mail-boxes in oak or walnut). Nevertheless, certain forms suffered from poor design (obtuse or sharp angles).

During this period, an effort was also made to modernize furniture design considered too conservative. But the artlessly modern chairs of the "New Campaign" booth of the National Agricultural Exhibition (1923) or the use of Soviet emblems could hardly be considered solutions to this problem and aroused more laughter and derision than anything else (see Ilf and Petrov's serial *Grandmother's Cupboard* and Mayakovsky's play *The Baths*).

Constructivism introduced the concept of furniture as the organizational element of the interior. In an interior design project, one drawing showed how an individual moved around in a given space, a second drawing showed the different relationships between types of furniture (bed, table, chairs, stove, etc.), and the two assembled drawings provided a complete study of the living processes of the habitat. In fact, these studies were most beneficial concerning the rearrangement of kitchens. Ginzburg believed that if one considered a chair not only in terms of its function as a seat but also from the viewpoint of its position and status within the interior space, it could be designed in a definitive manner.

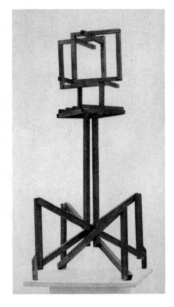

A. RODCHENKO, spatial construction in wood, 37 × 17¾ × 17¾" (94 × 45 × 45 cm) 1920.

The architect Sobolev developed this idea by proposing a definite correlation between the shape of a piece of furniture and its position in an interior. This would lead to the standardization that was a requisite of mass production. The following requirements had to be met: a maximum of rationalism, lightness, solidity, economy, minimal volume, and a kit-type assembly. Construction was necessarily industrial. Ginzburg and the Vesnin brothers nevertheless ran into difficulties, for their designs could not always be adapted to industrial requirements and had to fall back on craft production. Furniture designed by the Constructivists was generally either built-in, transformable, combinable, or portable; contemporary designers still draw inspiration from their ideas. Kitchen elements functioned as a partition between the kitchen and the dining room.

Another significant concept was that of the separation into areas (sleeping areas, eating areas, work areas, etc.). The theory, however, went beyond the practice. With the exception of the buildings designed by Ginzburg in Moscow and Saratov, and living quarters designed by Lissagor and Popov, actual interiors did not allow for such a rearrangement. The Constructivists had attempted to popular-

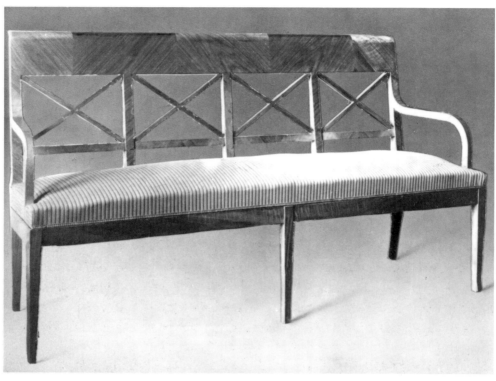

L. SAVELIEV, O. STAPRAN, divan, Moscow Hotel, circa 1930.

ize their ideas by means of the cinema. In 1927, a film by Chirokov entitled *How Do We Live?* showed Constructivist interiors (one-room apartments with kitchenettes, designed by Glutchenko). The apartment included a "private" area —for rest and work—located in an alcove, and a central section consisting of a dining area and living room. The kitchen was separated from the main room by a cupboard-partition with openings on both sides.

The art of interior architecture revealed its true potential in public buildings (mostly clubs and art centers) which were designed in keeping with the activities which were to occur there. Such interiors were divided into concert halls and rooms for given activities. Other kinds of interiors varied according to the nature of the unions which usually ran such enterprises. In the 1920–1930 period, such buildings tended to be larger and their organization more coherent than in the years 1918–1920 (Arts Center of the Moskovsko-Narvsky sector of Leningrad, by Gueguello and Kritchevsky, 1925–1927; the Kharkov Workers' Building by Dmitriev, 1927–1929). Conceived along the same lines as theaters, the rooms, corridors, classrooms, sports centers, and movie theaters were designed in relation to the shape of the central room. Anxious to break with former styles, architects were often content to offer a series of bare and austere constructions. The foyers, in contrast, were well-lit and spacious, in the form of an arc, with large bay windows opening to the exterior.

The main hall, particularly daring in design, was a fan-shaped amphitheater, with seats tiered up from the stage, broad aisles, improved acoustics and visibility, and free circulation of the public. The staggered boxes and paneled ceilings of the Leningrad Arts Center are equally worthy of interest.

Club interiors subsequently underwent more dramatic changes reflecting the Constructivist influence. Rather than a traditional fusion of the theater auditorium into a single volume with adjoining rooms, "differentiation" became the guiding principle—in other words, a free and asymmetrical composition of different, independent spaces grouped according to function.

In 1927–1929, Burov designed, in Cheliabinsk, a complex of five separate buildings sharing the same functions (a club center, a movie theater, a conference room for group discussions, a sports center, and a children's room).

Kornfeld's Art Center (1928–1938) in Moscow's Kievsky quarter is, to say the least, surprising. It combines two independent, almost antithetical spaces: on one side, a vast concert hall of 1,250 seats, and on the other, a multitude of small rooms reserved for a variety of activities. The two "sides" are joined by a series of passages. This is an illustration of the Constructivist principle of "interference of

E. LANCERAY, detail of the ceiling of the Kazan railroad station restaurant in Moscow, 1934.

spaces," that is to say, the opening of one space into another and the elimination of boundaries. The Moscow Arts Center in the Proletarsky quarter, designed by the Vesnin brothers, follows the same principle. It was to consist of two concert halls and several important spaces including exhibition wings and a restaurant. The large concert hall (not built) was to be a round amphitheater supported by an enormous arch (with a 125-foot span). The proscenium stage was extended outward by means of two wings, allowing for more direct participation of the spectators. The stage "interfered" with the seating portion of the hall, forming an ellipsoidal unit. The concert hall was surrounded by circular glassed-in foyers. The small concert hall was intended for chamber music, film showings, and conferences. The stage was supported by a triple-arched portal; the proscenium extended outward on descending lateral platforms. The roof was a cupola, embellished with three concentric corbie gables.

The foyer served as the unifying element. The open stairways at each end created an "interference" between the vestibule below, the gallery above, and all the other rooms. In addition, bay windows opened the foyer to the outside. The Stenberg brothers had chosen colors in shades of orange. The Vesnin brothers wanted this Arts Center to have a triumphal, luxurious aspect. The walls of the winter garden and sitting rooms were lined with marble; the furniture was massive, cubical. The globe and neon lighting was massive too, in contrast to the light and airy forms of the building.

Golossov designed the Moscow Communal Council Club on Lessnaya Street (1927–1929). It included such Constructivist elements as glass walls and spiral staircases. The building as a whole was a transparent cylinder.

The club buildings designed by Melnikov were a combination of the functional method, the formal coherence of the Constructivists, and his own artistic discoveries. Consisting of compact volumes whose interior could be altered by a simple interplay of partitions, flap doors, openings, and sliding floors, such buildings were truly mobile spatial modules. Melnikov applied these principles to the design of the Communal Council Club on Strminka Street, the Moskhim Factory Club, the Rubber Factory Club, the clubs of the Moscow Liberty and Bird of the Revolution factories, the Dulevo Club, etc. His imagination gave birth to spaces in the shape of fans, stars, and even of a cigar. Stage platforms as well as regular flooring could be raised to reveal swimming pools and hidden rooms. Such convertible structures, however, were not always successful and were sometimes rather bizarre.

Constructivist principles were also applied to lighting. The main trend was to include lighting sources within the construction of the interiors: insert lamps, luminous ceilings. Ceiling lights and bracket-lamps were often designed in a

Café Sport, Moscow, 1934.

LE CORBUSIER, N. KOLLI, stairwell of the Centrosoyouz building, Moscow,
1929–1936.

LE CORBUSIER, N. KOLLI, staircase, Centrosoyouz building, Moscow, 1929–1936.

A. VLASSOV, chess club, Pioneers Palace, Moscow, 1935.

"technical" manner which emphasized the asceticism of the walls and ceilings.

The interior organization of club centers was extremely complex. It was virtually impossible to achieve any sort of synthesis between the functional and the aesthetic, due to the fact that the furniture industry and aesthetic research were still largely undeveloped. Thus it was not rare to find unique museum pieces next to handmade benches and stools in pine, embroidered cushions and pink lampshades. The aesthetic unity of such clubs during the twenties and thirties was all but nonexistent. There is one notable exception: the craftsman Arutchian designed tables and rectangular chessboards for the Builders Club in Erevan. In 1928, Tugenhold criticized the lack of coherence in design; scientific data on color and light and their psychological influence were, in his opinion, too often neglected.[4]

The interior architecture of theaters was similar to that of clubs. Specific needs were defined by the different types of modern performances. The auditoriums had to accommodate mass rallies as well as sports competitions, meetings, and conferences. In addition, in order to make performances more dynamic and to involve the spectators more intensely, stages were built to emerge directly out of the tiered rows of seats.[5]

A. DAMSKY, three-branched chandelier, *Pravda* headquarters, Moscow, 1934.

The stage thus evolved from a proscenium to a more "egalitarian" amphitheater. The Vesnin brothers designed the project for the Kharkov Theater which earned them the first prize in the competition of 1931. Many projects, alas, were not realized or were modified over time, particularly in the case of interior architecture. Such modifications tended to be in the style of triumphant monumentality. Langbard conceived the project for the Opera and Ballet Theater of Minsk (1932–1938) in which, in contrast to the functional organization of space, the interior architecture was surprisingly luxurious.

Shchuko and Helfreih designed a Constructivist theater at Rostov-on-Don, made of glass and reinforced concrete, in the form of a tractor. But the slowness of the construction (1929–1934) caused the interior to be progressively transformed into a uselessly luxurious space with marble, fluting, pilasters, cornices, and balustrades in contrast to a dynamic exterior that was both open and functional. It is true that the interior decoration corresponded, chronologically speaking, to a reappraisal of Constructivism. In the adjacent rooms, marble walls, paintings and bas-reliefs, paneled ceilings, floors in mosaic, and massive leather sofas weighed down the overall design of the building. At the same time—the 1930s—that Constructivism was developing, a trend toward traditionalism began to emerge as well. For the latter, the heritage of the past was the measuring stick of creativity. Thus Joltovsky renovated the National Bank on Neglinnaya Street in Moscow, 1927–1929, in an Italian Renaissance style. The reinforced concrete roofing was masked by a groined vault. The entire conception was planned to give an idea of

V. SHCHUKO, V. HELFREIH, entrance hall of the Rostov Theater, 1924–1934.

V. SHCHUKO, V. HELFREIH, theater auditorium, Rostov Theater, 1929–1934.

E. LANCERAY, ceiling of the Kazan railroad station restaurant, Moscow, 1934.

luxury: columns in fake marble, mosaics, paneled or moulded ceilings, portals.

Shchussev began the construction of the Kazan railway station in Moscow in 1913–1914. The interior was continued from 1926 to 1933, so that while the exterior was in the old Russian style of seventeenth-century palaces, the interior vaults were reminiscent of the churches of Pskov, while the bay windows were in the "Muscovite baroque" style. The restaurant suggested the refectories of seventeenth- and eighteenth-century monasteries, and the vault was a monumental baroque fresco painted by Lanceray in 1933.

Fomin remained faithful to the Red Doric style. The interior of the Dynamo Association building (1928–1930), for example, was a renewal of classicism. The Doric order was simplified, with the bases and capitols of columns and pilasters decorated with simple gorgerins and annulets.

Joltovsky, Shchussev, and above all Fomin maintained that modern buildings in reinforced concrete were not incompatible with lavish decorations. "Such decoration is our architectural language," Fomin stated,[6] with "language" meaning "enrichment." "Soviet classicism," which reintroduced the basic three orders, became the rule of the day, lasting well beyond the 1930s.

Industrially produced furniture failed to satisfy either the Constructivists or the traditionalists. A competition aimed at improving the standards of private and public furniture was inaugurated in 1932. Designers were invited to submit projects in four different categories.

The first category consisted of multifunctional furniture. Such pieces were based on functional principles, but their complexity often made them unusable. A single piece of furniture could be used as a wardrobe, a bed, a table, and a folding partition. The second category included kitchen and dining room furniture. Smooth surfaces with right angles and uniform size allowed for easy standardization. The third category concerned prototypes: eclectic furniture embellished with Soviet emblems and abstract decorations (spots or lines of color). The fourth category included pieces of furniture having "straight lines and forms." Some of these pieces had been realized according to Constructivist projects conceived at the end of the 1920s—low, light, and rational pieces, or else pieces that were open, geometrical and devoid of ornamentation, and which tended to be both more massive and more luxurious.

During the second half of the 1930s, architects attempted to make interior design more expressive and thus to give more attention to details. Furniture was no longer required to be monumental but rather was adapted to the architectural space. Architects demanded the following from furniture: 1) A decrease in size; 2) The elimination of useless items of furniture (sideboards, high sofas, etc.); 3) The replacement of such items by practical and transformable furniture.

A. DAMSKY, ball chandelier, *Pravda* headquarters, Moscow, 1934.

A team composed of architects and artists (Borov, Zamsky, Jang, Damsky) was given the task of renovating the offices of the newspaper *Pravda*. Much attention was given to the question of color. The walls of the vestibule to the editorial office were ivory, the ceiling white, and the floor gray marble. Lateral parquet-floored landings were fitted out with leather seats and tables for visitors. A light green carpet softened the whiteness of the marble staircase. The color scheme emphasized the newspaper's colors, black and white; each floor had its specific colors, while the hallways were entirely done in white and black. The walls of the conference rooms were covered with panels in relief and frescoes; heavy, square armchairs went with horseshoe-shaped tables, and the circular hanging lamps and bracket-lamps were simple and elegant. The editor's office had a massive, E-shaped desk and walls covered with shelves.

During the 1930s, the Constructivists became increasingly interested in the aesthetic aspect of utilitarian objects. The furniture they designed was often upholstered with fabrics containing dynamic and colorful motifs.

The interior design of public spaces tended to be more coherent; luxury and monumentality were to reflect the heroic nature of the era and the joy of being alive.

From 1933 to 1935, Langman worked on the interior architecture of the Sovnarkom building in Moscow. His task was to create "a monument of the era." The style he used was classical and monumental, and the architectural elements, in particular the entrance halls and corridors, were deliberately heavy-handed. Pillars and columns, square or round, had simplified bases and capitols, the walls were massive, the ceilings weighed down with beams and panels; the staircase railings and elevator doors were in bronze. Everything, down to the most paltry ashtray, was to reflect the grandiose and official aspect of an administrative building. This same determination can be seen in the architecture of the Military Academy of Moscow, designed by Muntz and Rudnev in 1932–1937.

Concurrently, another more decorative current appeared, intended to suggest leisure activities and celebrations. One of the best examples of this style is the Khimky river terminal in Moscow, designed by A. Rukhlyadev (1932-1937). The building resembles a three-decker ship with an extremely high chimney. It is open to the outside by means of arcades, portals, terraces, and interior staircases. This same openness, however, disappears inside the building under the accumulated decorations—frescoes, mosaics, and heavily worked ceilings. The ceiling of the restaurant is pale blue; in the center, the panels are decorated with a seagull, while the side panels are each decorated with a different boat. The chandeliers are in the form of seashells.

The interior of the Hotel Moscow, designed by Shchussev, Saveliev, and Sta-

I. JOLTOVSKY, chandelier, Moscow, 1934.

E. LANCERAY, ceiling
fresco, Moscow Hotel, 1934.

pran in 1932–1935, was painted in gay and light colors. Shchussev chose a variety
of construction materials—marble, bronze, wood. In the restaurant, round tables
match the rounded columns, the upholstery of the chairs is in harmony with the
walls, and the parquet floor repeats the lines of the ceiling panels. Only master
craftsmen could have produced the Empire style furniture in rounded forms and
in different types of wood.

The Twelfth Workshop of the Moscow Soviet (Borov, Zamsky, and Jang)
designed the Foreign Book Store and several subway stations along the same lines.
The furniture seemed to be the result of a compromise between opposing theories.

A. SHCHUSSEV, L. SAVELIEV, O. STAPRAN, entrance of the Moscow Hotel, 1932–1935.

A. SHCHUSSEV, vault of the waiting room, Kazan railroad station, Moscow, 1926–1933.

Conference hall, Frunzé Military Academy of the RKKA, Red Army of Workers
and Peasants, Moscow, 1932–1935.

L. RUDNEV, entrance hall of the Frunzé Military Academy of the RKKA, Red
Army of Workers and Peasants, Moscow, 1932–1935.

K. MELNIKOV, concert hall of the Rubber Factory workers' club, Moscow, 1927.

Auditorium, cultural center of the Proletarian District of Moscow, 1930–1934.

B. IOFAN, design for the conference room of the Soviets' Palace in Moscow.

OUITS, O. PAVLENKO, detail of the decoration of the conference room of the
Supreme Soviet of Kirgizie, 1936.

Certain designers were now accepting polished surfaces, rounded corners, sculpture, and inlays. The new fashion was a combination of styles.

In each republic of the Soviet Union, the official style for public buildings took the national character into consideration. The Supreme Soviet of the Ukraine, in Kiev, designed by V. Zabolotny in 1939, was embellished with traditional decorations, particularly on the ceilings and gratings.

In the 1930s, the interior architecture of theaters reverted to more traditional concepts and to richer decoration, while preserving the type of interior structure established during the 1920s. Thus the Meyerhold Theater in Moscow, now Tchaikovsky Hall, is characterized by a discrepancy between the decor and the original design (architecture by Barkhin and Vakhtangov, interior design by Shchussev, 1932–1940). The amphitheater stage is completely open and juts forward by means of a parabolic platform. The daring of this design is lessened by columns and other nonfunctional decorative elements.

Such stylistic transformations can also be seen in Moscow's Red Army Theater, designed by Alabian and Simbirtsev in 1935–1940. The design is based on the five-point star. Despite their best efforts, the architects were unable to overcome the weaknesses of such an artificially conceived construction. Many of the foyers, staircases and passages were rounded. But the fan-shaped concert hall, with a semicircular balcony, was more successful. The height of the amphitheater was accentuated by a fresco by Bruno; the gigantic stage with its enormous portal and a curtain painted by Favorsky, is the work of megalomaniacs.

The Sotchy Theater designed by K. Chernopiativ in 1937 was also done in a classical style, but here functionalism was subordinated to decorativeness. Similarly conceived edifices are the Cultural Center of Kuibychev, designed by Trotsky and Katznelenbogen, 1937–1939, and the Officers' Building in Sverdlovsk by V. Emelianov, 1932–1941.

The Moscow subway stations, which began to be built in the early 1930s, also reflect the evolution of the artistic doctrine of the decade. The mere fact of turning an underground railroad into an architectural work was innovative. However, the sumptuousness of these underground palaces seems somewhat unjustified.

The subway stations opened in 1935 were modest and logical in conception, but those built in the second (1937–1938) and in the third sectors (1943–1944) were of a far more flamboyant style, with various shades of marble, majolica, moulding, and gilding. Chandeliers, bracket-lamps, and classical columns were lavish beyond reason. In only a three-year interval, Chetchulin designed stations that were radically different (Komsomolskaya, 1935, and Kievskaya, 1938). This

Lenin's Tomb, Red Square, Moscow. V. VESNIN, the Dniepr dam.

Foyer of the small theater of the cultural center of the Proletarian District, Moscow, 1930–1934.

V. VESNIN, A. VESNIN, foyer of the cultural center of the Proletarian District, Moscow, 1930–1934.

Entrance hall to the cultural center of the Proletarian District, Moscow, 1930–1934.

V. VESNIN, A. VESNIN, stairwell of the cultural center of the Proletarian District, Moscow, 1930–1934.

was also true of Fomin, who designed the Red Door station in 1935 and Sverdlov Square in 1938 (paneled ceilings, fluted pillars, Red Doric capitols, bas-reliefs in porcelain, etc.).

Among the more simply elegant stations, the House of Soviets station (now Kropotkinskaya) deserves to be mentioned. Designed by Dushkin and Lichtenberg in 1935, the central platform, bordered by two rows of columns, was spacious and well-lit. The sole element of decoration was the splayed capitol of each column which developed into a five-petaled flower on contact with the ceiling, a flower which was lit by hidden bracket-lamps.

Architects of subway stations generally sought the collaboration of artists and sculptors: ceramic panels by Lanceray for the Komsomolskaya station, mosaics by Favorsky and sculptures and frescoes for the Sverdlov Square, Revolution Square, Mayakovskaya, and Dynamo stations.

Mayakovskaya station is a good example of the synthesis between architecture and art (designed by Dushkin in 1938). Elliptical arches were reinforced with metal; the pillars were narrow. The silvery edges, medallions in mosaic executed by Deyeneka, and the cupolas gave this station a modern appearance.

As for housing, it too underwent a similar transformation toward the end of the 1930s and became both classical and national. Housing interiors were determined entirely by majestic facades. As the housing shortage persisted, enormous apartment buildings were built along the main streets.

Living space was increased; landings were lavish, decorated with moulding. Staircase railings were in fretwork; wooden doors were massive, wainscoted, and even sculpted. Certain vestibules were planned in the same way as vestibules of public buildings (columns, paneled ceilings, luxurious lighting). This was particularly true of the MKhAT House in Moscow, designed by V. Vladimirov and G. Lutsky in 1935–1937. The walls and ceilings of the apartments were decorated with increasingly mass-produced moulding. Such decoration, however, concerned only high-level buildings.

Generally speaking, there was virtually no coherence within furniture design: architects, cabinetmakers, and textile artists worked independently of each other.

Moreover, the production of the furniture industry was extremely irregular. Thus furniture designed by Saveliev and Stapran for the Hotel Moscow was never realized, and was replaced by pieces of furniture intended for private homes.

At the end of the 1930s, furniture design was reminiscent of "Russian classicism," intended primarily for high-level buildings. Built-in furniture existed only in a handful of buildings (the Bolshoi Artists' House, for instance), and usually consisted of built-in cupboards in hallways or entrances.

L. RUDNEV, monument,
Petrograd parade ground,
1918–1920.

In 1939, the Architecture Academy began a systematic approach to furniture design. The models used were the work of Russian artisans of the nineteenth century; the Academy rejected both Constructivism and the outrageous decoration of the traditionalists. At the beginning of the 1940s, armchairs were in Empire style, chairs were a strange mixture of Empire and Modern Style, and wardrobes were reminiscent of Constructivist designs but decorated with rosettes. During the war, architects abandoned such pursuits to participate in the rebuilding of cities and monuments. The third section of the Moscow subway network was completed in 1943–1945. The renewal of Soviet interior architecture was postponed until after the war.

NOTES

1. Regulations for the design competition of the Petrograd Workers' Hall, in *History of Soviet Architecture*. (1917–1925), p. 135.
2. One of these houses was described by Olga Bergholtz in her book *Stars of the Day* (1971). Built in order to combat the "former way of life," these apartments had no kitchen or front hall. Clotheslines were communal, as were relaxation rooms and playrooms. Lodgers brought their own dishes to the collective dining room and were given meal tickets. The building structure resembled the architecture of Le Corbusier. After a year or two, the inhabitants began to cook their meals on their windowsills. The collective dining room was unable to satisfy individual tastes. And collective life was growing tiresome.
3. The architect N. Kuzmin wrote articles and created idyllic projects in which collective living was carried to an extreme and individual existence reduced to "sleeping cubicles." His ideas were given the Constructivists' stamp of approval at the First Congress of the Union of Modern Architects in 1929.
4. *Pravda*, September 16, 1928.
5. See *Theory of Performance* by Meyerhold.
6. I.A. Fomin, "Creative Tendencies in Soviet Architecture and Problems of the Architectural Heritage" in *Architecture in the USSR*, no. 3–4, p. 16.

I. GOLOSSOV, Soviet Club, Moscow, 1927–1928.

V. KRINSKY, design for a newspaper kiosk, gouache on paper, 1919.

A. SHCHUSSEV, design for Lenin's Tomb, Moscow, 1929.

A. DUCHKIN, Mayakovskaya subway station, Moscow, 1938.
I. FOMIN, the Red Doors subway station, Moscow, 1935.

I. GOLOSSOV, design for the head office of Electrobank, Moscow, 1926.

I. LEONIDOV, skyscraper design, Moscow, 1930.

I. BAKANOV, lacquered box, *The Village Library*, Palekh, 1925.

A. KULIKOV, lacquered box, *A Scene from Country Life: Listening to the Radio*, 1926.
I. SEREBRIAKOV, lacquered box, *The Mtsypi*, 1931.

I. GRIPKOV, enameled tray, *The Bouquet of Flowers,* Jostovo.
D. OSSIPOV, enameled tray, *Tea Time,* Jostovo.

A. VOLTER, lacquered tray with a military motif, *Red Cavalry Soldier*, Jostovo, 1920.

VUKVOL, engraved walrus tooth depicting walrus hunting, circa 1930.
R. VIMA, cigar holder engraved in ivory, illustrating the arrival of a group of
explorers in the North Pole, 1935.

S. EVANGULOV, sculpted ivory, *Fish Drying,* 1931, MNI.
M. RAKOV, sculpted ivory, *Vrantel Island,* 1935, MNI.

Embroidered fabric with a traditional motif, Kirghistan, circa 1930.

Embroidered fabric with a traditional motif, Uzbekistan, 1934.
Embroidered fabric with a traditional motif, Uzbekistan, circa 1930.

M. BYTCHKOVA, *The Subway,* pillowcase, Mstiora, 1930.

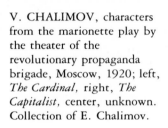

V. CHALIMOV, characters from the marionette play by the theater of the revolutionary propaganda brigade, Moscow, 1920; left, *The Cardinal,* right, *The Capitalist,* center, unknown. Collection of E. Chalimov.

E. KRYLOV, *V.I. Lenin,* carpet, Turkmenistan, 1930.

HANDICRAFTS

E. CHILNIKOVSKY, brooch with a floral motif, Veliki-Ustiug, circa 1930.
Metal box with a floral motif, Rostov-Jaroslavsky, circa 1920.

Lacquered Miniatures

T here are four crafts centers for papier-maché miniatures in Russia: Fedoskino (the Moscow region), Mstiora (Vladimir region), Palekh, and Kholui (Ivanovo region). The oldest center is Fedoskino; the most well-known, Palekh. The Palekh style emerged in the second half of the seventeenth century, influenced by the old schools of icon painting of Moscow, Stroganov, Yaroslav. Palekh craftsmen, working in Moscow, Kostroma, Makarievo, Kaliazin, Vololamsk, and at the monastery of the Holy Trinity in Zagorsk, had always restored ancient frescoes. Palekh iconography was famous for its traditional representation of faces and the refinement of its distemper techniques and gold colors.

After the Revolution, the icon painters began, little by little, to create secular papier-maché miniatures. During the 1920s, the Gostorg commissioned several items which sparked off a debate over whether to vulgarize the Palekh artistry. Gorky and Lunatcharsky came to the defense of the Palekh tradition with the argument that the crafts center must find its own path in the new era, that the poetical and fairy-like traditions of this art form should be preserved. Palekh artisans, indeed, were rapidly able to adapt the techniques of icon painting to the miniatures which were being produced at the time. Certain details required more attention: the depiction of volumes, oval or circular compositions, and the use of distempers for lacquered oil prints. Generally speaking, these miniatures used the same techniques as icon painting: non-porous hard surfaces, execution in four steps, and six layers of lacquer, which were polished afterwards to obtain a mirror-like sheen.

The master of the transformation from icon painting to miniatures was the self-taught artist Golikov. He was soon as thoroughly at ease with the black lacquer of boxes as he had previously been with the ivory backgrounds of icons covered with designs and arabesques (*Tea-drinking, 1922*). Later on, he discovered the idea of coating the black background of the boxes with a cherry color which made it easier to paint shiny miniatures with distempers (*The Feast, 1923*). In his early miniatures, the influence of the iconography of the Trinity can be seen, but gradually, Golikov switched to game scenes, idylls, or illustrations of songs (*Along the River, The Spinner, On the Mother-Volga*). Golikov even entered into the new artistic era with a series of lacquers on the theme of the "Red Laborer." He was also the author of a famous series of magical battle scenes. "The artist must show within his paintings the turmoil which has banished the past," he himself stated. Indeed, the horsemen, the rhythms, and colors suggest the turmoil of the era, but his paintings also call to mind the bas-reliefs of Roman sarcophagi, Italian Renaissance canvases or paintings by Rubens. In truth, as a former soldier himself, he was simply transcribing what he already was familiar with. Golikov was also fond of hunting scenes: exotic horsemen with golden spears, dogs and savage beasts depicted in moments of rage, ready to leap right out of the picture. This same imaginative vein can be seen on an unfinished box preserved at the Zagorsk Museum, *Igor's Joust*. Golikov usually began work on a painting directly, without any preparation or preliminary sketches. He composed flowers and arabesques from wildflowers he gathered for this purpose. Improvisation did not, however, keep him from creating decorations which were in harmony with the form of the object, as can be seen in his miniature friezes (the cigar-holder *Promenade,* 1925), his lacy frames (*On the Mother-Volga,* box, 1930), and his medallions (*The Tale of the Fisherman and the Fish,* box, 1925).

Vakurov was another master craftsman at the Palekh center. His specialties were painting with distempers and symbolic representations. On a 1936 box, *Tempest Bird,* he illustrated *The Song of the Tempest Bird* by Gorky with symbols of the Revolution: upon a red rock stands the silhouette of a worker armed with a pickax, gazing severely at the stormy waves breaking on a ship symbolizing Czarist Russia. Vakurov, like all Palekh artists, gave much attention to the story-line and complexity of a given subject. On the box *The Demons,* based on a story by Pushkin, the black lacquer represents night, spilling forth demons and horses with golden manes carrying the disgraced poet to his tragic end. The outlines are traced with gold, and the miniature shines with mysterious reflections.

The artists Bakanov, Markichev, Vatagin, Dydykin, Kotukhin, and Zubkov also worked at Palekh. In their miniatures, reality and fantasy exist side by side. People, trees, and houses have grotesque shapes; an abundance of gold and silver accentuates the emotional content of the pictures.

Folk tales were the favorite themes of Palekh artists, and in particular of Bakanov. On a 1930 powder box, the background depicts a legendary city on a decorative hilltop. In the foreground, slender, supple trees bend over the deep blue of a stream. In this landscape with a black sky, the red-shirted fisherman is miniaturized by cold, pearly colors. Among Palekh lacquers inspired by Pushkin, Bakanov's best piece was a box dating from 1934, *The Tale of the Golden Rooster,* reflecting both the icon-painting technique and the artist's familiarity with the Yaroslav frescoes. The miniatures produced at Palekh overshadowed even the artistry of the Fedoskino center, where papier-maché lacquerwork originated in Russia.

This art first appeared in 1795 in the Moscow region, in the village of Danilkovo (now Fedoskino) in the paper and cardboard factory owned by Korobov. In

I. FOMITCHEV, lacquered box, *The Defense of Vladimir Against Batu in 1238*, Mstiora, 1945.

K. KOSTERIN, lacquered box, *Kolkhoz Celebration*, Kholoui, 1934.

I. GOLIKOV, lacquered
glove box, *Two Troikas,*
Palekh, 1924.

the middle of the nineteenth century, the factory, then owned by the Lukutin family, expanded. Lukutin miniatures existed until 1904. Then its quality began to decline, and the factory closed its doors. Of the hundred or so craftsmen employed there, only a handful remained, forming an artisans' association which survived, with difficulty, for six years. In the simple and elegant Fedoskino miniatures, the forms in relief, the contrasting colors, and the heavy golds, silvers, and pearly lusters were of consistently outstanding quality. In addition, the technique employed at Fedoskino was unique. The painting of oils was part of a complex system in three phases: tinting, retinting, and touching up. Each coat of paint was covered with a coat of lacquer.

During the nineteenth century, Lukutin objects were characterized by deep black backgrounds, exceptionally hard lacquer, and original techniques: enamel cloisonné, "Scotch plaid" (imitating the fabric), "tortoise-shell," and ripples scored in the lacquer down to the metallic surface. The objects in question were snuff-boxes, small casks, chests, goblets, picnic boxes, match boxes, trays, dishes, and vases. During the second half of the nineteenth century, copies of famous Russian paintings served as the main sources of inspiration. This artistic tendency was associated with the name of Fedoskino, and continued even after the Revolution. Paintings by Perov, Vasnetsov, Chichkin, Makovsky, Savrassov, traditional scenes of troikas and people drinking tea, characterized Fedoskino objects until the 1930s. Classical Dutch landscapes and still-life paintings were then used as models (for example, A. Kruglikov's box *The Flowers,* repeated countless times over the following years). The Fedoskino craftsmen worked with painters who drew the sketches for the work. Modorov presented his travel sketches of the Far North, the Urals, and Central Asia for the series entitled *Life of the People of the USSR,* and Semenov executed them in lacquer (*On an Elk,* 1934; *Victory Over Illiteracy in the Far North,* 1936). Kruglikov executed others (*Nenet Encampment,* 1935; *Mongol on a Camel,* 1936; *Mongol Horsemen,* 1935). This series later inspired a line of mass-produced articles. Nonetheless, the Fedoskino output remained essentially artisan, often limited to prototypes and copies of newspaper photographs.

In 1930, following the example of Palekh, the Mstiora center began to produce lacquered objects as well. Before the Revolution, it had been the second most important center in the country, going back to the beginning of the eighteenth century. Within four or five years, Mstiora artists had created their own style of papier-maché objects, quite different from that of Palekh.

The tradition of icon painting was continued in the choice of colors, the drawings of mountains and palaces, and the use of unpainted spaces. Among other subjects were *The Birth of Christ* and *Nicholas the Miracle Worker*. The craftsmen were more independent in their depiction of saints' faces and in the way they placed figures. Their miniatures were painted with a kind of naïve realism similar to the traditional *lubok* images. This was even more visible in the icons they produced for mass distribution, executed by artists who maintained their independence, such as Bakuchinsky in the early 1930s. This new vein in Mstiora's production was also characterized by a certain independence concerning composition and a refusal of conventional techniques. Mstiora artists favored painting techniques; their miniatures were like tiny paintings or medallions on papier-maché box tops. In most cases, these miniatures were framed by small floral friezes with openwork and gilded colors. The colors were harmonious, in the old-fashioned tradition, with light, silvered touches. The Mstiora miniatures were closer to easel painting than those of Palekh. Whether the subject depicted was legendary, historical or mundane, its execution was always serene and lyrical.

The work by the center's oldest craftsman, Klykov, was the finest example of Mstiora's new style. At first, his work was in the "Novgorodian" style (*The Demon and Tamara, Tarass Bulba and his Sons,* 1928). The rather coarse stylization of human figures and landscape were in contrast with the refinement of the papier-maché object. Klykov realized his error and switched to the "Stroganov" style. The colors were lighter, the landscapes more precise and less weighty. The foreground figures were woodcutters, kolkhoz workers, workers (*Cutting Wood,* 1937; *Harvest,* 1936; *After the Siren,* 1936). Klykov liked to depict nature, scenes of repose, and leisurely activities: tea served under the veranda, ice-skating on frozen lakes, hunters and fishermen. The figures were often arranged on parallel planes, with pearly hills or faraway villages in the background. The world is seen from afar, with minuscule human figures. Occasionally, Klykov's compositions were divided into three parts, like a triptych, with trees separating the central sections. His work also included frieze-type compositions, a rhythmical succession of architectural elements or landscapes, allowing for much variety of detail.

The other artists of the old generation, Briagin and Kotiagin, were more conventional in style, with representations done in the "carpet" manner, that is to say, the action was suggested by "lines" or "steps." One of Briagin's boxes, *Elk Hunt* (1933), shows mountains rising in successive waves, with dynamic colors and rhythms suggestive of Persian miniatures.

Conventional mountains and palaces had their place among Mstiora minia-

A. KOTIAGIN, lacquered box, *The Legend of the Two Peasants*, Mstiora, 1933.

tures, as they had had at the Palekh center, but here such themes were airier and more picturesque. While the usual battle, hunting, and idyllic motifs continued to be painted, modern themes began to appear around 1922–1923: *Celebration at Kazakhstan* and *Harvest* by Briagin; *Unloading of Canal Boats, Peeling Onions, Repair Stations and Individual Exploitation, Peasant and Tractors* by Kotiagin.

Before the Revolution, the village of Kholui was the third center of icon painting in Russia. It introduced lacquered miniatures at a somewhat later date than Palekh or Mstiora. Until the 1940s, its production was centered around oil painting on canvas or jute. The Kholui center, which had originally specialized in inexpensive icons intended for sale at the monastery at Zagorsk, continued to produce simply-made icons of a pleasing naïveté and imitations of nineteenth-century academic religious painting. Only later did the textile canvases of Kholui appear, with sirens and simpering ladies against backgrounds of rose bushes.

After 1932, when the Kholui artisans' association converted its activities to papier-maché, some artists left to form their own association; they continued the creation of textile canvases until 1953. Only four remaining artists, Mokin, Puzanov, Kosterin and Dobrynin, attempted to assimilate the art of miniature painting. After 1932, they purchased undecorated Palekh objects which they then painted themselves. It was not until 1943 that Kholui produced its own articles. The work of these four artists gave rise to the Kholui miniature style, more concrete than that of Palekh, more decorative than the Fedoskino style. The artists themselves each had their distinctive manner. Mokin, who was also an easel painter, undertook difficult experiments: he painted typical Russian carpet arabesques or romantic landscapes on box tops. Kosterin, more limited in his palette and in his technique, drew inspiration from newspaper photographs. Puzanov, a refined and lyrical artist, reworked photographs or created stylized landscapes as he had previously done on icons. A professional school was founded in 1934, but did not really begin to bear fruit until the fifties and sixties.

Among the different crafts productions of lacquered articles, the metal trays of Jostovo should be mentioned. This crafts center originated around 1825 or 1830 in the factories owned by the Vichniakov merchants. Right up until the present day, the different articles it produced have remained faithful to traditional decoration and objects. Jostovo has always produced tea or kitchen trays in diverse standard shapes. The "Siberian" form is similar to trays from the Urals, rectangular with high borders. The "Gothic" form is suggestive of Gothic ribbed vaults. The "wing" form is easily recognizable by its undulating oval or rounded edges. The subject is always floral and freely executed. Bouquets, crowns, and garlands are drawn from fabric designs of the eighteenth and nineteenth centuries, porcelain from the Gardner factory, and still-lifes of indifferent quality. The mastery of Jostovo craftsmen developed steadily until they were able to improvise. The popularity of these low-cost trays meant that they had to be produced very rapidly; a Jostovo craftsman decorated five or six trays in a day.

Jostovo trays have black backgrounds and are decorated with large, multicolored flowers (roses, poppies, tulips) or with small flowers (cornflowers, daisies, bluebells). Within each bouquet, there is a standard rhythm of colors and lines. Such perfection is also the consequence of a particular technique by which the craftsman turns the tray on his knee as he decorates it, resulting in a fluidity of lines and colors and the compact aspect of the composition. The most talented artists in this domain were Leontiev, Leznov, the Kledov brothers, and Kurzin. A certain amount of experimentation did take place: backgrounds were not always black but could be red, blue, green, or ivory, which changed the composition of bouquets. New flowers appeared: clover, pansies, asters, dahlias. Leznov worked from sketches by such painters as Konchalovsky, Lhvostensko, Lange (*Flowers and Fruit in a Basket* and *Fruit and Vegetables* after Konchalovsky). He confided that this enabled him to paint more freely and more generously and that he was better able to perceive colors. Subsequently, Leznov created round trays: *Birds Among Flowers, Bouquet in a Basket with a Bird, Fruit in a Basket.*

Palekh, Mstiora, and Kholui experienced difficulties during the second half of the 1930s. The small artisans' associations producing for museums and exportation had gradually developed into industrial firms along the lines of Fedoskino. On the eve of the war, there were over fifty master-craftsmen at Palekh, one hundred and twenty-three at Mstiora, sixty-five at Kholui, and over a hundred at Fedoskino. Mass production based on a limited number of prototypes appeared; some of these were copies of paintings, like the Fedoskino articles.

In addition to this routine production, special orders from within the USSR as well as abroad encouraged the creation of unique pieces: decoration of sanatoriums, rest homes, clubs, department stores; theater decoration; book illustrations.[1] Palekh undertook porcelain decoration as of 1929.

This secondary production was not always the most successful, because craftsmen were obliged to transpose their techniques onto other supports very different in size. Panels were particularly badly done—the artists concentrated on detail but forgot that such panels were supposed to be primarily decorative.

During the war, activity slowed down. Fedoskino stopped its production from 1941 to 1942, due to the proximity of the front. Kholui also closed its doors for a time. Heroic themes were the order of the day: a box by Ovtchinnikov had sides bearing the following illustrations: *The Battle of the Alexander Nevsky Against the Swedes on the Neva,* 1944, *Moscow Liberated from the Poles by Minin and Pojarsky,* and *The Battle of Borodino.* The cover depicted an episode from World War II, the battle of the Dniepr. In 1945, the Tretyakov Gallery organized an exhibition devoted to Russian lacquered miniatures.

NOTES

1. Palekh: Pioneers' House in Leningrad, 1936; Crafts exhibition at the Tretyakov Gallery in Moscow, 1937; panel for a sanatorium in the Moscow area, 1938; renovation of the Elisseyev department store in Moscow, 1938; panels for Yaroslave, Ivanovo, and Sverdlovsk; theater decor for *The Song of Stepan Razin,* Leningrad, 1934; *Ruzlan and Ludmila,* for the Leningrad puppet theater, 1932–1933; illustrations for tales by Pushkin, 1937.
    Mstiora: Sanatoriums in Sotchy and Kislovodsk, 1937. Panels for clubs and for the exhibition at the Tretyakov Gallery, Agriculture Pavilion at the National Agricultural Exhibition, 1939; panels for the "Crafts Art" store in Moscow, 1939.
    Fedoskino: Panels for the exhibition at the Tretyakov Gallery.

N. TSIBIN, lacquered powder-box, *Summer Troika,* Fedoskino, 1928.

A. TCHUCHKIN, wood sculpture, *The Laborer*, Bogorodskoye, 1924.
I. STULOV, traditional wood sculpture, *How the Bear Broke the Shaft*, 1943.
Traditional sculpted wood toy, *The Blacksmiths*, Bogorodskoye.

Traditional Statuettes and Toys

T raditional decorative statuettes are part of everyday life, and as such, it is difficult to include them within the category of sculpture. It is through traditional forms of expression that the craftsman defines his feelings and thoughts. Even tradition, however, evolves. It was thus that certain toys began to be appreciated for their decorative qualities: for example, the clay toys made in Viatka, wood carvings made in Bogorodskoye, and the majolica toys made in Opochnianskoye. Magical qualities had been attributed to certain traditional sculptural objects in the past—chiseled ivory pieces from Tchukotka, sculpted wood and stone from Tuva, amulets, and so forth—which were now gradually absorbed into the category of decorative sculpture. A third type of traditional sculpture came into being with the growth of industry in the eighteenth century. It included ivory miniatures from Tobolsk and cast objects from Kassli. Lastly, there was the sculpture derived from traditional thematic tableware including Ukrainian ceramics and Georgian glazed black ceramics.

During the 1920s and up until the middle of the 1930s, the production of statuettes was practically nonexistent or else was in the process of being totally restructured. The Tchukotka and Tuva centers were still impermeable to the new art of the Revolution.

The Tchukotka ivory sculptors worked outside the organized production framework, and it was not until 1931 that such craftsmen as Vukvol, Onno, Vukvutagin, Khalmo, Aiz, Aromke, Rochlin, and Keinitegrin organized an ivory sculpting workshop at Uelen.

They specialized in walruses, whales, and reindeer. Walrus bodies were tapered rather than modeled, with carved notches for the mustaches. Tchukche statuettes existed in order to be touched. Like an amulet, the statuette was worn around the neck or carried in a pocket or a pouch. During this same period, in the wood carving center of Bogorodskoye and the ivory sculpting center of Tobolsk, traditional concepts were being adapted to modern artistic demands.

The decorative statuettes of Bogorodskoye (in the Zagorsk region, not far from Moscow) were originally used as toys for children or game pieces for adults. This dual orientation—toy or bibelot—had existed as early as the eighteenth century. Now, at the beginning of the twentieth century, the work of the Bogorodskoye craftsmen experienced the influence of the "Zemtsvo" schools and workshops.

During the 1920s, production of traditional "articulated" or "rocking" toys continued. But toy making was not the principal activity at Bogorodskoye. During the 1930s, Bogorodskoye sculptors began to create complex compositions with several human figures. New habits needed to be acquired in order to meet the demands of realism. Although they had rejected tradition, Bogorodskoye craftsmen had not turned their backs on professionalism. At the Leipzig fair in 1928, Bogorodskoye was particularly noted for its toys, figurines (a series of Mujiks), and group compositions on pedestals. These were unique objects, original and expressive, with traditional subjects such as horse-and-carts, unchanged since the beginning of the nineteenth century (troikas of one or two horses, barouches, wagons). Sometimes a figurine subject was identical to that of a toy: horse and wagon, each on a separate pedestal, were coarsely carved in the manner of inexpensive toys, but in a more expressive manner. New models were also presented—a typical tabletop sculpture represented a team of horses pulling a cart, but with less conventional horses and more refined harnesses, although the riders wore traditional clothing. Another sculpture showed a woman's elegant horse and carriage, and yet another, a mujik carrying wood. Other statuettes were larger in size than the horse-and-cart type sculptures, showing brave young men who resembled Stepan Razin, or traditional animals and birds (lions, horses, etc.) similar to the hollow-ware of the eighteenth and nineteenth centuries. Blacksmiths were popular subjects.

Compositions of several figures included peasants, carpenters, woodcutters, or a peasant family seated around a table. The horse-drawn plow was occasionally replaced by a tractor, and traditional "little soldiers" by infantrymen of the Red Army. But new themes were not a priority with Bogorodskoye craftsmen; their main concern was the revival of technical mastery and traditions. Although mass production had already been launched in this domain, craftsmen like Chuchkin, Stulov, and Boblovkin also created unique and original pieces of work. Before the Revolution, Chuchkin had favored complex compositions such as *The Stairway of Life*, *Village Meeting*, *Napoleon on Poklonny Mountain*, and *Linen Making*. Boblovkin's main subject was birds, transforming their wings, feathers and tails into ornamental motifs; such sculptures were static rather than suggestive of movement. Stulov, author of such compositions from the 1930s as *The Trumpet of the Red Army* and *Chapayev on Horseback*, gave these new themes a certain romanticism. He also created traditional models such as *Horse-Drawn Sleigh*.

At the beginning of the 1930s, the Bogorodskoye professional school was feverishly producing designs and prototypes. In 1931, the Toy Museum was transferred from Moscow to Zagorsk. Professional sculptors came to collaborate with craftsmen.[1] New techniques, new compositions, and new subjects were discovered as a new generation of young craftsmen came of age.

At the end of the 1930s, the center was in the midst of preparations for the National Exhibition of Traditional Arts and Crafts. The exhibition's artistic directors encouraged the participating craftsmen to work from nature. The latest directives concerning themes even temporarily allowed work based on folk tales. It was thus that, until the early 1940s, Bogorodskoye produced unique group compositions intended for exhibitions and museums.

Around this time, a talented craftsman named Erochkin began to draw attention. He was skilled in all the different genres produced at Bogorodskoye—articulated toys (*Mowers*, 1935–1937), group compositions on pedestals surrounded by trees or other common objects (*The Tale of the Fisherman and the Fish*, 1936, *The Master and the Worker*, 1938–1939), simple compositions representing human figures, houses, trees, furniture (*The Tale of the Three Bears*, 1943–1945, *The City of the Birds*, 1936–1939), and single figure sculptures (*Peasant with Ax*, 1935). Erochkin was as interested in modern themes as he was in traditional subjects.

Like many artists of the 1920s and 1930s, he preserved traditional forms and compositions while giving his figures a modern appearance. In *Mowers*, the peasants wear jackets, long pants, and berets, but all the rest of the composition is strictly traditional. In *Red Army Patrol on Horseback*, 1939, the traditional "little soldiers" are conventional enough, but they wear Budenny caps and long greatcoats. What was important for Erochkin was not what differentiated the new from the old, but rather what the two had in common.

In the second half of the 1930s, Zinin also created original pieces of work, in particular articulated toys (*The Fisherman, Butting She-Goats*). In 1936, he sculpted a group composition, *The Armed Wagon of Tchapayev*, in which he departed from Bogorodskoye principles. The action is tense and dramatic—horses are galloping, a soldier is trying to restrain them while another is firing his machine gun and Tchapayev is aiming his revolver. The ensemble is naïve and naturalistic.

Chichkin specialized in group compositions based on themes of traditional pleasures. Silhouettes of girls with their suitors, merchants, peasants, and children were arranged at random in the vicinity of merry-go-rounds or food-stands. Such toys were often musical. A little key was turned, tiny hammers hit a cord, and a simple melody started up, in perfect harmony with the subject.

Stulov was undoubtedly the most interesting sculptor at Bogorodskoye. A talented craftsman, he gradually developed into a genuine artist. In 1932, he began to create traditional toys with new themes (*Kolkhoz Team, Red Cavalry*), followed by decorative sculptures in the thirties and forties. Animals were one of his favorite subjects: *Falconer*, 1936, *Tetras Hunter*, 1937, *The Shepherd*, 1938, *The*

I. STULOV, wood sculpture, *The Heron*, 1936.

Shepherd and the Ewe, 1940, *The Stork,* 1949, *Masha and the Bear,* 1942–1943, *How the Bear Bent the Shaft,* 1943. These statuettes became part of the classical repertory of Bogorodskoye because, in spite of their economy, the forms were well-designed and attractive.

Erochkin's and Stulov's work represented two different trends at Bogorodskoye. The Erochkin trend used traditional themes, while the Stulov trend sought to emphasize the differences between the sculpture of yesterday and of today.

Another crafts center which also underwent a kind of renaissance during the 1930s was Viatka (or Dymkovo), whose specialty was clay sculptures. Among the different sorts of figurines produced at Viatka were clay whistles of an extremely ancient design, still manufactured today. These included sheep, goat, duck, rooster, and turkey motifs. Today, these figurines are not considered to be toys, as industrial toys are now more solid, hygienic, and less costly than Dymkovo clay objects. Decorative sculpture was also produced at Dymkovo, similar to the classical whistles it produced. A favorite motif was that of a woman in national costume, with kokochnik (high coiffure), blouse with puffed sleeves, ruffled apron, and bell-like skirt: *Peasant Woman With Bucket, The Child's Nurse, Woman and Little Dog.* In the early 1930s, thanks to the impetus given by the artist Denchin, Dymkovo toys became popular again.

At the time, almost all artists at Dymkovo were producing plaster figurines. The Dymkovo style was almost invariably the same. Even in the 1930s, no new themes or techniques were introduced; rather, Dymkovo craftsmen turned to the past for inspiration. In the work produced at Dymkovo, there is almost no trace of individuality, with the exceptions of a few highly original sculptures.

Mezrina, too, produced traditional compositions and sculptures. These were assorted toy whistles—ducks, sheep, horses, reindeer, bears, cows, mountebanks on goats, women, and nursemaids. The style of these toys was genuinely archaic: simplified forms, bold transitions from one form to another, vivid and simple colors. Kochkina's compositions were more varied—peasant women and a horse beside a well, a toy peddler, milking cows. Kochkina enjoyed giving her female figures—nursemaids, peasant women carrying buckets—wavy hair, as well as arched eyebrows and heart-shaped mouths. Mezrina's figures had eyebrows with more severe lines, with rounded mouths and cheeks.

Konovalova created interesting compositions of seamen on boats, sailors rowing, and so on. Bezdenezhnykh's fertile imagination had a wider range of subjects: *Woman Milking a Cow, The Squire, The Shepherd, The Harvest, The Barnyard, Masha and the Bear, Cabbage Harvest, The Harvester, Girl and her Suitor, Musicians on a Bench and Dancer, Breeder of Reindeer, Sale of Toys, Tea-drinking,* etc. Such toys were relatively tall, around fifteen to twenty inches (40–50 cm) which gave them a more

I. STULOV, wood sculpture,
Red Army Procession,
Bogorodskoye, 1930.

elegant line. Three basic forms could be distinguished which contributed to the overall roundness of the silhouette: a circle for the kokochnik (headdress), with the woman's face in the center; a second circle which included the bust and the waist, with rounded forms for the puffed sleeves and arms in semicircle; and lastly, a third circle consisting of a bell-shaped skirt. These three forms became heavier toward the bottom, and the proportions were successfully rendered. The sense of volume was emphasized by costume details—collars, cuffs, ruffles—as well as by an increased number of accessories. Under Bezdenezhnykh's influence, Dymkovo statuettes became progressively longer, higher even than statues intended for modern interiors. It was thus that they became museum pieces or gifts.

Tobolsk ivory miniatures appeared during the second half of the nineteenth century. The ivory came from mammoth tusks.

During the 1920s, an effort was made to get this ruined industry back onto its feet. Only a few craftsmen remained—Terentiev, Denissov, Peskov—who sculpted pipes, cigar-holders, and brooches out of mammoth tusks. Production was minimal, the subject matter almost always having to do with animals. A few of these carved objects represented reindeer, elks, dogs.

In the 1930s, another trend emerged at Tobolsk—traditional miniature subjects and compositions (*Harnessing the Reindeer, Ostiak on Skis*). These decorative sculptures retained their traditional authenticity. Figures stood out on curved tusks or blades cut out of mammoth tusks. Such objects were easy to hold and touch. Hair, clothing, and facial features were finely chiseled. Reindeer antlers, harness details, and bows and arrows were carved in openwork. These finely polished horns and tusks were as beautiful as gem stones.

Such objects were not always traditionally executed, as can be seen in the miniature *Ostiak on Skis*. Usually, this inhabitant of the Far North was shown to be an exhausted hunter. In the 1930s, on the contrary, he was depicted as strong and confident. During the second half of the 1930s, production of miniatures of animals, Ostiak life, and chess pieces continued, but preference went to human figures. Compositions consisted of one or several figures, with dynamic gestures, exaggerated musculature, and heavy body proportions. The search for new forms slowed down, and there was little evolution.

In 1936, Lopatin created a miniature entitled *Ostiak Hunter.* The hunter is shown on skis, carrying a bow and arrow and accompanied by his dog. However, he is not seen pursuing an animal, but remains calmly in an upright position. His clothing is embroidered and edged with fur. He is on the lookout, his expression attentive, almost dreamy. All these were new elements in Tobolsk sculpture.

Truly remarkable articles of forged work were produced at Kassli. They are linked to the names of famous artists of the late nineteenth and early twentieth centuries. During the first two decades after the Revolution, this craft stagnated. Only moulds dating from before the Revolution were used, based on creations by Lanceray, Klodt, Liberich, and Auber. Contemporary work was extremely rare. This was equally true of the stone statuettes produced at Perm and Gorky. Forged artwork, like stone statuettes, did not experience any kind of renewal until after the Second World War. This was also true of Ukrainian ceramics and wood-carvings, stone statuettes from Tuva, and ivory engravings from Kholmogor, Tchukotka, and Yakutie.

NOTES

1. O. Balandin, N. Bartram, V. Vatagin, E. Teliakovsky, B. Lange.

V. DENISSOV, ivory sculpture, *Returning from Fishing*, Tobolsk, 1936.
M. RAKOV, ivory sculpture, *Hunting in the Arctic*, 1936.

Sculpture in Ivory

I n 1917, only four craftsmen remained at the renowned crafts center of Kholmogor—Perepelkin, Uzikov, Guriev, and Petrovsky. Reviving their art form was a long and difficult process. In 1929, the older craftsmen founded an ivory carving workshop in order to train young artists. It was only in 1930 that a Lomonossov artisans' association and professional school were founded.

By the second half of the 1930s, the nucleus of craftsmen had enlarged and the center's activities had been significantly diversified. All sorts of gift objects were now made—brooches, barrettes, hairpins, combs, signet rings, buttons, etc. Openwork subjects in mammoth or walrus tusks were used to decorate cases, powder boxes, and cigar holders. In addition to this mass production, large, finely worked articles with openwork reliefs were created for exhibitions and museums. Although these were also utilitarian articles, the handiwork was of such high quality, having often taken several months of work, that they acquired the status of precious objects. Miniatures were the most prized of all.

At the beginning of the 1940s, the artistic style of such objects began to evolve, as did the forms, motifs, execution, and subject matter. Little by little, craftsmen ceased imitating classical art and began to draw inspiration from nature, the surrounding environment, new elements of Soviet life, and folk tales. New rhythms and simplified interpretations characterized the work of Guriev and Uzikov.

S. EVANGULOV, ivory sculpture, *Fur Hunter*, 1933.

During the 1930s, artists from Moscow assisted the Kholmogor craftsmen by supplying them with models. Rakov, for instance, in his openwork subjects, depicted the types of work, animals, and nature of the Far North. All parts of the composition were balanced and rhythmical. The openwork background played an important role by creating the rhythmical decoration and organization of the composition. Rakov rejected the "Empire" style whorls and cross-hatches which were practically obligatory at Kholmogor, while perpetuating the traditional subjects of the craft: *Reindeer Hunt, Hunting in the Far North, Harpoon Fishing, Crafts of the Far North,* etc. Tchukotka ivory sculptures and carvings had always served as souvenirs and gifts, even before the Revolution. Figurines depicting animals and idols of the Far North, paper cutters with sculpted handles, and walrus tusks decorated with small carved scenes, were bought by foreign sailors who carried these objects to America by way of Alaska.

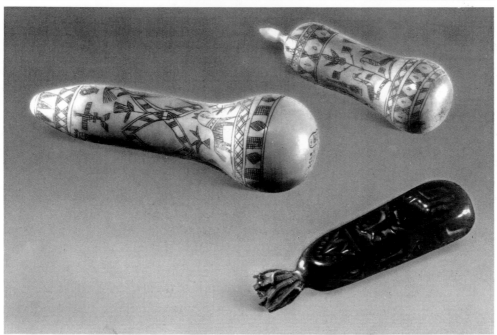

M. TCHIRKOV, metal plaque depicting the city of Veliki-Ustiug, 1923.
Uzbek *naskadu* in the form of gourds, circa 1920.
EMKUL, engraved ivory walrus tooth, *The Tale of the Wicked Soul of Kale*, detail,
Tchukotka, circa 1940.

Such sculpted ivory objects were linked to the very roots of Tchuk art. Local folklore was full of stories of hunting, festivities, and the breeding of reindeer, scenes which were engraved in color on walrus tusks. Cruel hunting scenes were depicted with the serenity and simplicity of epic poems. As for day-to-day tasks such as the preparation of nets, fishing, or the care of reindeer, these images of typical and extremely vital events were depicted with great sensitivity. Folk tales, legends, and popular beliefs were also shown—the heroes of Tchuk epic poems, for example, represented the positive and negative forces of nature. Color and design brought rhythm to the construction; the figures were regularly spaced, arranged in friezes. Such carvings were similar to the chain-stitch embroideries done by vari-

V. UZIKOV, candy dish in sculpted ivory, Kholmogory, 1936.

ous peoples of the Far North.

Before the 1930s, when the sculpture workshop at Uelen was founded, ivory work had a familial, domestic character. By the second half of the 1930s, Tchuk artists were participating in exhibitions, creating specially commissioned pieces that were, on occasion, rather unusual. The miniaturist craftsman Vukvol, for instance, had to create a panel in plastic, entitled *Scenes from the Life of a Tchuk Kolkhoz* (Exhibition of Traditional Folk Art—Tretyakov Gallery, Moscow, 1937). Vukvol was able to adjust to the required large dimensions, but the abundance of details characteristic of Tchuk carvings was incompatible with the overall harmony of such a large composition.

In 1935, Vukvol designed a snuffbox decorated with a scene from contemporary history, the rescue of the shipwreck at Tcheliusin. Vukvol was not at ease with this type of shape, and the harmony of the drawings is less successful than on walrus tusks. The mass-produced articles at Uelen were the same as at Kholmogor: pipes, cigar holders, hairpins, barrettes, and other accessories intended for city dwellers. This type of production made it possible for the craft to survive, but it was of inferior quality. Decorative objects, such as walrus tusks covered with colored engravings depicting the day-to-day life of the Tchuks, were more interesting.

Wood Carvings

Khokhloma, near Gorky, is the most important wood-carving center in Russia. At the end of the nineteenth century, Khokhloma wooden peasant dishes were famous for their shape and expressive brushwork. It must also be said that these wood carvings tended to go somewhat overboard in the pseudo-Russian style then in fashion and overdid such motifs as arabesques and dragons. These designs were foreign to traditional art, but had been introduced by artists from the *zemstvo* (local council), Durnovo and Matveyev, who encouraged the use of arabesques.

During the twenties and thirties, Khokhloma artists tried to shake off the Art Nouveau influence by using innovative decors and shapes. In addition to dishes made on a lathe, they began to manufacture pencil cases, desk objects, sewing boxes, trays, serving dishes, decorative vases, furniture, and even kiosk facades.

During the 1920s, artists like the Krassilnikov brothers continued to use floral designs at their workshop in Novo-Pokrovskoye, while at Khokhloma, this type of production was considered to be inferior. Bakuchinsky insisted that authentic popular designs needed to be revived. Artists using the pseudo-Russian style therefore turned to traditional designs.

In 1936, Khokhloma objects created by "the new traditionalists" were exhibited in Moscow. They went on to the Tretyakov Gallery where they met with great success. The only criticism made was that they tended to contain an overabundance of detail. In the middle of the decade, the brushwork became freer and more vivid, and ornamental motifs became increasingly varied. Stylized birds, fish, flowers, and berries were introduced into the decor. In the Koverminsky region, craftsmen preferred the naïve designs referred to as "little leaf": branches of flowers and berries, usually wild strawberries and apples, were painted in delicate brush strokes on the gilded surface of bowls, small casks, spoons, and shelves. Red and black floral motifs unfurled rhythmically around tendrils or stood in vertical groups on vases. Notes of color were repeated, completing the basic motif and accentuating the link between the design and the object.

A new technique was introduced, in which the artist traced the outline of the floral design, then painted the background in red, black, green or brown. He then added delicate lines of color to the leaves, petals, and grass.

During the twenties and thirties, unique pieces were also created at Khokhloma. A. and N. Podogov presented a gate entitled *Springtime,* which earned much renown, at the Exhibition of 1937. The silvery-green background, unusual for Khokhloma work, was punctuated with the black silhouettes of starlings and the white clusters of wild cherry flowers. Such concrete execution was new. Another gate, *Autumn,* in red and gold tones, was executed by Tiukalov and Krassilnikov.

During the 1930s, Khokhloma artists created the frescoes of the Folk Art Theater of Moscow, the Pioneer House in Gorky, and the Gorky Pavilion at the Agricultural Exhibition of 1939.

The Gorky region remained the center for wood sculptures and carvings. The traditional objects of Khokhloma continued to be manufactured, as well as the famous nests of dolls made in Semionov, consisting of from three to thirty dolls. The region was also renowned for its wooden toys from Fedossevo, children's furniture, and other such objects. Decoration was often reminiscent of the lubok style, joyous and naïve.

Farther north, far from the big cities, traditions were even stronger. Thus the sculpted spinning wheels of Arkhangelsk and Mezen preserved principles of elaboration and decoration dating from the nineteenth century. On the other hand, symbolical motifs were also accompanied by more concrete and contemporary subjects. Generally speaking, craftsmen from remote areas continued almost out of inertia to create objects stemming from a peasant tradition that no longer existed. It was not until the 1950s and 1960s that this phenomenon came to light. Sculpted wood from Abramtsevo developed in the Zagorsk region (Moscow province). All sorts of small, everyday decorative objects were created there. Production of sculpted furniture slowed down, in comparison to the beginning of the century. Medicine chests, shelves, ladles, small boxes, vases, and dishes were created along Polenova's principles: engravings were concentric, with floral motifs, geometric, and flat. During the twenties and thirties, the most talented sculptor at Abramtsevo was Vornoskov, from the village of Kudrino. Before the Revolution, he had worked on Polenava's designs. Vornoskov and his four sons gave their name to a kind of sculpture in flat relief and founded a new crafts trend at Abramtsevo. At the end of the 1930s, Abramtsevo produced decorative panels of high quality. For the exhibition at the Tretyakov Gallery in 1937, the Vornoskovs produced, for example, a gate entitled *Guarding the Frontiers of the USSR.* In 1940, the Abramtsevo artisans' association consisted of more than two hundred craftsmen.

Among traditional Russian art forms, one of the most ancient and widespread was the creation of everyday objects out of brick bark. In the North, Siberia, the Far East, and Central Russia, pails, cradles, baskets, and boxes were made in this

Chiseled wooden dish in a stylized geometrical motif, Kossov, 1940.
N. VEPREV, sculpted wooden dish, *The North*, Chemogode, 1937.

manner. The bark was decorated according to several different techniques: stamping, openwork, veneer, drawing.

The most renowned type of birch bark work was the "Chemogodiye birch" or drilled bark. Voronov believed that this type of work dated from the nineteenth century. Executed by peasants, it was intended for city dwellers. Other authors have found a similarity between "Chemogodiye birch" and iron openwork which has existed since the sixteenth century. It is also possible that this craft dates back as far as the Slavic Middle Ages. Before 1917, Veprev, master of this craft, had prefigured artists whose talents were revealed during the 1930s and 40s: Uglovskaya, S.A. and L. Vepreva, Jilina, Balagurovskaya, Mussinskaya, Ostrumova.

A. Veprev's chiseled bark resembled lace motifs: *Hare Hunt,* 1938, *Lion Hunt,* 1939, *Customs Officer and His Dog,* 1939. Human figures and animals blended into the floral design to such a point that the forest took on a fairytale aspect. Under Veprev's influence, other craftsmen added fish, birds, and animals to their designs, but they were far from being his equals.

L. Veprev presented an elegant decorative dish, *The North,* at the Paris International Exhibition in 1937. The openwork motifs were suggestive of Kholmogor ivory, which was a slight contradiction considering the simplicity of wood. The border, with its medallions and geometrical cross-hatches, was reminiscent of "Empire" compositions.

Wood work was common in the Ukraine. The "dry sculpture" technique was practiced in the regions of Kiev and Poltava. These were flat reliefs and hollowed out geometric designs, often in triangle. This technique enabled such everyday items as buffets, boxes, spoons, saltshakers, and other peasant objects to be decorated. During the 1920s, Ukrainian carvers pursued this tradition. New objects appeared in the 1930s, intended as gifts or exhibition items: wall plates, inkstands, panels, and decorative vases. Motifs took on certain modern characteristics, inspired by new aspects of technology. For example, a wall plate by Lopatin was bordered by tractors in relief. In the center, sheaves of wheat and harvesters created a harmonious composition. Kisslenko combined traditional motifs of five-branched stars with sheaves inspired by modern graphism.

Certain craftsmen participated in the decoration of public buildings. Alimjan Kassymdjanov, Suleyman Khodzhayev, Turayev, and Abduvakil Issayev decorated the Pioneer's House in Tashkent. The result was rather surprising, as the building's modern architecture was poorly adapted to traditional designs.

Mention should also be made of an ancient Uzbek crafts tradition, that of dishes made out of hard colocynth or bitter apple plants. At the beginning of the twentieth century, colocynth dishes were no longer used. But in Samarkand and Bukhara, snuffboxes made in small colocynths were a great success during the

A. VEPREV, chiseled wooden chest, *The Foxhunt*, Chemorog, 1938.

twenties and thirties. Craftsmen worked on the plant when it was still in the ground, tightening it in some places and marking it in others, thus obtaining motifs in relief. It was then decorated using a variety of techniques: it could be engraved with the help of a sharpened awl, or painted in black with pigment obtained from burned and ground peach pits. The craftsman Khikoyatoy inscribed his own poems on snuffboxes. Toch painted scenes. The snuffboxes by Essambey Khamrayev were more ornamental.

Pottery

There was a severe lack of tableware at the end of the Civil War. Small pottery workshops were set up to help alleviate the situation. The objects produced were coarsely executed and undecorated. However, like all traditional crafts, pottery could not disappear entirely. The Ukraine, Central Asia, and the Daghestan produced outstanding everyday pottery. At the end of the nineteenth and in the early part of the twentieth century, *zemstvos* (local councils) played an important role in keeping Ukrainian crafts alive. The main centers were Opochnia, Mirgrod, Mezhigorye, Dybintsy, and Glinskoye.

After the Revolution, new centers and specialized schools were created. The teachers were artists of experienced craftsmen like Massiuk, Kramarenko, Zhdanko, and Pavelnko.

The technical school in ceramics at Mezhigorye had an excellent reputation, earning success and diplomas at the Paris Exhibition of 1922 and the Moscow Exhibition of 1923. In the early part of the 1920s, the school produced pitchers, plates, vases, and sculpted pieces representing animals (roosters, sheep, etc.). The work was carefully executed, with shiny glazes; the most popular colors were brown and green. Surfaces with decorations in relief rarely bore designs. Although traditions were respected, Mezhigorye pottery was produced for an urban market, with severe and practical shapes for the cups, teapots, and vases, similar to work in porcelain.

Pitcher, *Khelada*, Georgia, 1938.

In the thirties, shapes and designs began to change. Craftsmen no longer produced copies of nineteenth-century work, but created their own variations of traditional pottery. Valuable inspiration came from contemporary artists. One of the most original craftsmen of the period was Gontchar, who came from the village of Krichentsy. His decorative sculptures, similar to traditional clay toys, were renowned. In 1937, he executed a large vase decorated with reliefs depicting parachutists, with small airplanes in a frieze around the neck of the vase.[1] In the 1930s, most craftsmen approved of modernizing the tradition. The Gerassimenko brothers from the village of Bubnovka worked at the monastery in Kiev. Their pottery was embellished with multicolored designs. Larger and flatter than most traditional pottery, the Gerassimenkos' dishes were similar to urban tableware. They also designed services, which was completely new at the time. Their choice of elegant and sober colors, browns and blacks, yellows and greens, against light brown

Cruet, *The Sheep*,
Mezhigorye, 1921.

backgrounds, helped to simplify and give rhythm to the floral motifs. As in Ukrainian embroidery, flowers symbolized the joy of being alive.

In Asia, the traditional ceramics centers were Richtan, Samarkand, Bukhara, and Khiva. The potters in this region were Tadzhiks and Uzbeks. in Tadzhikistan, until the 1950s, pottery preserved archaic forms dating from before the crafts era. As in early times, only women were potters. Motifs were symbolical (protection against the "evil eye," wishes for prosperity), but the aesthetic appearance predominated. Women sometimes decorated pottery for their own amusement, but most pieces were undecorated. In Uzbekistan, on the contrary, pottery was an urban phenomenon, executed by the men. Women participated only in subaltern tasks. Potters were respected, even venerated. Clay pottery was considered pure in the ritual sense of the word; the pots were used for water and for grains.

One of the best craftsmen of the 1920s and 1930s was Miralliev. After 1932, he taught in the Tashkent workshops. The goal of these workshops was, among other preoccupations, to go beyond the limits of a caste craft that was ultimately too hermetic. Experimental workshops were created, and motifs were diversified and modernized. Cotton flowers, five-pointed stars, and other Soviet emblems appeared on dishes. Portraits or compositions of human figures were introduced, thus perturbing the traditional decorative system. These often awkward innovations were not long-lasting.

T. KAMAL, dish decorated with a peacock.

The most successful items were traditional bowls and dishes. These were usually decorated by means of a chasing-chisel, but Miralliev as well as Rakhimov and Aminov also worked by hand, with a brush. These artists, who had received a higher education, subsequently became Uzbek pottery specialists. In the 1930s, many craftsmen worked on restoring the medieval buildings of Central Asia. At this time, new faïence workshops were opened in Tashkent and Samarkand. Khazratkulov, Umarov, and Djurakulov recreated the ceramic tile facings of the tombs and *medersas* of Samarkand. Pottery was widespread in the Daghestan and particularly in Balkhar, where women prepared and decorated clay dishes. This pottery was quite simple, using the archaic, unglazed columbine technique. The women prepared the pottery during the summer, to be baked in wintertime. The men sold it all year round throughout the Daghestan.

NOTES

1. Preserved at the Museum of Ethnography in Leningrad.

Metal

n the 1920s, the situation of metalwork was as alarming as it had been at the end of the nineteenth century. The production of artistic metalwork was not as indispensable as that of pottery or wood. In addition, metals were harder to obtain.

Kubatchi, in the Daghestan, was one of the most original metalworking centers. For centuries, the entire population had made and decorated weapons, armor, helmets, ornaments for horses, and, in lesser quantity, jewelry and accessories for men's and women's clothing. Some craftsmen created dishes in hammered bronze or copper. At the beginning of the twentieth century, the main production consisted of silver tableware and jewelry. In the early twenties, materials and commissions were scarce. Metal craftsmen were forced to look for work elsewhere or else had to change professions. In order to help this crafts technique, the Economy Soviet of the Daghestan commissioned ordinary articles for the Exhibition of Decorative Arts in Paris in 1925. The Kubatchi crafts center was thus introduced to an outside market and able to survive economically.

An effort was also made to adapt accessory and jewelry decorations to pieces of larger dimensions. Akhmedov, a master of filigree, created a naïve-styled silver inkstand in the form of a derrick, in 1922.[1] Of all the craftsmen working in metal, Akhmedov was best able to reconcile tradition with modern and urban taste. He created a number of objects for exportation in 1925–1926, including an inkwell whose form resembled that of a traditional Kubatchi lamp. The motifs were suggestive of niello-work, the typical Kubatchi decoration, with complicated interlacings of stylized stems and leaves. In the 1930's, craftsmen continued to copy national tableware on objects intended for other types of use. Pepper grinders were made in the form of local jugs ("mutchals"), sugar bowls in the form of ancient caldrons. Such procedures, however, were unable to resolve the problem concerning the variety of articles offered by Kubatchi. It was for this reason that craftsmen turned for inspiration to European and urban tableware. This enabled them to sell on the domestic and foreign markets a choice of chased or traditional niello-work articles including teapots, milk pitchers, goblets, and cigar holders. Around the middle of the 1930s, the choice of items expanded to include picture frames, powder boxes, and brooches. This transformation was dictated by the needs of the market—exportation, gifts, exhibitions, and museums.

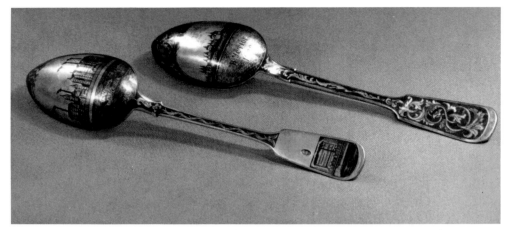

Little silver spoons, Veliki-Ustiug, 1928.

Kubatchi work was shown at the most important international exhibitions—in Paris in 1937, where it received a grand prize, and in New York in 1939. Kubatchi became wealthier and more organized, with a more complex production. In 1935, for example, the Museum of the Peoples of the USSR commissioned a silver leaf engraved with the decree concerning the elimination of illiteracy in the Daghestan. This unique piece of work was executed in a variety of techniques—niello-work, hollow-engraving, gilding, and, to a lesser extent, chasing on iron or on ivory, and filigree. Even the background was chiseled in places.

Among the younger jewelers, one of the most talented was Alikhanov, the son and student of Akhmedev. At 17, he participated in the New York Exhibition. He also illustrated books on national folklore. After the war, he directed a school of engraving techniques. At this time, the work of Alikhanov and his contemporaries was at its peak. Hammered copper Uzbekistan tableware is also worth mentioning. During the 1920s this craft was active at the Bukhara, Samarkand, and Kokand centers.

The Nordic art of niello-work experienced a new period of development during the 1920s and 30s. At the end of the nineteenth century, a single craftsman, Kochkov, possessed the secrets of niello-work in the village of Veliki-Ustiug. He transmitted his knowledge to his grandson and disciple, Tchirkov, a talented engraver whose goal was to revive this traditional art form. In 1929, Tchirkov organized an experimental workshop in Veliki-Ustiug. The students he trained there worked until 1933 in the Northern Niello-Work Collective. Tchirkov continued the tradition of niello-work designs on bracelets and oblong silver boxes. One of his specialties was variations on the Veliki-Ustiug panorama, a popular subject from the nineteenth century. These engravings done in the lubok tradition had a naïve charm. The Northern Niello-Work Collective was able to achieve a certain modernism, unlike many other traditional art forms, because it almost immediately found an outlet. It executed commissions for the domestic market as well as for export, and participated in international exhibitions, with the result of achieving a permanent stability, as much for the range of articles it offered—brooches, passe-partout mountings, goblets, powder boxes, dessert spoons—as for its engraved designs. However, despite its perfect craftsmanship, its production lacked inspiration. For many years, all work was executed according to the designs of a single artist, Chilnikovsky. The niello-work designs of Veliki-Ustiug were similar to the graphic work of illustrated books. In the 1920s, modern themes like factories and smoking chimneys were introduced. During the 1930s, themes became more narrative, with more detailed human figures. However, the major part of its production preserved Empire or Art Nouveau-style floral compositions.

The enamel-work of Rostov had a somewhat different destiny. In the 1920s and 1930s, artists and illustrators assisted the Rostov craftsmen in reviving their art. Before the Revolution, Rostov production consisted of small icons and crosses which no longer had a market in Soviet Russia. But it was imperative to preserve the technique of painting on enamel with a silver support. New articles were introduced—badges, powder boxes, cases, frames, and jewelry. The bouquets, garlands, and compositions were similar to the painted designs on porcelain, perhaps because the director of the Rostov artisans' association was Tchekhonin, who was also extremely active in the revival of porcelain.

NOTES

1. Offered to Lenin by the oil workers of Baku, the inkwell is preserved at the Lenin Museum in Moscow.

A. AKHMEDOV, cigarette case in a stylized floral design, with the emblem of the USSR in the center, Kubatchy, 1929.

Textiles and Carpets
Embroidery

During the 1920s, the restructuring of traditional textile work occurred with more or less success according to the different regions concerned. The cottage industries of weaving, embroidery, lace, and carpets were transformed into cooperative unions, and the main embroidery centers—those of the Moscow region, Ivanovo, Gorky, Kaluga, Novgorod, Riazan, and Smolensk—were renovated. Each region had its specific style.

Kresttsy embroidery had the refinement of silver chasework, with its openwork design made of interlacing threads. The pillow lace of Gorky, on the other hand, was transparent, soft to the touch and complex in design, like a snowflake. Ivanovo embroidery was simpler and more severe, with transparent stitching and geometric designs in cross-stitch. Embroidery from Mstiora near Vladimir used a raised satin-stitch; its floral motifs formed bouquets and garlands against a background of white cambric. In Riazan, Smolensk, Orel, and Kaluga, peasant traditions had been preserved in the stitch techniques as well as in the designs. The ancient "interlacing of colors," typical of Tarussa, was pursued.

In the twenties and thirties, peasant embroidery was introduced into urban clothing. The artist Gumelevskaya played an important role in reviving Kaluga embroidery. In the Kaluga region, Tarussa developed into one of the main centers for traditional embroidery.

From the 1930s onward, embroidery found a dependable outlet in urban clothing. Two trends coexisted. On the one hand, artists working in artisans' associations attempted to adapt elements of festive peasant clothing to modern lifestyles. Blouses with puffed sleeves were a great success at exhibitions, but were, unfortunately, useless in everyday life, especially as their rich embroideries were extremely costly. On the other hand, a new tendency in urban fashion—dresses, suits, blouses—used traditional embroidery to add variety to essentially industrial and stereotyped garments.

At the end of the 1930s, the great majority of artisans' associations had ceased producing hand embroidery. Thematic motifs and geometric patterns were replaced by stereotyped designs inspired by motifs dating from the early part of the century. In addition, the work was now mechanized.

Hand embroidery continued to be produced in small centers in Ivanovo, Kaluga, Riazan, and Gorky. Production was of unique pieces intended for exhibi-

tions. Tablecloths, curtains, and panels were embroidered in the ancient Russian tradition. An effort was also made to reflect modern life. In the Ukraine, the embroidery centers of Tchernigov, Poltava, and Vinnitsa were grouped into cooperatives after 1919. The traditional principles concerning technique and design as well as presentation of the article were preserved. Ukrainian embroidery remained active in peasant life as well as in urban settings.

Embroidery from Pechetilovka, Klembrovka, Sorotchintsy, Poltava, and Dikanka had the best reputations during the twenties and thirties. Women's blouses, men's shirts, napkins, and hand towels were produced in these centers. In the late 1920s and early 1930s, urban artisans' associations appeared in the Uzbekistan and in the Tadzhikistan (in Samarkand, Chahrissiab, Tashkent, Tchust, Margelan, and Bukhara), producing traditional embroidered panels and skull caps. These were so much in demand that machines were introduced (the tambour or embroidery frame).

During the 1930s, embroiderers were called upon to execute commissions that were far from traditional for the different aspects of modern and urban civilization. They produced panels, drapes, and curtains for theaters, clubs, museums, and exhibitions, embroidering such emblems as red stars, hammers and sickles, sheaves representing the different republics, airplanes, dams, cotton, fruit, and grains. These elements were often poorly adapted to traditional motifs. Among the articles produced in this domain, the most well known are Sapozhnikova's *Fireworks in Moscow*, 1943, and Dmitrieva-Chulpina's *Onward Towards the West*, 1945.

Lace

The most important lacemaking centers were Vologda, Orel, Kirov, Leningrad, Riazan, and the Karelian and Tatar regions. Vologda and Elets, the largest centers, employed four thousand lacemakers. All the lacework was produced by cooperative artisans' associations.

Until the middle of the 1930s, all production was intended for export, with the obvious consequences concerning assortment, technique, and material. Vologda lace was tightly constructed, with geometric designs; Elets lace was light, airy, with rounded and star-shaped motifs. Bedspreads, napkins, pillowcases, tablecloths, and ruffs were made, generally executed in an Art Nouveau style. These articles were greatly in demand, and the stylization of the floral motifs became increasingly monotonous. Elements of specifically Soviet art began to be introduced. The organization of new professional schools was dependent on the Kalinin School in Moscow. At the end of the 1930s, designs on napkins, pillowcases, and bedspreads became more inventive as well as more concrete. The lacemakers of Vologda received the grand prize in Paris in 1937; the Elets lacemakers won the gold medal. Lacemakers, like other crafts artists, were interested in finding new floral motifs; concurrently, they began to introduce Soviet emblems into their work. They also created thematic compositions. These innovations, however, met with little success. Zvezdina's *The Cavalry,* intended for the International Exhibi-

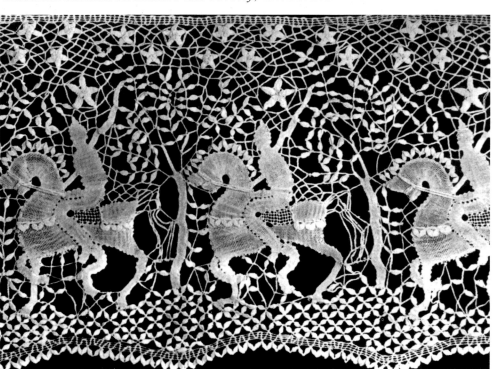

E. ZVEZDINA, *The Cavalry,* lace frieze, Kirichi, 1939.

E. DMIETRIEVA-CHULPINA, *The Conquest of the West,* wall embroidery, Mstiora, 1945.

tion of New York in 1939, was one of the best pieces of this type. It was an epic composition whose regular succession of horsemen gave the impression of perpetual movement.

Printed Cloth

In nineteenth century Russia, hand-printed cloth had already been replaced by industrially produced printed calico.

In the early 1920s, however, textile factories functioned only intermittently, so that the handmade cloth of little villages was greatly in demand. In the North and in the Urals, where industrial fabrics had greater difficulty of access, craftsmen known throughout the area traveled from village to village offering their services. Hand-printing remained, however, within the limits of individual craftsmanship, and it diminished steadily with the rise of industrial textiles. The traditional craft was preserved only within an artisans' association, working under Povstiany's guidance (The "Exportnabivtkan" association, 1930s). The motifs created were not only traditional but also innovative thanks to their printing and stencil techniques. The cloth produced was intended for export. In the Ukraine, two artisans' associations identical to the one previously mentioned had been founded at the end of the 1920s, in Rechetilovka (Clara Zedkin's workshop) and in Poltava (Lessia Ukrainka's workshop). In addition, individual craftsmen continued to produce hand-printed cloth. In the Ukraine, Povstiany was active in the revival of this crafts tradition.

Fabric intended for clothing was printed with small, geometric or floral motifs. For tablecloths and hand towels, the colors were blue and white, with motifs identical to those used for embroidered hand towels.

In Central Asia, hand-printed textiles had long been highly developed in the Uzbekistan. During the 1920s and 1930s, the output was divided between small workshops and cooperative artisans' associations. Traditional designs were produced for strips on everyday clothing and the linings of overcoats. Craftsmen also produced more elegant prints for decorative tablecloths and bedspreads, with remarkable floral and geometric motifs. Uzbek designs were strict, with warm colors, consisting most often of three basic colors: black, madder-red, and cream. The background color was always a fundamental element; for cloth sold by the meter, it was light-colored, with darker drawn-thread silhouettes standing out against it. For other pieces of cloth, a red arabesque was incorporated into a background of piping, stamps, and medallions. Against this colored background, the design was in white or black. The appearance of new articles in the everyday life of peasants encouraged textile craftsmen to look for new inspiration. As in Russia and the Ukraine, they introduced greater realism into both design and color. It was in this spirit that the panel entitled *The Fireworks* by Povstiany and Abdugafurov was created for the Tashkent Theater.

E. POVSTIANI, handmade cloth.

Cotton towel with a traditional geometric motif. Krovelets, Ukraine, 1939.

Hand Weaving

On the eve of the Revolution, hand weaving persisted only in areas that were far from any industrial structure. During the years 1917–1920, the dearth of fabric was advantageous to hand weavers. Linen, hemp, wool, and cotton became indispensable. The traditional centers for hand weaving were Moscow, Ivanovo, Riazan, and Kostroma, which were organized into artisans' associations in the beginning of the 1920s. Jacquard fabrics and other motifs were reserved for the domestic market; very little was exported.

At first, inexpensive cloth was mass-produced. The production was of mediocre quality due to the lack of raw materials and dyes. During the second half of the 1920s, weaving associations introduced mechanization. Folk and hand weaving persisted only in Riazan and Vologda. Mechanized weaving was most developed in the Ukraine. The main centers, Krolevets, Dekhtiari, Boguslav, and Rechetilovka, specialized in finished products with multicolored motifs. The experimental schools of Kiev and Krolevets helped to support the profession and were instrumental in reviving forgotten techniques as well as creating new designs and articles for urban use. Each center produced specific items. Krolevets weavers produced tablecloths, towels, curtains, and cushion covers. The large designs had geometric or floral motifs, in solid colors, usually red. The background was always white. Occasionally, such motifs as red stars, inscriptions, commemorative dates, and Soviet emblems were introduced.

In Dekhtiari, weavers continued to create the traditional "plakhta," a rectangular, brightly colored panel generally made into a skirt. In the 1920s, the "plakhta" began to be used for interior decoration, on bedspreads, cushion covers, and tables. This shift in function influenced the fabric content. There were fewer details and more emphasis on overall design and color contrast. The highly decorative "plakhtas" preserved the harmony of traditional woven cloths.

In the Uzbekistan, the first artisans' weaving associations appeared at the beginning of the 1920s in Andijan, then in Samarkand, Urgut, Kitab, and other towns. The organizations into artisans' associations as well as mechanization served to modify the familial structure of hand weaving workshops. Striped and multicolored cottons and silks were produced. Stripes were transversal; designs and colors were identical to those produced previously by families of weavers. The designs degenerated, however, with the disappearance of vegetal dyes and their replacement by chemical dyes, which implied new production methods.

Carpets

The main carpet production centers were traditionally situated in Central Asia, the Caucasus, the Urals, and Moldavia. The beginning of the 1930s marked the reorganization of carpet weaving into artisans' associations which helped to bring about a revival of its activity. It was only at this time that the situation of agriculture was once more able to provide the necessary raw materials.

Immediately after the Revolution, carpets began to be exported, which brought about a reorganization in the production of strongly-woven wool carpets. Family production, however, was considerably reduced, as was the variety of carpets. Most carpets were made in artisans' associations which used traditional motifs. These were woven by memory, varying the basic motif.

Exportation required the copying of certain models as well as special technical designs. The technical design was applied to a quarter of the carpet. A perfect symmetry was obtained by turning the carpet during the weaving procedure. While weaving was simplified and accelerated by this method, the possibilities of variations were reduced. Skilled weavers used the technical design only for the basic composition, and filled in the details by memory. Some artists tried to introduce thematic scenes or portraits, or else elements of modern life, but the results were not satisfactory.

In Central Asia, carpet weaving was highly developed in Turkmenia. During the 1920s and 1930s, carpets were still an indispensable element in Turkmenian habitats. Each woman knew how to spin, dye, and weave the wool. The technical and artistic quality was excellent. Turkmenian carpets were finely-grained and soft, with sober and refined motifs in madder-red or garnet-red.

Little by little, the Soviet state took away the monopoly on exportation from private exporters. In the early 1930s, seventeen-thousand home weavers were called upon to realize large-sized wool carpets in Tekin, Pendin, and Yomud styles.

Tekin carpets were characterized by stark boundaries between the central motif and the borders. The composition of the center motif consisted of a basic repetitive octahedral design, placed horizontally and divided into other smaller motifs. Rosettes were inserted between the different motifs. Dominant colors were dark red and orange, white, green or dark blue for details. Interior motifs were large, contrasting with the small designs of the borders.

Pendin carpets were quite similar to Tekin carpets, but with cherry-brown and reddish-orange colors. There were no white motifs or diagonally ordered light and dark colors.

Prayer rug, Azerbaidjan, circa 1930.

Yomud carpets were similar to Tekin carpets in their use of colors, but their motifs were arranged in checkered patterns. The background consisted of a network of diamond-shapes.

The most common carpets were executed in the "bechir" style, with floral motifs and large dimensions similar to Caucasian designs.

Ensi carpets, used as door hangings, had preserved certain obvious national traits—the central square was placed closer to the top, leaving a wider bottom border.

Realistic elements were included in the traditional decor—human beings and animals, grapes, fruit, and cotton. Krylov, an artist from Achkhabad, even introduced contemporary events and portraits.

A series of these carpets was prepared for 1936. The first thematic carpets were presented at the Paris and New York Exhibitions. One of these carpets showed the Achkhabad-Moscow horse race, another depicted national dances. Such thematic carpets were not very popular.

At the end of the 1930s, the artist Tsivchinsky opened an experimental workshop in Alma-Ata for the production of thematic carpets. But the weaving techniques as well as the thematic composition were foreign to traditional Kazakh art; in fact, these were Russian and Ukrainian contributions. Pictorial panels of rather mediocre quality were also realized: *Amangueldi,* 1937, *Sports Event,* and *A Decade of Kazakh Art,* 1940, all compositions by Tsivchinsky.

In the Caucasus, the ancient art of carpet weaving was familial but also organized into workshops. It played a dominant role in the economy. Family production consisted of wool carpets, reversible carpets, and rugs. Techniques, varieties, and motifs were extremely varied. Azerbaijani carpets were not made along the principles of contrasting colors. In general, they were light in color, with colored backgrounds. Their designs tended to be more intense, with original, even rare shades of color—blue-gray, pink, light brown, and light green.

The artist Kerimov introduced thematic compositions and portraits, using medieval miniatures as his source of inspiration. His best creations use motifs from the poems of Nizami (1940) and the portraits of the poets Firdussy (1934) and Chota Rustavely (1937). The colors were light and gay.

The Daghestan was an important carpet weaving center. Daghestani carpets were more sober than Azerbaijani carpets. The design construction of the central part consisted of medallions. The border was divided into three strips. Decoration was floral, geometric, or realistic.

Armenian carpets were divided into two groups. The first group was similar to Azerbaijani carpets, realized by weavers living in the border areas. Such carpets were woven in Chirvan, Kuba, Kazakh, and Karabakh styles. The dominant colors were reds.

The second group consisted of more original carpets, with large motifs in the style of ancient Oriental fabrics. The floral composition was arranged vertically. Within the extraordinary flowers and leaves were dragons, roe-bucks, and other animals shown in running herds or in combat. Borders were narrow.

In the 1930s, indigenous artists created new designs, inspired by Armenian miniatures. These were known as the Erevan and Idjevan carpets.

The Ukraine and Moldavia were the two most important producers of two-sided carpets in various fibers. Production was stimulated by demand. Artisans' associations were organized in Rechetilovka, Dekhtiari, Klembrovka, and Opochnia in the Ukraine, and in Tiraspol and Kichinev in Moldavia.

Motifs in Ukrainian carpets tended to be very geometric. There were not always borders. In the center, stars or diamond-shapes were repeated against a black or solid color background. Sometimes there was not even a background; the carpet was composed of several surfaces of colors with geometric designs. In Central Ukraine, floral motifs were identical to the motifs on hand towels—flower branches, bouquets, and garlands against a black or light-colored background.

Thematic compositions were created; recourse to classicism helped to avoid any mistakes in this domain. A series of carpets on the theme of work were exhibited at the Exhibition of Ukrainian Craft Arts, in Kiev and Moscow in 1936. The most beautiful carpets were the closest in inspiration to traditional designs: *Young Dobvass* by Ovtchinnikov and *The Dance* by Tsivtchinsky.

Moldavian carpets were highly contrasted, with stylized birds and flowers. Such carpets had originated in monasteries, with a technique that remained close to embroidery styles of the late nineteenth century. Generally speaking, the art of carpet weaving tended to become standardized: local differentiations became less distinct, and the original colors were altered by the use of chemical dyes. An overall simplification was the main consequence of mass production in this domain.

Index

Acknowledgments

The editor thanks: I. Alpatova, L. Andreeva, I. Bibikova, M. Botcharov, E. Iakovleva, B. Kapralov, V. Kazakova, B. Koromislov, I. Krioukova, O. Popova, I. Riazantsev, V. Rojankovski, I. Souslov, T. Strijenova, V. Tolstoy, V. Vygolov for collaborating with the authors of this book. Thanks also goes to those persons who helped in the research—S. Beziaev, N. Coleno, N. Gremiachkina, H. Gryasnova, I. d'Hauteville, S. Leboulenger, V. Manine, L. Musement, and G.A. Ter-Gazaryants, président de la VAAP—and particularly to the photographers G. Guinzbourg, I. Markine, I. Palmine, J.-M. Tardy.